THE NEW
ACADEMIC
GENERATION

THE NEW ACADEMIC GENERATION ⇉⊹

A PROFESSION IN TRANSFORMATION

Martin J. Finkelstein
Robert K. Seal
Jack H. Schuster

THE JOHNS HOPKINS UNIVERSITY PRESS
Baltimore and London

All rights reserved. Published 1998

Printed in the United States of America on acid-free paper

9 8 7 6 5 4 3 2 1

The Johns Hopkins University Press
2715 North Charles Street
Baltimore, Maryland 21218-4363
The Johns Hopkins Press Ltd., London

Library of Congress Cataloging-in-Publication Data
will be found at the end of this book.

A catalog record for this book is available from the British Library.

ISBN 0-8018-5886-0

CONTENTS

List of Figures and Tables   ix
Preface and Acknowledgments   xi

ONE   CONTEXT: THE FACULTY AT A CROSSROADS   1
A Faculty Perspective   1
Two Notable Developments   4
In Summary   5

TWO   TAKING THE MEASURE OF A
NEW ACADEMIC GENERATION   7
Studying the Professoriate: A Historical Note   9
Scope of Inquiry   10
Identifying the New Academic Generation   11
The Seven-Year Sort   12
The 1993 National Study of Postsecondary Faculty   15
Data Analysis Procedures   15

THREE   DEMOGRAPHIC CONTOURS
OF THE NEW ACADEMIC GENERATION   17
The New-Faculty Cohort: Its Size and Venues   17
    Size of the Cohort   18
    Institutional Venues   19
    Program Area   21

Demographics and Background   23
    Age   23
    Rank   24
    Gender   26
    Race/Ethnicity   29
    National Origin (Citizenship)   32
    Socioeconomic Status (Parents' Education)   35
    Marital Status   37
    Missing Data: Religion   38
In Summary   39

FOUR   THE PREPARATION AND CAREERS
    OF THE NEW ACADEMIC GENERATION   43
Educational Background   44
    Level of Highest Degree   44
    Source of Highest Degree   46
    Undergraduate Honors   47
    Graduate School Support   48
Career Experience   50
    Age at Award of Highest Degree and
        at Appointment to Current Position   50
    Previous Employment History   51
    Tenure Status   54
    Job Satisfaction   58
    Career Satisfaction: The Global Measures   61
In Summary   63

FIVE   THE NEW ACADEMIC
    GENERATION AT WORK   65
Distribution of Faculty Effort   65
The Work Week   70
    Paid and Unpaid Activities   70
    Office Hours and Student Contact   72
Teaching Strategies   73
    Primary Instructional Methods   73
    Other Instructional Methods   74
Involvement in Research and Publication   76
Concurrent Employment   80
In Summary   83

SIX   THE ATTITUDES AND VALUES
       OF THE NEW ACADEMIC GENERATION   85
       Faculty Roles and Rewards   85
       Instructional Duties   90
       The Campus Environment   91
           Undergraduate Education   91
           Equity Issues   93
           Work Pressures   95
       Campus Facilities and Resources   96
       In Summary   100

SEVEN THE NEW ACADEMIC GENERATION
       AND THE FUTURE OF AMERICAN
       HIGHER EDUCATION   101
       Summary of Intercohort Comparisons   102
       Implications for the Future Faculty and Their Work   104
       In Conclusion   111

       Appendix A: Extended Tables   113
       Appendix B: Selected Comparisons of
                   New- and Senior-Faculty Cohorts   179
       Appendix C: 1993 National Study of Postsecondary
                   Faculty: Faculty Questionnaire   183
       Notes   211
       References   221
       Index   227

FIGURES AND TABLES

Figures

1 Faculty categories   12
2 Cohort size and gender distribution, full-time faculty   18
3 Cohort differences in race / ethnicity, full-time faculty   29
4 Cohort differences in citizenship, full-time faculty   33
5 Cohort differences in the proportion of native-born
    white males, full-time faculty   40
6 Cohort differences in the proportion of native-born
    white males in liberal arts fields, full-time faculty   41
7 Cohort differences in types of appointments, full-time
    faculty   56

Tables

1 Institutional type   21
2 Academic program area   22
3 Age   23
4 Academic rank   24
5 Gender   27
6 Race/ethnicity   28
7 Citizenship   32

7A Country of birth: Ten most frequent responses   34
7B Country of birth for permanent residents:
    Ten most frequent responses   34
7C Country of birth for temporary residents:
    Ten most frequent responses   35
 8 Father's educational level   36
 9 Mother's educational level   36
10 Marital status   38
11 Native-born white males   39
12 Native-born white males in the liberal arts   41
13 Level of highest degree   45
14 Doctorate source   47
15 Undergraduate honors   48
16 Graduate school support   49
17 Age at award of highest degree and at appointment to
    current position   50
18 Previous employment sector   52
19 Previous employment primary responsibility   53
20 Previous employment history: Post–highest degree
    and pre–current position   54
21 Tenure status   55
22 Job satisfaction   60
23 Global career satisfaction   62
24 Actual and preferred distribution of effort   66
25 Weekly hours spent on paid and unpaid activities   71
26 Weekly office hours and student contact hours   72
27 Primary instructional methods used   73
28 Other instructional methods used   75
29 Involvement in research and publication   78
30 Concurrent employment   80
31 Concurrent employment sector   82
32 Perceptions of faculty roles and rewards   86
33 Perceptions of instructional duties   90
34 Perceptions of campus environment: Undergraduate education   92
35 Perceptions of campus environment: Equity issues   93
36 Perceptions of campus environment: Work pressures   95
37 Perceptions of campus facilities: Space issues   96
38 Perceptions of campus facilities: Computing resources   97
39 Perceptions of campus facilities: Other support   98

PREFACE AND
ACKNOWLEDGMENTS

American colleges and universities are positioned at the leading edge of a remarkable transformation as higher education enters upon—some would say lurches into—an era of cascading technological changes and increasingly intense competition for funding. But nowhere is the change more emphatic than in the composition of the new entrants into the faculty. Higher education, of course, is always in flux, as are the characteristics of the faculty who occupy the core of the academic enterprise. Indeed, the story of American higher education, spanning three and a half centuries, can be told in substantial part by recounting just who made up the faculty over time and what was the mix of their responsibilities. Arguably, however, the extent to which the faculty's demographic profile has changed in very recent years is unprecedented. These changes are dramatic, certainly in some crucial respects, and, as we argue in this book, their long-term implications are profound.

Our study attempts to capture this ongoing transformation, to describe its many dimensions, and to suggest what significance for higher education inheres in these shifts. The primary vehicle for our analysis is a national survey of faculty, the 1993 National Study of Postsecondary Faculty (NSOPF-93), conducted by the U.S. Department of Education's National Center for Education Statistics (NCES). Because it is the largest national survey of faculty that has been undertaken in a quarter century, its robust sample size permits detailed analyses not feasible with the more commonplace smaller surveys. Our strategy has been to describe the characteristics of the relatively new entrants into academic careers—those who will reshape American colleges and universities for years to come—and to compare them to their more settled, more senior colleagues. This exercise has revealed some surprising results.

We believe we have identified and substantiated important trends that challenge the widespread perception that American colleges and universities change at an unhurried rate. Our findings will be relevant to anyone, whether within or outside higher education's precincts, who seeks to understand better the complex workings of the astonishingly multifaceted higher education system (or nonsystem, as the case may be). We also offer guidance for devising strategies for the strengthening of the faculty and, thereby, higher education itself.

We are indebted to numerous persons for having encouraged and facilitated our work. This list must begin with those who provided financial support for our research. Our collaboration had its beginnings with NSOPF-93. After the National Opinion Research Center at the University of Chicago (the contractor to the U.S. Department of Education) completed its tasks of conducting the survey and developing a massive electronic data base, the Department's NCES contracted with several researchers who had submitted proposals to probe the data and to submit reports on specific topics.

We proposed to examine the characteristics of the new generation of faculty, especially in comparison with their more senior faculty colleagues, and to assess the implications of whatever differences surfaced. We submitted our draft report, a monograph entitled *New Entrants to the Full-Time Faculty of Higher Education Institutions*, in December 1995. We initially presented our findings the following month at the American Association for Higher Education's annual conference on Faculty Roles and Rewards (Magner 1996).

This book is an outgrowth of that earlier report, a much-expanded analysis and interpretation of our original inquiry. NCES was the catalyst, having provided initial funding and subsequently authorizing us to make use of our original monograph as a basis for this book. We are grateful to NCES and especially to Linda J. Zimbler, the NCES program officer who was our principal contact throughout the early stages of work on our monograph, and to Valerie Martin Conley, the liaison to NCES who advised us regarding the data presented in our tables.

We are grateful to the Teachers Insurance and Annuity Association–College Retirement Equities Fund (TIAA-CREF) for its support of our ongoing research aimed at better understanding the work and careers of American faculty members and our efforts at improving the lives of faculty and thereby the academy. That support significantly facilitated our work on this project.

We acknowledge with appreciation the two external reviewers for The Johns Hopkins University Press who read our manuscript with care and made very helpful suggestions. Although their names are unknown to us, their expertise was manifest. We especially give thanks to Jacqueline Wehmueller, senior editor at the Press, whose encouragement was unstinting and efficiency greatly appreciated. We wish also to express our appreciation to Lee Sioles at the Press and to Peter Strupp of Princeton Editorial Associates, both of whom were very helpful in the latter stages of production.

Office staffs have contributed their indispensable assistance, especially Gwen Hoyt at Claremont Graduate University and Georgianna Maroulakos at Seton Hall University. Several doctoral students assisted in important ways, especially Jesús F. Galaz Fontes, Guy Gerbick, and Lilian Metlitzky at Claremont and Constance Willett at Seton Hall. We are deeply grateful to them.

As is the case with all time-consuming projects, family members have accommodated us with more than a little patience; we are most appreciative for their unselfish support.

THE NEW
ACADEMIC
GENERATION

ONE

CONTEXT:
THE FACULTY AT A
CROSSROADS

Decades serve as convenient—if artificial—delineators of history's flow. Most of the way through this last decade of the twentieth century, it can be said that these years have not been particularly kind to faculties employed at American institutions of higher education. There are so many faculty members—no fewer than a million, if all categories are included—and they serve in so many varying capacities in their "small and different" worlds of institutional types and academic fields, that generalizations about "the faculty" are hard to come by.[1] Yet, from the faculty's vantage point, several developments underscore the proposition that for the faculty this has not been the best of times.

A Faculty Perspective

Consider this array of interrelated factors, which, from the perspective of many faculty members, presses upon them and threatens—or has already disrupted—traditional features of academic life:

- The assessment movement, launched with vigor during the previous decade, continues to gain momentum and signals to the faculty that they are to be held more strictly accountable for what they do and for the results of their efforts.

- The academic labor market has been a strong buyer's market for several decades in most fields. The current market continues to constrain access for aspirant faculty and to limit mobility for existing faculty.
- Tenure, a virtually unassailable centerpiece of academic convention for decades, readily withstood the scrutiny that followed the turbulent 1960s. Yet it has recently come under renewed attack; the prospect looms that one state legislature or governing board may decide to strike tenure a lethal blow and that an ensuing domino effect may follow.
- Expectations of the faculty, by most accounts, have risen steadily, as institutions and their patrons stress "productivity." The prevailing buyer's market in turn enables institutions to avoid renewing non-tenured faculty with reasonable assurance that the departed can be readily replaced with new prospects eager to please.
- Institutions of higher education, anxious about preserving a measure of flexibility amid the uncertainties of a rapidly changing environment and driven to be ever more cost conscious, have increasingly resorted to making non–tenure track appointments. As a consequence, the number of part-time and off-track full-time appointments appears to be expanding rapidly relative to that of "traditional" full-time, tenured or tenurable appointments.
- Faculty compensation, which had increased steadily in terms of real (adjusted) salaries throughout the previous decade, in 1990–91 suffered its first decline in nine years, experienced similar declines for 1992–93 and 1996–97, and has hovered near or below the break-even point for the first seven years of this decade.[2]
- Reliable data about the faculty role in governance are scarce, particularly concerning whether the principle of "shared governance" is being eroded. Yet anecdotal evidence abounds about "top-down management" styles and institutional strategic decisionmaking that relegate the faculty to a more peripheral role.

In addition to these developments, the faculty seems not to have fared well in the estimation of the public and of policymakers whose opinions about higher education are consequential. The perception appears to be widely shared among them that faculty members lead privileged, protected lives, often pursuing agendas incongruent with students' needs—in a word, say their critics, out of touch with the "real world." On the whole, the faculty of the 1990s have become more and more accustomed to hearing themselves characterized as a part of the problem, as a central feature of the academy that needs to be "fixed" if the higher education enterprise is to maintain viability (and market share) in the coming era.

Above and beyond this litany of developments and perceptions are two hard realities that have had significant effects on higher education and especially on the faculty in recent years—one a principal cause, the other a powerful effect. The cause is the scarcity of resources essential to meeting higher education's needs, combined with the almost universal expectation that higher education's ability to compete for support with other sectors, from K–12 schools to corrections, is likely to weaken further. The effect is the dominant dual strategy adopted so widely—and not surprisingly—by higher education administrators and governing boards: to contain costs and to maintain as much organizational flexibility as possible in an era of growing uncertainties, volatile student interests, and the spectre of technologies that will revolutionize higher learning. Neither cause nor effect originated in the 1990s, nor indeed in the United States,[3] but the several-year recession that began at the outset of this decade seriously eroded the resources available to higher education and fueled the strategic responses just described.

This is not to argue that the 1990s have been a time of unrelenting crisis for the academic profession or even that this decade has constituted a period of uniform setbacks. The record is more mixed. It is to say, however, that a number of trends are evident that, if further extrapolated, will alter the nature of academic life in significant ways and on balance will bleaken the outlook for the academic profession—at least in terms of traditional academic work and careers—unless certain correctives come into play.

We do not argue that the well-being of the faculty is coterminous with the health of the far-flung higher education enterprise. Higher education is, of course, larger than the faculty. The two are inextricably linked, but the time when the faculty could credibly assert that "we *are* the university" is long past. Thus the tension between faculty self-interest and the broader interests of higher education's institutions, perhaps invariably in some degree of conflict with one another, may well be intensifying.

However one reckons the overlap between "the faculty" and "higher education," it is inarguable that the former is and will be central to the future of the latter. That is, who the faculty are and what they do define higher education's center; that much is axiomatic. Sometimes, even oftentimes, that proposition drifts out of focus as institutions of higher education wage their offensive and defensive campaigns across many fronts. Yet it is indisputable that no college or university can accomplish its missions without a dedicated and competent faculty. Thus to repeat: who the faculty are and what they do are the heart of the enterprise.

These observations provide a context within which the analyses and interpretations that make up our study should be viewed. The point is that the academic profession near decade's end is under pressure—mounting pressure, it appears to us—and this reality contributes to the importance of being able to answer such key questions as the following:

- In what ways are the faculty changing in terms of who they are and what they do?
- What do these changes portend for the future of the academic profession and for the institutions that employ them?

Chapter 2 describes how we have gone about trying to answer such questions. But before we begin that examination, it may be useful to expand on several of the themes just outlined.

Two Notable Developments

Contributing to this complex and rapidly evolving environment for higher education, two events—one a published work, the other an ongoing project—have gained prominence in reconceptualizing critical elements of academic life.

The first is an imaginative effort to rehabilitate teaching and the second is the movement to examine anew how academic appointments (and thus careers) are structured. It will be relevant to consider the significance of each, for they are possibly the two most influential arguments currently reshaping faculty life. In the long term, these two develop-. ments may have a profound impact in reconfiguring who the faculty are, their career trajectories, and indeed the very nature of the academy. As noted, each development is captured by—symbolized by—a specific publication (as in the first case) or a program generating a series of position papers (as in the second).

The decade began with Ernest L. Boyer's *Scholarship Reconsidered: Priorities of the Professoriate.*[4] This thin volume is probably the most widely read treatise on higher education in recent years. In it Boyer urges that traditional notions of what constitutes scholarship should be expanded to encompass several other types of intellectual activity. This is not the forum to restate the Boyer thesis. Suffice it to say here that the notion of reconceptualizing (meaning, for his purposes, broadening) what should be regarded (and rewarded) as "scholarship" was a creative response to the building pressure on the faculty to revitalize teaching and to rescue teaching from the neglect that so many critics perceived it had endured.

In effect, a consensus had begun to form that the pendulum had swung as far as was tolerable in the direction of prizing research (presumably at the expense of teaching in some institutions). The stick was being wielded by the overseers. The Boyer thesis provided another, more palatable, carrot-like route: acknowledgment that other forms of intellectual activity, reaching beyond "discovery research" and publishing, are valuable and worthy of being counted as scholarship when done well.[5] The question arises: to what extent has there been a response by institutions and their faculties to the heightened expectation that some effort will be shifted from research to teaching? We believe that our data in Chapter 5 provide a window onto that phenomenon—and a reason for concern.

A second portentous development that is affecting higher education is the changing pattern of academic appointments. A project known as "New Pathways," begun in 1995 by the American Association for Higher Education, has been very influential in prompting a reconsideration of traditional academic appointments.[6] Whether tenure will withstand the increasing scrutiny remains to be seen. What is clear already, however, is that the deployment of instructional staff has been undergoing a dramatic shift. For one thing, many more part-time faculty are being hired relative to full-timers—roughly double the proportion, from about 22 percent of all faculty in the early 1970s to at least 42 or 43 percent at present.[7] Moreover, the pattern of full-time appointments is changing markedly. Our data show that more recent appointments of full-time faculty are often made outside the traditional tenured or tenure track realm (see Chapter 4). New Pathways thus symbolizes, and is a driving force behind, efforts to infuse more flexibility into the types of faculty appointments. The results are already evident, and they are beginning to recast nothing less important than how higher education is done.

In Summary

It is indisputable that higher education is entering a period of turbulence. Change, of course, is a constant for higher education, but the rate of change is by all accounts accelerating. Our inquiry has taken place within this context of change—change that presents opportunities and poses threats. Of two things everyone can be certain: in this process, nothing in higher education will be unaffected, and the work and careers of the faculty will undergo a powerful transformation.

The evidence of the beginnings of that transformation is manifest in the following chapters. Specifically we identify a number of changes that, taken together, indicate an important shift in who the new faculty are, that is, how they differ from their more senior colleagues. Our thesis holds that these differences portend substantial changes in academic life: who the faculty of the future will be, how academic careers will be constructed, and what the relative attractiveness of such careers will be.

The following chapter describes how our study was conducted and in so doing identifies several key issues crucial to any efforts to study "the faculty." Subsequent chapters present the results of our analyses of the demographic characteristics of the faculty (Chapter 3), their careers (Chapter 4), their work patterns (Chapter 5), and their attitudes (Chapter 6). Finally, in Chapter 7, we explore the implications of our findings for higher education and accordingly for those who are, and will be, responsible for developing appropriate public and institutional policies.

TWO

TAKING THE MEASURE
OF A NEW
ACADEMIC GENERATION

Powerful pressures are already at work that will reshape American higher education over the next several decades (Kerr 1994, 1997; Dolence and Norris 1995; Kennedy 1995; Noam 1995; Lenzner and Johnson 1997). Among those forces most frequently cited are the demographic shifts that will promote an increasing focus on multiculturalism; technological developments that will assuredly revolutionize instruction and scholarly communication (and will prompt the emergence of new education/information providers); and economic (and political) constraints that will require increased emphases on productivity improvements and cost savings.

Less frequently discussed are the characteristics and orientation of the faculty members who will be on the front lines—and who thus will determine on a daily basis, as a function of their competencies and commitments, just how well the higher education system adapts to new realities. Starting in the mid 1950s, many thousands of faculty members, often without doctoral degrees, were hired to staff the rapid expansion of higher education (Smelser and Content 1980; Youn 1984). By the early 1970s, however, a new cohort of faculty members, more research oriented than their predecessors, had begun to leaven the mix. It is these "teacher-scholars" who have largely reconfigured our current system in the image of their own collective career aspirations and values. Now a new academic generation—

their successors—has begun to emerge, a product of different pressures and priorities. In some respects they can expect to be less influential in the face of the powerfully determinative demographic, technological, and economic forces that are transforming higher education. And yet, despite the environmental constraints, this cohort of recent hires, particularly in view of its large size, is certain to play a significant, long-term role in determining how higher education evolves in the United States. Accordingly, if we understand who these new faculty members are and what values they bring to their classrooms, laboratories, and studios, we will have provided an important lens through which to bring more clearly into focus higher education's uncertain future.

In the following pages we attempt to provide answers to a host of questions about the future faculty:

- What do we know about this new academic generation? Who are they?
- From where do they come?
- What sorts of careers are they planning for themselves?
- How are they balancing their teaching, research, and service roles?
- What are the orientations, values, and experiences that they bring to their work?

Central to the present inquiry, we also ask how the new faculty compare, along all of these dimensions, to that dominant earlier cohort that molded higher education for two decades and whose imprint still dominates.

- Are the recent entrants in effect clones of the masters who trained them? Or, if not clones, are they at least reasonably faithful disciples?
- Alternatively, is a new breed emerging—an academic generation whose characteristics, both demographic and attitudinal, clearly distinguish them from their predecessors?
- If that is the case, are those changes so pronounced that the new cohort can be expected, despite the limitations imposed by external conditions, to infuse higher education with different values and directions?

On the answers to these questions hinge to a considerable degree the future of the academic profession and hence the outlook for the American academy itself.

The 1993 National Study of Postsecondary Faculty (NSOPF-93) allows us to delineate this new academic generation—which we have defined as the cohort of full-time faculty members in the first seven years of their academic careers—and to examine how this subgroup compares with their seniors on a wide variety of demographic, career, and work variables.

Studying the Professoriate: A Historical Note

Although the higher education literature does not include any general studies describing the generational process whereby the national corps of college and university teachers regularly renews itself, several more focused studies are useful in describing the faculty regeneration process. These span institutional studies of faculty cohorts at Harvard, Dartmouth, and Michigan in the late nineteenth century and at the University of Minnesota in the 1970s (Corcoran and Clark 1984) and a few more contemporary studies, albeit with a narrower focus, including Bess's (1973) comparison of faculty and student life cycles, Rice's (1980) analysis of two cohorts of Danforth Fellows, and Finnegan's (1993) examination of entering cohorts of faculty at comprehensive colleges and regional universities.

What have we learned from studies such as these? Most generally, higher education tends to change slowly in its aggregate characteristics. From time to time, however, there have been substantial, almost revolutionary changes in the cohorts of entering faculty over even as little as a single generation (in an era of expansion) or over two or three generations (in less dynamic periods).

The nineteenth century provides abundant examples of generational discontinuities or breakthroughs. Harvard, for example, moved from a faculty dominated by temporary tutors to one dominated by discipline-trained professors in the first quarter of that century. Later, within a decade following the Civil War, Dartmouth (Tobias 1982), Williams (Rudolph 1956), Bowdoin (Packard 1882), and even the emerging state universities in the Midwest, such as Michigan (Creutz 1981), all, through a bunching of new hires in a very brief period, had substantially changed the balance of their faculties—and thereby transformed the character of their institutions. As larger numbers of institutions completed their individual transformations (fueled by the enrollment expansion of the last decade of the nineteenth century, the accelerating pace of specialization, and the growth of a research-oriented ethos that displaced the English college model to a considerable degree), the national character of the American faculty was discernibly changing. Both a new organizational form, the university, and a new national professional guild, the American Association of University Professors (AAUP, founded in 1915), were well established within two generations (Geiger 1986).

Following the turn of the century, the pre–World War II period, within the span of a single generation, gave rise to the academic infrastructure in terms of doctoral production (a fivefold increase between 1920 and 1940), as well as to second-order specialization in the disciplines for the mammoth postwar expansion (Berelson 1960). In not quite a ten-year period between the mid-1960s and the mid-1970s, the size of American college and university faculties nearly doubled (Cartter 1976). The sheer magnitude of this new generation—newly inclusive of Jews and Catholics (Steinberg 1974) and women (Lipset and Ladd 1979), and conditioned by the research ethos of their graduate education—came to dominate their campus cultures and escalated the trend of research university mimicry that has defined the last half century of American higher education (Jencks and Riesman 1968).

The most recent generation—the new hires of the late 1980s and 1990s—are the subjects of this volume. They have penetrated higher education throughout the system but often have been confronted with a significantly more limited opportunity structure. What have we learned about them? And how have we learned it?

Scope of Inquiry

In the following chapters we describe the methods we employed to identify the new generation cohort and the more senior cohort and the analytical procedures used to make these comparisons. Following a description of the basic contours of the new generation (their size and institutional venues), we turn successively to four multifaceted dimensions of the academic profession for which intergroup comparisons were drawn:

- Demographic and background characteristics, including gender, race/ethnicity, citizenship, socioeconomic background, and marital status.
- Career characteristics, spanning graduate school experience, previous employment history (sector and type of responsibility), source of highest degree, type of current appointment (tenurable or off-track), and job satisfaction.
- Work characteristics, including percentage of time spent in teaching, research, and service (both actual time spent and preferred allocations); teaching load; instructional methods employed; office hours and informal contact with students; involvement in research, publication, and grant preparation; and concurrent employment (that is, outside work).

- Attitudes and values, covering attitudes about faculty roles and rewards and levels of satisfaction with various facets of their academic careers, including two measures of their overall satisfaction.

Throughout the text, comparisons are undertaken with appropriate controls that permit breakouts by gender, by institutional type, and by academic program area, in order to permit finer understandings of the respondents' backgrounds and careers. Finally, drawing on these data, we present our conclusions, suggest implications for the future of higher education, and offer guidance for the effective management and nurturance of this enormously important national resource—the American faculty.

Identifying the New Academic Generation

Crucial to our analyses throughout this book are the methods by which we identified the new and senior cohorts of faculty. Based on the variables included in the NSOPF-93 survey instrument (see Appendix C), we selected four criteria to define membership in the subgroup of new-generation academics:

1. Academic status: having faculty status.
2. Type of appointment: full-time as distinguished from part-time.
3. Principal activity: identified by the respondent as teaching, research, or administration (in the latter case, at the level of program director, department chair, or academic dean) during fall 1992 (the academic term during which the NSOPF survey was in the field).
4. Duration of faculty experience: seven years or less in a full-time faculty position (including current appointment and any previous academic employment).

These decision rules underpin our entire analysis, for we have purposely excluded two significant populations of faculty members from our purview.

First, current part-time faculty members, as noted, were excluded. This meant bypassing a very sizable and very important segment of the contemporary faculty.[1] However, the thrust of our inquiry has focused on the changing characteristics of the "regular" full-time faculty—the core faculty, as we think of them—and accordingly the part-timers, despite their burgeoning presence in the conduct of postsecondary education, were not included.

Second, we excluded full-time employees in higher education who had some status as "faculty or instructional staff" but who did not satisfy our criteria as outlined. Our selection process yielded 514,976 individuals, or fewer "cases" than the National Center for Education Statistics (NCES)

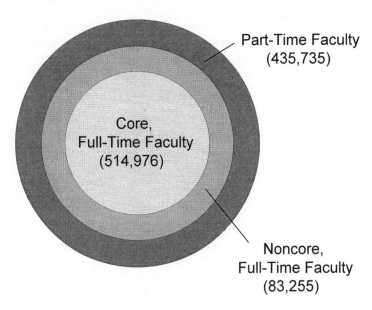

Part-Time Faculty
(435,735)

Core,
Full-Time Faculty
(514,976)

Noncore,
Full-Time Faculty
(83,255)

FIGURE 1. Faculty categories

national estimate of full-timers. What should we make of these non-core, full-time faculty members, who account for almost one in seven (13.9 percent) of the full-time faculty as reckoned by NCES? Essentially, they were excluded because we chose to limit our analysis to "core," full-time faculty members. Our procedure accordingly excludes some individuals who may have faculty status on their respective campuses but whose principal (or exclusive) responsibilities differ from those of teaching faculty. Who are they? They include on some campuses, for example, librarians, counselors, student services personnel, and other nonteaching professionals whose faculty status may be conferred by a collective bargaining agreement or by other campus policies.[2] Our decision to exclude them in no way disparages their importance, but again reflects our decision to concentrate on the core faculty. Figure 1 depicts the balance among these faculty groups.

The Seven-Year Sort

Beyond the exclusion of those two categories of personnel, a third decision was basic to our examination: our strategy to separate out for analytical purposes faculty whose experience exceeded our seven-year limitation. That is, faculty members were disqualified from our new-entry cohort if they already had accumulated more than seven years of full-time teaching experience at one or more higher education institutions. In this fashion we eliminated persons who had eight or more years of full-time teaching in higher education even though they may have been relatively new (even brand new) to their current institution. Conversely, we included in the new-entry cohort persons who may have been impressively senior in some respects; such "new" faculty might include, for instance, a retired diplomat who is appointed to a full professorship or a senior research scientist moving from a corporate or governmental laboratory to the academy. But if they had taught in higher education for fewer than seven years on a full-time basis, they were judged for our purposes to be "new" in terms of their academic experience and socialization into the profession.

As a cutoff point, seven years—or any other number, for that matter—is an arbitrary choice. But we reasoned that persons hired as recently as 1986 were, as of 1992, still relatively young in their careers and, further, that use of a cutoff lower than seven years would unduly constrict the size of the new-entry cohort. Conversely, we felt that use of a value of more than seven years would, for analytical purposes, undesirably increase the proportion of that cohort that was becoming well established, already beginning to attain promotions and tenure—in a word, encroaching upon midcareer. Thus seven years seemed to us a better breakpoint than any other.

A similar set of criteria was used to define an appropriate comparison group of senior faculty: having faculty status, holding a full-time appointment, and having teaching, research, or administration (at the level of program director, department chair, or academic dean) as one's principal activity. There was one difference: in order for a faculty member to attain membership in the senior cohort, the number of his or her cumulative years in full-time faculty positions, including current and previous positions, needed to be greater than seven. And so our inquiry compared faculty cohorts whose basic status was essentially the same except for seniority in the profession (and the perquisites "appertaining thereto").

Seven years is, of course, a readily recognizable career marker in the academy, for it is the traditional length of a probationary period after which, in the "pure" academic personnel system, a faculty member is either "up or out." (The applicable professional standard, formulated long ago by the AAUP, called for a tenure decision to be made in the sixth year; in the event of a negative decision, a seventh year was provided as a "terminal year" [American Association of University Professors 1995].) We arrived at our seven-year sort independently of the normative probationary period, but it is not purely happenstance that our best sense of when a particular stage of career maturity is reached coincides with the AAUP-prescribed seven-year norm.[3]

Because the method we used to demarcate the new and senior cohorts is so central to our analysis and interpretation, a further word may be useful to clarify why we did not rely simply on chronological age, or perhaps alternatively on *total* years of teaching experience (rather than just full-time teaching experience), as the variable to delineate the two cohorts. We chose full-time teaching experience because to our way of thinking that measure comes closest to capturing the richly textured process of becoming integrated or socialized into the profession (or, to use an old-fashioned concept, admitted into the guild).

Chronological age speaks to one's entire life experiences, but, as we have suggested, a person more senior in "life experience" who is nevertheless a relative neophyte in the distinctive academic milieu needs time to adapt to new surroundings, to form work patterns, and to develop job-related attitudes. Eight or more years "in the saddle," we contend, is an adequate formative period—if one still short of achieving grizzled veteranhood.

Similar reasoning has led us to discount part-time teaching experience, albeit not without misgivings. Our decision rests on an assumption that the substantial majority of part-timers are not as intensively absorbed into academic careers as persons for whom postsecondary teaching and scholarship define their exclusive or predominant professional endeavors. One test of our logic is the clear evidence that only a small fraction of part-time faculty members seeks full-time academic appointments. This finding is at odds with the common image of part-time faculty members (for instance, cabbies with Ph.D.'s in English literature) as would-be academic careerists who are frustrated by their inability to find full-time academic work in an unrelentingly harsh academic labor market. There are, to be sure, many such able persons who have been frozen out of the academic marketplace, many of whom, having turned to other pursuits, no longer teach even part time (and accordingly no longer show up in surveys of part-time faculty as aspirants to full-time academic appointments). But decades of surveys (Tuckman 1978; Tuckman and Pickerill 1988; Gappa and Leslie 1993) have consistently shown that the substantial majority of part-timers do not aspire to full-time appointments. Thus to count part-time teaching experience for present purposes, given the wide variation of such experiences in both intention and intensity, would in many instances distort the construct of being a core faculty member.

In summary, by applying these three decision rules—excluding part-time faculty, excluding noncore full-timers, and sorting by seven or fewer years of full-time teaching—the universe of potential subjects for analysis has been trimmed appreciably in order to enable us to focus on the vital heart of the academic profession. The segmentation of the core faculty into two cohorts has enabled us to isolate the new generation and to understand in what ways and to what extent they diverge from their "elders," and thereby the extent to which they bring to their tasks different capabilities and priorities. It is in those discontinuities (as well as in the continuities) that we will find important clues to the future of the profession of professors and, indeed, the future of the American academy.

The 1993 National Study of Postsecondary Faculty

A brief description of the NSOPF-93 is necessary to establish the nature of the data base upon which we relied. The NSOPF-93 survey was conducted in 1992–93. It represented a substantial expansion over the first NSOPF cycle, which had been conducted in 1987–88. NSOPF-88 had surveyed 480 colleges and universities, about 11,000 faculty members, and another 3,000 academic department chairs. NSOPF-93 was much more ambitious; this expansion of scope was possible because it was more generously funded than its predecessor.[4] The 1992–93 survey was distributed to 974 colleges and universities (all nonproprietary) and 31,354 faculty members. Ultimately, 817 institutions (83.9 percent) participated. Of the 31,354 faculty surveyed, 1,590 individuals were found to be ineligible; of the 29,764 eligible faculty, 25,780—a remarkable 86.6 percent—provided usable responses. A sample so large, amplified by the weighting techniques employed by the National Opinion Research Center and NCES, has yielded numbers (cells) sufficiently large to permit comparisons along the dimensions identified earlier.[5] The NCES's initial report, *Faculty and Instructional Staff: Who Are They and What Do They Do?*, appeared in October 1994; it provides basic demographic data and describes the project's data-gathering and analysis methods (National Center for Education Statistics 1994).

Data Analysis Procedures

Data from NSOPF-93 were analyzed using SPSS-PC+. Once the comparison groups had been determined, frequency distributions were generated for variables taken directly from the survey and for derived variables.

Imputation variables were considered when frequency counts were below a reasonable level. To correct for oversampling of certain underrepresented populations and for nonresponses, the sample was weighted by the NCES to produce estimates of the total faculty population. For our analysis, only weighted estimates are reported.

For each comparison group, simple frequencies (for categorical variables) or means (for continuous variables), or occasionally medians, were computed. Then cross-tabulations or subgroup means were calculated. In most cases, all bivariate relationships were recalculated to highlight the effects of institutional type, program area, gender, and, occasionally, age—especially when these factors are known from previous research to have substantial effects or correlations with the focal variable.

THREE

DEMOGRAPHIC CONTOURS OF THE NEW ACADEMIC GENERATION

The new generation of American academics is strikingly different from their more established senior colleagues. The contrast between the two cohorts is especially evident in several key demographic categories: race/ethnicity, nativity, and especially gender. Another important difference is seen in the greater infusion of new faculty, compared with faculty veterans, into fields outside the liberal arts.

To probe the differences between the two cohorts, our profile of new entrants to the academic profession is divided into two sections. The first discusses the size of the cohort and their distribution throughout their institutional and academic field venues. The second section presents basic demographic data describing them. In each case, their characteristics are compared with those of their senior colleagues.

The New-Faculty Cohort: Its Size and Venues

The new-entrant cohort is much larger than might be expected, as explained later in this section. The distribution of its members differs in important ways from that of their senior colleagues both by type of institution and by academic field.

Size of the Cohort

Applying our selection criteria (as detailed in Chapter 2), we find that the new academic generation numbers 172,319 full-time core faculty. This compares with 342,657 full-time faculty in the senior cohort or almost precisely twice as many as in the new-entry faculty. Put another way, these new entrants constitute fully one-third (33.5 percent) of the 514,976 total full-time core faculty and instructional staff employed by colleges and universities.[1]

Thus, as depicted in Figure 2, a very considerable infusion of new blood is apparent. This will strike some observers as surprising, for the recent past is widely perceived to have been a time of stasis rather than dynamism in the academic marketplace; it has been commonplace to think of higher education as being gripped by market conditions that have forestalled new entries in significant numbers. The facts, however, reveal a steady stream,

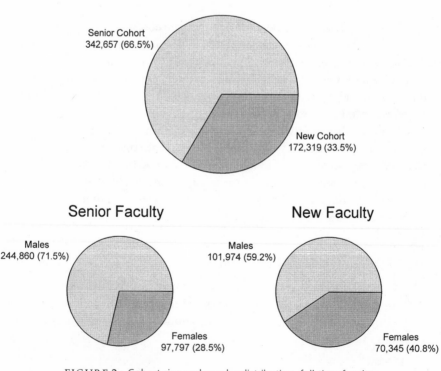

FIGURE 2. Cohort size and gender distribution, full-time faculty

no mere trickle, of new faces, amounting cumulatively to a very sizable contingent of faculty members.[2]

It is important to note, additionally, that the total of 172,319 faculty making up the new cohort in fact substantially undercounts the number of faculty members who were actually appointed to full-time faculty positions during the seven-year period 1986–92 upon which we have focused our attention. This is because our analysis necessarily is based on a snapshot of the faculty in place during the fall 1992 term, when the NSOPF survey was in the field; this approach thereby excludes the numerous persons who had been hired at some point during the seven-year "window" but who had exited, voluntarily or otherwise, by the fall of 1992. We cannot measure the incidences of tenure denials and nonrenewals of term appointments (pertaining to those persons who failed to latch onto a full-time faculty position at another institution) or of voluntary departures (including persons who were counseled out or who, for whatever other reason, chose to leave academe). However, we estimate that they numbered in the tens of thousands. Accordingly, the actual number of new faces who entered the full-time ranks indicates even more academic labor market activity—that is, more new hires in any given year—than the 172,319 figure would suggest.

Institutional Venues

It is instructive to look at the distribution of these new entrants among types of institutions and to compare their institutional settings to those of the senior cohort.[3]

As of 1969, nearly half (47 percent) of all full-time faculty were employed at universities, about two-fifths (39 percent) at other four-year colleges, and about 15 percent at two-year community colleges. But major shifts within higher education were under way; a decade later the proportion of full-time faculty at universities had declined to one-third while the two-year community colleges' share had jumped to one-quarter and the proportion at four-year colleges (other than universities) had swollen to nearly half (Trow 1975; Stadtman 1980). In more recent years, though precise comparisons are elusive because institutional categories shift, it appears that the relationship among institutional types in terms of the number of full-time faculty has stabilized.

In turning to the infusion of new hires as seen in our analysis of the 1993 NSOPF, we find that a very large proportion of the more recent new hires—the new cohort in our study—are located in the doctorate-granting institutions; in fact, almost half of the new entrants (over 77,000 or 44.8 percent of the total) are found in these universities (Table 1*). Note that the Carnegie scheme, as adopted largely by the National Center for Education Statistics (NCES) for the NSOPF surveys, distinguishes between two types of doctorate-granting institutions: Carnegie "research universities" account for 29.5 percent of all new-entry faculty members and those doctorate-granting institutions that are not classified as "research universities" employ another 15.3 percent. Comprehensive (that is, master's-granting) universities account for an additional 23.2 percent, liberal arts colleges for only 7.4 percent, and public two-year colleges for 19.3 percent.

This intake of new faculty in such large numbers is manifest across all types of institutions. In fact, expressed as a proportion of all faculty in a given institutional sector, in no type of institution do the new-entry faculty compose less than 30 percent of the core faculty. Particularly intriguing is the strong presence of a new cohort in the research universities; there the newcomers account for 35.9 percent of the existing full-time faculty, including a remarkable 41.4 percent at the private research universities—creating a veritable sea of new faces. This situation leads to an interesting phenomenon. The *proportion* of research university faculty has been declining as the other sectors have grown more rapidly in enrollments and faculty. But the turnover rate at the research universities has been quite high, resulting in a regenerated faculty that is very different from the top-heavy distribution characteristic of research university faculty throughout the 1980s. Note, too, that new members consistently constitute larger proportions of the faculty at the private institutions compared with their public counterparts. Thus at research universities the very high proportion of new-cohort faculty at the private institutions (41.4 percent) is sub-

---

*The scheme we use for numbering tables is as follows: Abbreviated tables, located in the text, are numbered 1–39. All other tables amplify the basic text tables; they are located in Appendix A and are preceded by an A. Thus text Table 2 reports the distribution of faculty members by aggregated academic program areas, shown for each cohort, while appendix Table A-2 further breaks out that distribution by specific program areas. Text Table 4 shows the distribution of academic rank by faculty cohort while appendix Table A-4 further breaks out rank by several key variables, namely gender, institutional type, and academic program area.

Occasionally an appendix table is followed by a further refinement of that table in order to focus attention on one aspect of particular interest. Thus for example Table A-4, which includes a breakout of rank by gender, is followed by Table A-4A, which focuses explicitly on one academic rank (full professor) within a single faculty cohort (the new faculty). Several special-focus tables that cover a single topic are labeled sequentially, for example A-22A through A-22C or A-29A through A-29D.

All tables are derived from U.S. Department of Education, National Center for Education Statistics, 1993 National Study of Postsecondary Faculty, "Faculty Survey."

Table 1 ⇒+ Institutional Type

	All faculty		New faculty		New faculty as percent of all faculty	Senior faculty		Senior faculty as percent of all faculty
	Number	Percent	Number	Percent		Number	Percent	
All institutions	514,976	100.0	172,319	100.0	33.5	342,657	100.0	66.5
All research universities	141,593	27.5	50,866	29.5	35.9	90,727	26.5	64.1
Public	108,309	21.0	37,085	21.5	34.2	71,224	20.8	65.8
Private	33,284	6.5	13,782	8.0	41.4	19,502	5.7	58.6
All other doctorate-granting institutions[a]	76,207	14.8	26,361	15.3	34.6	49,845	14.6	65.4
Public	50,581	9.8	17,028	9.9	33.7	33,553	9.8	66.3
Private	25,626	5.0	9,333	5.4	36.4	16,293	4.8	63.6
All comprehensive institutions	131,418	25.6	39,929	23.2	30.4	91,490	26.7	69.6
Public	93,877	18.2	28,017	16.3	29.8	65,860	19.2	70.2
Private	37,541	7.3	11,912	6.9	31.7	25,630	7.5	68.3
Private liberal arts institutions	37,426	7.3	12,662	7.4	33.8	24,764	7.2	66.2
Public two-year institutions	103,529	20.1	33,283	19.3	32.1	70,246	20.5	67.9
All other institutions[b]	24,803	4.8	9,217	5.4	37.2	15,586	4.5	62.8

Note: Details may not add to total because of rounding.
a. Includes medical schools.
b. Includes public liberal arts, private two-year, and other specialized institutions except medical schools.

stantially higher than their presence at public research universities (34.2 percent). And at the private doctoral and comprehensive institutions, the percentage of new faculty is higher, although only marginally, than that at their public counterparts.[4]

The overall lesson is clear: The new faculty are everywhere. And in substantial numbers.

Program Area

The liberal arts base of the academy is shrinking—and the attrition continues. Between 1969 and 1976, the proportion of students enrolled in professional and occupational majors soared dramatically from 38 percent to 58 percent, while the proportions majoring in the humanities and the physical sciences plummeted by about half: from 9 to 5 percent in the former and from 7 to 4 percent in the latter. During this same period, while the faculty distribution, despite shifting student interests, remained relatively stable among the broadly defined fields, one could already discern an incipient shift toward the professions and away from the liberal arts core: the proportion of faculty in the professions rose gradually from about one-third to three-eighths while their numbers in the liberal arts eased from two-thirds to three-fifths (Stadtman 1980).

That trend has accelerated. Viewed by program area (Table 2), the *majority* of the new generation of faculty members have academic homes *outside the traditional liberal arts*.[5] That is to say, the humanities and social and natural sciences *together* account for less than half (only 44.0 percent) of the new entrants (rising to 49.1 percent when fine arts faculty are included.)[6] Among the liberal arts faculty members, the natural scientists compose the largest single subgroup in both cohorts, accounting for 20.0 percent of all the new-entry faculty (or 40.8 percent of all new liberal arts faculty). The humanists (13.0 percent), social scientists (11.0 percent), and fine arts faculty (5.1 percent) constitute the balance of the new liberal arts faculty. The significant development here is the perceptible decline in the liberal arts' share of new appointments.

By way of contrast, the liberal arts faculty (including the fine arts) constitute well over half (55.1 percent) of the senior cohort. This six-point decline in "market share" reflects an ongoing trend and speaks to the hastening dilution of the academy's traditional liberal arts curriculum core. It is also noteworthy that the diminution of the liberal arts spreads across all four broad categories, with the biggest dropoff—from 15.8 to 13.0 percent— evident among the humanists.[7]

Table 2 ⇌ Academic Program Area

	All faculty		New faculty		New faculty as percent of all faculty	Senior faculty		Senior faculty as percent of all faculty
	Number	Percent	Number[a]	Percent		Number[a]	Percent	
All program areas	503,141	100.0	166,045	100.0	33.0	337,096	100.0	67.0
Professions	165,382	32.9	59,966	36.1	36.3	105,416	31.3	63.7
Business	39,442	7.8	13,293	8.0	33.7	26,149	7.8	66.3
Education	35,152	7.0	11,326	6.8	32.2	23,826	7.1	67.8
Engineering	25,116	5.0	9,278	5.6	36.9	15,838	4.7	63.1
Health sciences	65,673	13.1	26,069	15.7	39.7	39,604	11.8	60.3
Liberal arts and sciences	266,944	53.1	81,297	49.0	30.5	185,647	55.1	69.5
Fine arts	31,045	6.2	8,394	5.1	27.0	22,651	6.7	73.0
Humanities	74,779	14.9	21,504	13.0	28.8	53,275	15.8	71.2
Natural sciences	103,382	20.6	33,141	20.0	32.1	70,241	20.8	67.9
Social sciences	57,738	11.5	18,258	11.0	31.6	39,480	11.7	68.4
All other program areas	70,815	14.1	24,782	14.9	35.0	46,033	13.7	65.0

Note: Details may not add to total because of rounding.
a. Missing: 6,274 (3.6 percent) new faculty and 5,561 (1.6 percent) senior faculty.

A finer breakout by academic fields reveals further variations (see Table A-2).[8] "Winners" and "losers" become more visible. Among the former, for instance, are faculty in communications, in the health fields (first professional degree programs, nursing, and "other health sciences"), and in computer science. All of the humanities fields have suffered setbacks, history most emphatically. A significant shift is taking place among the natural sciences: the number of biological scientists swelled (from 6.7 to 7.9 percent) while the number of their colleagues in the physical sciences shrank proportionately. Among engineering faculty, chemical engineers have surged in number—the new-cohort chemical engineers actually outnumber their senior colleagues—while civil and mechanical engineers have lost some ground. Business faculty, whose numbers had expanded sharply through the 1970s and into the 1980s, stabilized and even receded as enrollments in undergraduate and master's-level business programs dropped off sharply (Schuster 1994).

Demographics and Background

Who are the new academic generation in demographic terms and what do we know of their social backgrounds? How do they compare to their more seasoned colleagues? Based on NSOPF-93 data, we are able to examine the variables of age, rank, gender, race/ethnicity, national origin (citizenship), socioeconomic status (parents' education), and marital status. These characteristics enable us to see in sharper relief just how distinctive this new generation is.

Age

The American faculty has been graying over the past quarter century. In 1969 nearly one-third (30 percent) were under 35, in contrast to 10 percent by 1988 (Blackburn and Lawrence, 1995, 33).

Among all faculty in 1993 (the two cohorts combined), 48 is the mean and median; four of every nine faculty members are 50 or older and one in eight is 60 or older. The cohort of new entrants is, naturally, younger than their more experienced counterparts (Table 3). Their mean age is 42 and

Table 3 ⟫ Age

	Mean	Median	Mode
All faculty	48	48	51
New faculty	42	40	37
Senior faculty	51	51	51

their median age is 40. Almost half (about 45 percent) are between 35 and 44. New they may be, but they are not, on average, a notably youthful lot. In comparison, the senior cohort averages 51 years of age (mean, median, and mode). These measures vary little by institutional type or program area.

The new-entry women (mean age 41.8) tend to be slightly younger than their male counterparts (mean age 42.3), and the senior-cohort women on average are several years younger than their senior male colleagues (49.3 versus 52.0). (See Table A-3 for further details, including breakouts by five-year age bands.)[9] The large number of new appointees in the doctorate-granting institutions tend to be somewhat younger than those recently appointed in other categories of institutions; the mean age of new-entry faculty in those venues is 41.3 (compared, for instance, with 43.6 at the community colleges). Viewed by program area, the new social scientists tend to be younger (mean age 40.6) than their peers in other fields.

Viewed through another lens, the difference in age *between* cohorts is slightly greater for the social scientists (about an eleven-year gap) than among the other groups. Among the senior faculty, there are notably fewer humanists younger than 45: 16.0 percent compared with a range of 21.7–26.0 percent in the other areas.

Rank

American faculty over the past quarter century have "seniorized" not only in age but also in academic rank (Bowen and Schuster 1986), with 54.1 percent of all full-time faculty having attained the senior rank of either full or associate professor by 1992 (National Center for Education Statistics 1995) compared with only 42.3 percent in 1969 (Bayer 1973).

The new generation naturally differs from the senior cohort in their attainment of the higher academic ranks. About two-fifths (42.6 percent) of the new entrants are at the assistant professor level (which is also the modal rank) (Table 4). One-fifth of the new entrants hold the rank of

Table 4 ⤳ Academic Rank

	Number	Percent	Academic rank						
			Professor	Associate professor	Assistant professor	Instructor	Lecturer	Other	Not applicable
All faculty	514,976	100.0	32.1	24.0	23.1	13.2	2.0	2.6	3.0
New faculty	172,319	100.0	11.9	15.0	42.6	20.1	3.2	4.8	2.4
Senior faculty	342,657	100.0	42.3	28.5	13.3	9.8	1.5	1.5	3.2

Note: Details may not add to total because of rounding.

instructor; of these, most are at the community colleges (Table A-4). At the higher range, over a quarter of the new cohort has already attained either the rank of associate professor (15.0 percent) or even full professor (11.9 percent).

There is a big and important difference between the two cohorts in the proportion appointed to the three traditional "ladder" ranks (assistant, associate, and full professor): only 69.5 percent of the new cohort hold such appointments compared with 84.1 percent of the senior cohort—a highly significant dropoff. (Some of the difference is attributed to the substantial number of new-entry community college faculty appointed to the rank of instructor [55.0 percent] compared with only 33.4 percent holding the rank of instructor among the community colleges' senior faculty cohort.)[10] Note, too, that apart from the special case of the community colleges, the percentage of senior faculty at research, doctoral, comprehensive, and liberal arts colleges who hold a rank other than professor, associate professor, or assistant professor ranges narrowly between 5.5 and 8.3 percent. This contrasts sharply with the comparable percentages among their new-cohort colleagues, which fall between 21.0 and 23.7 percent, except at the doctoral institutions, where the percentage is 16.7. The widespread phenomenon of these appointments throughout the new cohort of faculty suggests a resourcefulness in creating different types of ranks, very likely intended to minimize the number of tenurable appointments. (For corroborative evidence, see also Table 21 on tenure.)

The distribution of the two highest ranks by gender is strikingly uneven. Thus the proportion of men in the new cohort who have attained the rank of full professor (16.6 percent) is more than three times that among women (5.2 percent). Appointments at the associate professor level also have gone disproportionately to men, whereas at the assistant professor level the proportion of each cohort is essentially the same for both genders. This leaves as a partial explanation for the shortfall of women in the higher ranks the phenomenon of significantly larger percentages of new-cohort women who are appointed as instructors or lecturers. Indeed, almost twice as many of the new-cohort women (31.1 percent) as their male counterparts (17.9 percent) are instructors or lecturers. (Remember, these are all full-time appointments.) Among the senior-cohort faculty, comparable differences separating men and women in the distribution by rank are manifest, but, at least for the rank of full professor, the men's greater seniority surely has some explanatory power.

Table A-4A shows that those new faculty members who have already reached the topmost rank, as full professors, are disproportionately concentrated (well over half) in professional fields and to a lesser degree in the natural sciences. In these faculty clusters many faculty would seem to have been hired on at an advanced rank, presumably, in the case of the former, having had nonacademic careers as professionals (e.g., lawyers, public officials) or, in the case of the latter, as seasoned scientists with postdoctoral experiences. Most striking is the fact that among full professors, male new-cohort faculty outnumber their female counterparts by nearly five to one. This finding might be explained in part by the disproportionate number of new-cohort women in the liberal arts colleges, which are generally quite small institutions, and in the community colleges, where traditional academic ranks sometimes do not exist (see Table A-5 and note 10). Even so, the differences in the rate at which recently hired men and women reach the top academic rung on the ladder must raise questions about continuing gender inequities, despite the recent hiring of large numbers of women.

It is noteworthy, too, that almost two-thirds (65.1 percent) of these new-to-academe full professors are at least 50 years of age. About one in five is 60 or older.

Considerable differences are evident among the academic fields regarding the proportion of new-entry faculty who are appointed to one of the top three ladder ranks (excluding instructors for present purposes). The highest percentage is for the social scientists (79.1 percent) with the natural scientists close behind (76.2 percent). By contrast, only 62.1 percent of the humanists hold those ranks, probably reflecting a considerable number of non–tenure track appointments for foreign language and writing specialists.

Gender

Since 1969, women have slowly and steadily increased their overall presence in the academy from about 20 percent to just over 30 percent by the late 1980s (Gappa and Uehling 1979; Dwyer, Flynn, and Inman 1991). Among the most dramatic and portentous findings derived from the NSOPF-93 survey is the remarkable surge in the proportion of academic appointments—across all institutional types and program areas—that have gone to women in recent years. Women have made remarkable gains in obtaining faculty positions; they constitute nearly 40.8 percent of the new generation of faculty (Table 5). This contrasts sharply with the much less extensive presence of women (28.5 percent) among the more experienced faculty cohort. Indeed, so many women have entered the academic work force during this relatively brief period that the new cohort of women now constitutes 41.8 percent of all full-time women faculty. In other

Table 5 ⇒ Gender

	Male	Female	New females as percent of all females
All faculty	67.4	32.7	
New faculty	59.2	40.8	41.8
Senior faculty	71.5	28.5	

Note: Details may not add to total because of rounding.

words, two of every five women in the core faculty entered into full-time faculty work during this recent seven-year interval.

Analyzed by institutional type (Table A-5), new-entry women are found to outnumber the newly hired men both at liberal arts colleges (50.7 percent) and at community colleges (53.2 percent). Although women account for only one-third of the new hires at doctorate-granting universities (research and doctoral universities combined), the data nonetheless establish impressive progress: at those institutions the ratio of females to males among new entrants is 1:2 in contrast to 1:4 among the senior faculty cohort in the research universities and 1:3 at the other doctorate-granting institutions. In fact, so many women have been hired recently at the research universities that, in consequence, close to half of their full-time women faculty (47.9 percent) belong to the new-entry cohort. At the comprehensive (master's-granting) institutions, the women account for 43.7 percent of the new cohort, in stark contrast to 29.5 percent among the senior faculty. In the catchall category of "other institutions," which consists largely of professional programs, women are not well represented (only 25.5 percent of the senior cohort); however, women have been hired at a greater rate in recent years, such that almost half (46.1 percent) of all women faculty in the category of "other institutions" are members of the new cohort.

An interesting public-private comparison is evident. Whereas the public and private research universities and comprehensive institutions appear to be hiring women and men, in roughly equal numbers, among the other doctoral institutions nearly 38 percent of the new cohort is female at the public campuses but only 24 percent at the private campuses. This may reflect relatively more intense political pressure on public doctoral institutions to diversify their faculty.

Viewed by program area, we find that women have made substantial advances in virtually all fields (Table A-5A). Among the new-entry cohort, women obtained a clear majority of all appointments in education

(64.4 percent), law (54.8 percent), the humanities (53.9 percent), and the health sciences (51.9 percent). They fared least well in engineering, but even in that historically male enclave the proportion of women among new entrants (12.0 percent) contrasts strikingly with the proportion of women among the more experienced engineering faculty (a mere 1.6 percent).[11] In every category except agriculture/home economics the proportion of new-entry women, compared with their senior counterparts, is higher; indeed, their proportion nearly doubled in the social sciences and fine arts and expanded substantially in the humanities and natural sciences, as well as in the sizable residual category, "all other programs."

Expressed another way, the number of new-entry women is so sizable that they now constitute

- 74 percent of all women faculty in engineering
- 45 percent of all women faculty in social sciences
- 45 percent of all women faculty in natural sciences
- 42 percent of all women faculty in fine arts
- 40 percent of all women faculty in education
- 38 percent of all women faculty in humanities
- 36 percent of all women faculty in business

Proportions aside, the largest actual numbers of new-generation women are found in the health-related fields (constituting 19.2 percent of all women new hires in all fields). Women are least numerous in engineering (1.6 percent of all newly hired women), occupational programs (1.4 percent), and agriculture/home economics (1.2 percent).

This is not to suggest that equity for women has been achieved, as further analyses (including Tables A-21 and A-21A) suggest. However, the degree of progress made by faculty women in recent years is indisputably impressive (for contrast, see Farley 1982).

Table 6 ⚌ Race/Ethnicity

			Race/ethnicity				
	Number	Percent	American Indian / Alaskan Native	Asian / Pacific Islander	Black not Hispanic	Hispanic	White not Hispanic
All faculty	514,976	100.0	0.5	5.5	4.9	2.5	86.6
New faculty	172,319	100.0	0.5	7.7	5.7	3.1	83.1
Senior faculty	342,657	100.0	0.4	4.4	4.6	2.3	88.3

Note: Details may not add to total because of rounding.

Race/Ethnicity

Racial/ethnic minority representation in the American professoriate hovered during the 1970s at around 6–7 percent (Lipset and Ladd 1979; Exum 1983), increasing to about 10 percent by 1987 (National Center for Education Statistics 1990). Against this backdrop, the new entrants are considerably more diverse in terms of race and ethnicity than their predecessors (Table 6 and Figure 3). The growth in the number and proportion of non-Caucasian faculty, although less dramatic than that of female faculty, is nonetheless significant, rising steeply from 11.7 percent minority faculty among the senior cohort to 17.0 percent among the new entrants. Whites, at 83.1 percent, still compose by far the largest share of new faculty hires, though their proportion is substantially less than it is among the senior generation (88.3 percent).

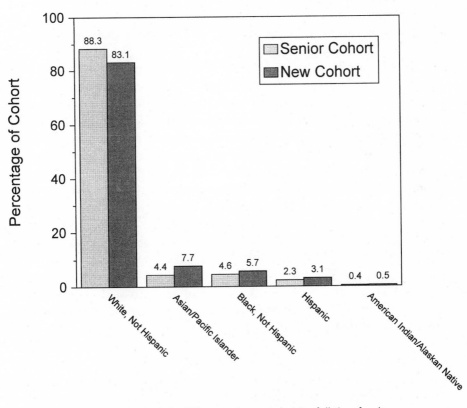

FIGURE 3. Cohort differences in race/ethnicity, full-time faculty

Although the aggregated categories reported here obscure important differences within racial groupings, faculty of color have increased their proportion in all four broadly defined minority categories.[12] Expressed another way, the new cohort accounts for 42.1 percent of all faculty of color (roughly 29,000 of the total of 69,000 faculty of color). The biggest change is found among Asian / Pacific Islander faculty, who account for a 3.3 percent greater share among new hires than among their senior counterparts, rising from 4.4 to 7.7 percent. In fact, the new-entry Asian / Pacific Islander faculty make up almost half (45.6 percent) of the total newly hired faculty of color.[13]

In controlling for gender (Table A-6), we find that Asian / Pacific Islander men are the new generation's biggest gainers, almost doubling from 4.8 percent among all senior men to 9.3 percent of the new-entry cohort of men. Note, too, that among the racial minority groups, women outnumber men among recently hired African American / Black faculty (roughly 5,100 to 4,700). But males constitute the majority in all the other new-entry groups. Even so, in all five racial groups, new-entry women have markedly improved their share compared with their proportion among their senior counterparts.

Female faculty of color, who accounted for 31.1 percent of all faculty of color in the senior cohort, have recently fared better; that is, women constitute 38.4 percent of all new-entry faculty of color. (Indeed, among non-Asian faculty of color, the proportion of women jumped from 36.6 percent of senior faculty of color to nearly half [47.4 percent] of the new faculty of color.) Viewed differently, the number of female faculty of color in the new cohort very nearly equals the number of such faculty in the senior cohort (about 11,200 versus 12,400). In fact, the new-entry cohorts of Asian / Pacific Islander and of Hispanic women actually outnumber their counterparts in the senior cohort. Meanwhile, the percentage of white women rose, too, from a little less than a quarter of the entire senior cohort (24.9 percent) to more than one-third (34.3 percent) of all the new hires.[14]

Viewing the distribution of faculty of color by institutional type (Table A-6), it is clear that gains have been made across all institutional types. At the doctorate-granting (research and doctoral) and comprehensive institutions, nearly one in five of the new cohort are faculty of color (between 18 and 19 percent at each). On the doctorate-granting campuses, the faculty of color nearly doubled in share from 10.4 percent of the senior cohort to 18.2 percent of the new faculty (18.2 percent at the research universities; 18.4 percent at the doctoral institutions). In fact, there are very nearly as many faculty of color on the doctorate-granting campuses in the new cohort (about 14,100) as in the senior cohort (about 14,600).

Perhaps the most striking datum at the research universities is that 11.5 percent of the entire new faculty cohort is Asian / Pacific Islander (almost doubling their proportion in the senior cohort). Less substantial but nonetheless significant gains are evident for minority faculty at the comprehensive and liberal arts institutions. In contrast, a much more modest increase in the proportion of faculty of color took place at the community colleges, edging upward from 13.7 in the senior cohort (highest among the five institutional types) to 15.0 percent of the new-entry faculty.

Examined by broad program areas, differences are less pronounced. In fact, the range is very narrow within the senior cohort (10.1–12.8 percent), although it widens somewhat among the new-entry faculty, from 14.6 percent of the social scientists to 17.9 percent of the natural scientists and among faculty in the professions. The gains are widespread; that is, the proportion of Asian / Pacific Islanders, African Americans / Blacks, and Hispanics increases from the senior to the new cohort in each of the five program groupings (with the single exception of African Americans / Blacks in the fine arts).

However, lest advocates of diversity rejoice prematurely, it should be made clear that disaggregating the broad program areas demonstrates a continuing skewed distribution of faculty of color. And that skewed distribution continues to reflect longstanding patterns of ghettoization of Black faculty in education and a few fields of the social sciences, concentration of Hispanic faculty in a few fields of the humanities and social sciences as well as education, and the proportionate overrepresentation of Asian faculty in the natural sciences, mathematics, and engineering (Gilford and Snyder 1977; National Research Council 1978, 1989). As seen in Table A-6A, although disproportionate concentrations continue, there is evidence of greater dispersion. For example, among Asian / Pacific Islander faculty, 27.3 percent of the senior cohort held appointments in engineering and mathematics, but for the new cohort the proportion in those two fields totaled only 20.9 percent. Patterns among Black and Hispanic faculty are not as distinct. It is noteworthy, however, that minority faculty appear to be gravitating in larger numbers toward teaching in first professional degree programs; those program areas rank second among new-cohort Hispanic and Asian / Pacific Islander faculty and fourth among Black faculty. The growing presence of minority faculty in business programs is also more evident.

In sum, the new-generation cohort is notably more diverse than their predecessors. This is manifest across all institutional types and program areas.

National Origin (Citizenship)

Reflecting the ascent of foreign-born professionals in the United States since the Immigration Reform Act of 1965 (Heller 1987; Bouvier and Simcox 1995; Davis 1997), a sharp rise is evident in the number of faculty members who are not native-born U.S. citizens: more than one in six new entrants (16.9 percent) compared with only one in nine (11.5 percent) among their senior colleagues (Table 7 and Figure 4).[15] When institutional type is factored in (Table A-7), we find that by far the largest influx of foreign-born faculty (including naturalized U.S. citizens and both permanent and temporary residents) has occurred at the research universities, amounting to a substantial and rapid increase. In fact, over one quarter (26.7 percent) of new entrants at these institutions are not U.S. natives compared with 17.0 percent among their senior counterparts. Thus at these institutions more than one in five new-cohort faculty (20.6 percent) have either permanent or temporary resident status—a far greater proportion than is found among faculty at other types of institutions. Their presence diminishes as one moves to institutions offering the baccalaureate degree and to the community colleges. Even so, the proportion of nonnatives is greater among new entrants in all institutional categories.

Males account for substantially more of this influx. When program area is taken into account, we find cohort-specific patterns: among the senior cohort, non-native-born faculty are fairly evenly distributed across academic fields, falling within a range of 11.9–14.4 percent of the faculty in each (with the exception of the fine arts). Among new entrants, however, a sharply

Table 7 ⇒ Citizenship

	Number	Percent	Citizenship			
			Native U.S. citizen	Naturalized U.S. citizen	Permanent resident	Temporary resident
All faculty	514,976	100.0	86.7	6.7	5.4	1.2
New faculty	172,319	100.0	83.1	5.3	8.8	2.8
Senior faculty	342,657	100.0	88.5	7.4	3.7	0.4

Note: Details may not add to total because of rounding.

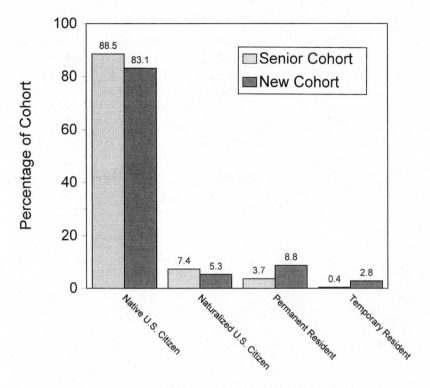

FIGURE 4. Cohort differences in citizenship, full-time faculty

increased presence of non-native-born faculty is evident among natural scientists in particular; in fact, one in four (24.7 percent) new-entry natural
scientists is not native-born. For other faculty the percentage is much
lower—about 15 percent. (These figures exclude the fine arts faculty, who
are considerably more likely to be U.S.-born [94.9 percent of the senior cohort
and 88.6 percent of the new cohort], but there, too, the influx of faculty from
other nations is evident.)

    In considering country of origin, it is important to understand that nat-
uralized U.S. citizens and permanent residents may have immigrated to
the United States at an early age, resided here for a long time, or both, often
attenuating the cultural diversity they bring to their respective colleges and
universities. Nevertheless, the surge in diversity by place of birth is noteworthy.

    To what extent do the new faculty who are not born in the United States
come from countries of origin different from those of their senior colleagues?
The patterns are changing. Looking at country of birth (regardless of current citizenship), one finds that India and the United Kingdom are the two

leading sources in both cohorts (Table 7A).[16] Both China and Japan have sharply increased their representation; both are countries of origin for larger numbers of new faculty than for senior faculty. One indicator of volatility is seen among the temporary residents' countries of origin (Table 7C); only two countries (Canada and India) are among the top ten on both the new-faculty and senior-faculty lists. In other words, eight countries appear anew among the new temporary residents' countries of origin. (By way of contrast, only three countries emerge anew among the permanent residents' birthplaces [Table 7B].)

In order to examine further the phenomenon of the increasing presence of Asian / Pacific Islander faculty in the natural sciences, Table A-7A shows that they account for nearly 9 percent of all new-cohort faculty in

Table 7A ⇒ **Country of Birth: Ten Most Frequent Responses**

All faculty		New faculty		Senior faculty	
Country of birth	Number	Country of birth	Number	Country of birth	Number
India	8,307	India	3,633	India	4,674
United Kingdom	7,616	United Kingdom	3,158	United Kingdom	4,457
China	5,398	China	2,736	Canada	3,007
Canada	4,832	Canada	1,825	West Germany	2,790
West Germany	3,936	Japan	1,441	China	2,662
Japan	2,331	West Germany	1,146	Taiwan	1,123
Taiwan	2,164	Taiwan	1,041	Philippines	1,074
Iran	1,712	Greece	882	Czechoslovakia	1,014
Korea	1,472	Iran	822	Italy	926
Italy	1,425	Korea	711	Japan	889

Table 7B ⇒ **Country of Birth for Permanent Residents:**
Ten Most Frequent Responses

All faculty		New faculty		Senior faculty	
Country of birth	Number	Country of birth	Number	Country of birth	Number
United Kingdom	4,117	United Kingdom	2,323	India	1,992
India	3,684	India	1,692	United Kingdom	1,794
Canada	2,182	China	1,454	Canada	1,256
China	1,923	Canada	926	West Germany	1,013
West Germany	1,360	Japan	613	China	468
Japan	979	Greece	514	Iran	397
Iran	775	Taiwan	489	Japan	367
Taiwan	710	Iran	378	The Netherlands	360
The Netherlands	613	Lebanon	352	South Africa	315
Nigeria	419	West Germany	347	Australia / New Zealand	274

Table 7C ⇒ **Country of Birth for Temporary Residents: Ten Most Frequent Responses**

All faculty		New faculty		Senior faculty	
Country of birth	Number	Country of birth	Number	Country of birth	Number
China	666	China	658	India	277
India	560	Japan	512	United Kingdom	267
Japan	537	Australia / New Zealand	500	Rumania	90
Australia / New Zealand	500	Canada	284	Canada	87
Canada	371	India	284	Bangladesh	70
United Kingdom	296	France	225	Nigeria	60
France	225	Finland	155	Lebanon	55
Taiwan	180	Taiwan	154	Poland	52
West Germany	168	West Germany	148	Mexico	40
Finland	155	Korea	138	Singapore	34

mathematics (8.8 percent) and computer science (8.7 percent) and 6.3 percent of the new-cohort engineering faculty, but a far smaller proportion (2.7 and 3.4 percent, respectively) in the biological and physical sciences.

Socioeconomic Status (Parents' Education)

Historically, an academic career has always appealed to the children of the relatively well-to-do. Throughout the eighteenth and nineteenth centuries, compensation was so low that full-time academics were prototypically individuals "of independent means" (McCaughey 1974). Today's academics are still drawn from predominantly well-educated, middle class backgrounds. (For a glimpse into the exceptions, that is, academics from working class backgrounds, see Ryan and Sackrey 1984 and Tokarczyk and Fay 1993.) Whereas one-fourth of respondents in 1969 reported having working class parents, another fourth had fathers with baccalaureate degrees (twice the proportion in the general population) and yet another fourth had fathers with graduate school experience (some nine times the proportion in the general population) (Lipset and Ladd 1979). The new academic generation springs from even higher socioeconomic origins than did their senior colleagues, as defined by their fathers' educational level (Table 8). Only 19.8 percent of the new career entrants reported fathers with less than a high school education, in contrast to 28.5 percent of their more experienced colleagues whose fathers did not complete high school. A further indicator: 40.2 percent of new entrants' fathers had earned at least a bachelor's degree compared with 31.6 percent of the senior cohort's fathers.

Table 8 ⯈ Father's Educational Level

Father's Educational Level

	Number	Percent	Less than high school diploma	High school diploma	Some college	Associate degree	Bachelor's degree	Master's degree	Doctorate / professional degree	Other	Don't know
All faculty	514,976	100.0	25.6	24.8	11.6	2.0	14.9	8.0	11.5	0.9	0.7
New faculty	172,319	100.0	19.8	24.7	11.6	2.0	17.1	10.0	13.1	1.1	0.6
Senior faculty	342,657	100.0	28.5	24.8	11.6	2.0	13.9	7.0	10.7	0.7	0.8

Note: Details may not add to total because of rounding.

Table 9 ⯈ Mother's Educational Level

Mother's Educational Level

	Number	Percent	Less than high school diploma	High school diploma	Some college	Associate degree	Bachelor's degree	Master's degree	Doctorate / professional degree	Other	Don't know
All faculty	514,976	100.0	22.1	34.7	13.4	4.2	15.0	7.1	1.8	1.1	0.5
New faculty	172,319	100.0	18.2	34.7	12.7	4.5	16.7	9.1	2.3	1.4	0.4
Senior faculty	342,657	100.0	24.1	34.7	13.7	4.1	14.2	6.1	1.6	1.0	0.5

Note: Details may not add to total because of rounding.

When the variable of a faculty member's age is introduced (Table A-8), we find among both the new-entrant and senior cohorts that fathers' education decreases as the faculty members' age increases. This finding strongly suggests that cohort socioeconomic differences are largely attributable to differences in age. New career entrants are, naturally, proportionately younger, and their fathers' greater educational persistence reflects the general increase in educational attainment (and concomitant movement into the middle class) among their parents' generation during the post–World War II period. However, some intergroup differences remain even after controlling for age; this observation suggests that academic careers are increasingly attracting entrants from higher socioeconomic backgrounds. This trend may well be a function of modest levels of academic compensation vis-à-vis some other professions, a condition that would enable relatively affluent career-choosers to afford academic careers more readily than those who come from less affluent backgrounds.[17]

When gender is taken into account, socioeconomic differences between new and senior cohorts persist. This finding suggests that the higher proportion of women among new entrants does not account for the higher average socioeconomic status of the new entrants. Academic women have historically been drawn from higher socioeconomic strata than men (Finkelstein 1984), but those differences may now have disappeared: among the cohort of new women academics, about 40 percent of the fathers have earned at least a baccalaureate degree, compared with approximately 41 percent of the men's fathers. Comparing the pattern of education of faculty members' mothers to that of their fathers, one finds that about 10 percent more mothers had only a high school education and about 10 percent fewer had earned doctorates or professional degrees (Table 9). As with the fathers of new-cohort faculty, the mothers of new-cohort faculty have been better educated than the mothers of the senior faculty (Table A-9).

Marital Status

New career entrants are significantly less likely to be currently married than their senior colleagues: 71.8 percent compared with 77.0 percent (Table 10).

When the findings are analyzed by age group, we find that differences in marital status between cohorts largely disappear (Table A-10). For example, among those 35–44 years of age, 73.9 percent of the new academics are married, compared with the 74.1 percent of their senior counterparts who are married. However, some differences in marital status persist, especially in the significantly higher proportion of new entrants

Table 10 ⇒ Marital Status

			Marital status					
	Number	Percent	Never been married	Married	Living with someone	Separated	Divorced	Widowed
All faculty	514,976	100.0	11.0	75.3	2.3	1.3	8.9	1.3
New faculty	172,319	100.0	14.9	71.8	3.0	1.4	8.1	0.8
Senior faculty	342,657	100.0	9.0	77.0	2.0	1.2	9.3	1.5

Note: Details may not add to total because of rounding.

reporting divorces. This finding suggests that in large part marital status differences between cohorts, as might be expected, are attenuated when age is taken into account.

When we control for gender, we find that males in both cohorts are much more likely to be married (78.4 percent of new entrants and 83.2 percent of seniors) than their female colleagues (62.2 percent of new entrants and 61.5 percent of their senior colleagues). Women in both cohorts are more likely than their male colleagues to report that they are "living with someone" and about twice as likely as their male colleagues to be divorced. However, whereas new-faculty males are less likely to be married than their senior counterparts (not unexpected given the differences in age), new-faculty females, in contrast, are slightly more likely to be married than their senior colleagues.

Although this picture represents, in some sense, a continuation of the historical trend (Fulton 1975; Freeman 1977; Finkelstein 1984), the data do suggest some clear attenuation of gender differences. A generation ago, academic women were only half as likely to marry as academic men. A major factor in their decision to forego marriage has always been, of course, the gender-specific concomitants of marriage, such as housework and child-rearing. Studies a generation ago, when the initial rise in marriage rates for academic women began, report greater conflict between work and family roles for academic women (Finkelstein 1984, 211). These conflicting pressures may indeed help explain the demonstrably higher incidence of divorce among new-entry women faculty.

Missing Data: Religion

Historically, reporting data on faculty members' religious backgrounds and preferences was de rigueur. After all, religion—specifically Protestantism—had been a powerfully determinative force that had molded higher education on these shores since its inception. For nearly three centuries the salience of religion was unmistakable, extending its influence to determining (and limiting) just who the faculty were. But change occurred rapidly after World War II, especially by the 1960s, as religion came to serve less and less as a gatekeeper to the professoriate (Steinberg 1974; Lipset and Ladd 1979). So it is that in recent years faculty members' religious orientations have proved less fascinating to the gatherers of faculty data, and thus no item on religion was included in the NSOPF-93 survey or its 1988 predecessor. For monitors of higher education, and of societal trends more generally, this data vacuum is unfortunate.[18]

In Summary

The new generation of academic career entrants is readily distinguishable from their senior colleagues. First, they are more diverse demographically than the previous generation, most dramatically in terms of the substantial increase in the proportion of women (40.8 versus 28.5 percent). Second, greater racial diversification is evident (16.9 percent minority versus 11.7 percent). This is most notable in the increase of Asians / Pacific Islanders (from 4.4 to 7.7 percent); indeed, Asian males account for 9.3 percent of all newly hired males. Third, there has been a significant increase in the proportion of non-native-born faculty among the new entrants (16.9 versus 11.5 percent). Fourth, in terms of their academic program affiliations, a considerably larger proportion of the new entrants hold appointments outside the traditional liberal arts (51.0 percent) compared with their senior colleagues (44.9 percent).

The changes in each of those categories can be seen as substantial, even dramatic. The extent of the demographic shift can be captured in even more emphatic terms when described as follows: white, male, native-born faculty constitute 58.6 percent of the senior cohort. But among the new academic generation, the percentage of native-born white males—in a sense, the "traditional" faculty in American colleges and universities— has plunged to 43.2 percent (Table 11 and Figure 5). Indeed, significant

Table 11 ⇌ Native-Born White Males

	As percent of all males in cohort	As percent of all males and females in cohort
All faculty	79.3	53.4
New faculty	73.0	43.2
Senior faculty	82.0	58.6

FIGURE 5.
Cohort differences
in the proportion
of native-born
white males, full-
time faculty

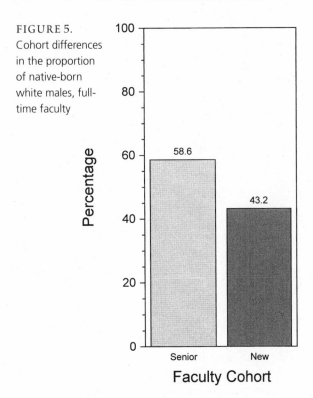

Faculty Cohort

differences between the two cohorts hold across all institutional types and program areas (Table A-11).

Using these three descriptors of gender, race, and nativity, the different makeup of the two cohorts—the extent of change that has taken place—is evident across all institutional types (Table A-11). Among institutional types, the proportion of "nontraditional" faculty (that is, those other than native-born white males) among the new cohort is greatest at the community colleges (61.9 percent) and liberal arts colleges (59.0 percent) and least at the doctoral (non–research university) institutions (52.8 percent), especially, among them, the private doctoral institutions (46.2 percent).

Curiously, among the research universities, historically a bastion of white males, the extent of change is especially palpable at the public institutions, where the proportion of native-born white males has declined sharply from 66.0 percent of the senior faculty cohort to 46.2 percent among the new faculty. The least change appears to have occurred at the private research universities, where the percentage of native-born white

**Table 12 ⇒ Native-Born White Males
in the Liberal Arts**

	As percent of all males in cohort	As percent of all males and females in cohort
All faculty	40.9	27.6
New faculty	34.6	20.5
Senior faculty	46.9	33.5

males has shrunk only from 53.4 percent in the senior cohort to 41.4 percent in the new cohort. Similarly, the extent of change is more pronounced at the public doctoral campuses compared with their private counterparts. Considerable change is also evident at the liberal arts colleges.

The smallest percentage of new-cohort native-born white males, as noted, is found on the public two-year campuses: only three of each eight faculty members. The heterogeneity of the American faculty—by gender, race, and nativity—is swiftly becoming a reality.

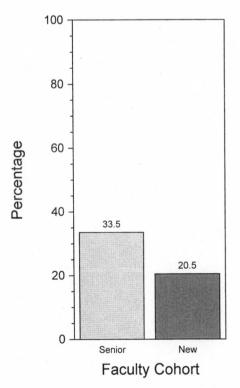

FIGURE 6. Cohort differences in the proportion of native-born white males in liberal arts fields, full-time faculty

The increasing diversification of the faculty is also seen across all program areas (Table A-11). Change is modest in some historically male-dominated areas, for example, business and engineering. But in the fine arts, the percentage of native-born white males has plunged from 64.1 percent in the senior faculty cohort to 37.8 percent among the new faculty. Among the natural scientists, the comparable percentages changed from 66.2 to 46.4 percent.

A further indication of dynamic change becomes clear when a fourth variable is factored in: whether or not a faculty member is teaching in a liberal arts field. Seen through this lens, a remarkable datum emerges: only one-fifth of the new-cohort faculty (20.5 percent) are identifiable with the group characteristics of faculty members who have dominated American higher education over much of its history: native-born white males teaching in the liberal arts. This level contrasts with 33.5 percent of their senior counterparts (Table 12 and Figure 6). As more egalitarian hiring practices prevail and as higher education responds increasingly to students' interests outside the traditional liberal arts, the once prototypical faculty members—white males, native-born and ensconced in the liberal arts—are becoming ever scarcer.

A summary of the most significant changes is presented in Appendix B.

FOUR

THE PREPARATION AND CAREERS OF THE NEW ACADEMIC GENERATION

To what extent, and in what ways, is the demographic diversification of new career entrants to faculties of higher education reflected in the patterns of their emerging careers? And how do the careers of these newcomers compare with those of their more experienced colleagues? Based on the NSOPF-93 survey, we can examine a wide array of variables, including the level of their highest degrees earned, the types of institutions that granted their highest degrees, undergraduate honors, kinds of graduate school support, their ages upon receipt of their highest degrees and appointment to their current positions, their previous employment history (by employment sector and functional responsibility), their tenure status, and finally the degree to which they report satisfaction with their jobs and their careers.[1]

By the way of context, the post–World War II period had seen the consolidation of the "lockstep" academic career path: the Ph.D. was awarded in one's late twenties or early thirties (with variations by field), followed directly by the securing of an academic appointment. (Often this initial academic employment occurred after the successful job seeker had been advanced to candidacy but before he had received his degree; this practice led to the status of "ABD," meaning "all but dissertation.") By the mid-1970s, however, in response to the tightening academic job market, the National Research Council (1978) was already reporting the increasing popularity of postdoctoral appointments for new Ph.D.'s, espe-cially in the natural sciences (such appointments absorbed some 40 per-cent of newly minted life scientists). What had developed in the 1960s as a device for enhancing preparation for faculty careers had come to func-tion a decade later as a "holding pattern" (Zumeta 1985). Young Ph.D.'s, caught in the squeeze of increased supply amid declining opportunities, were reporting less certainty about their eventual employment; they increasingly gravitated to a variety of postdoctoral appointments as interim employment while seeking permanent jobs (National Research Council 1978, 76).

Throughout the 1980s and well into the 1990s, the academic market-place, in most fields, has translated into limited opportunities for prospec-tive faculty members seeking a traditional tenure-track appointment (El-Khawas 1986; Schuster 1995) and, for those who managed to obtain such appointments, both the prospect of extended probationary periods (Sibley-Fries 1986; Chait 1997) and formidable pressures to demonstrate produc-tivity, at least in many institutions (Bowen and Schuster 1986; Finkelstein and LaCelle Peterson 1992; Olsen and Sorcinelli 1992). That is the acade-mic environment within which the new-cohort faculty have entered upon their careers.

Educational Background

Level of Highest Degree

An account of recent history provides a useful perspective. In 1969, about two-fifths of the faculty held the doctorate. These included about three of each five faculty members at research universities and elite liberal arts col-leges; one of four at the less selective liberal arts colleges; and about 5 per-cent at the two-year community colleges (Bayer 1973; Trow 1975). Just a decade later, following the tightening of the academic labor market that enabled colleges and universities to be considerably choosier in their hir-ing, the proportion of faculty doctorate holders climbed overall to about three-fifths (National Education Association 1979) while among new hires it was just over one-half (52.9 percent) (Atelsek and Gomberg 1978). By 1992, about 57 percent of faculty members reported holding the doctorate while another 9 percent held professional degrees, including J.D.'s and M.D.'s (National Center for Education Statistics 1995).[2] It would appear that about the same proportion of faculty hold the doctorate now as was the case a generation ago, when the "declining" labor market first ratcheted up the qualifications for new faculty hires.

Our analysis indicates that new faculty are more likely to hold a master's or bachelor's as their highest degree (38.3 percent) compared with the senior cohort (31.5 percent) (Table 13).[3] However, direct comparability between the two cohorts is not possible because the corresponding shortfall of doctorates among the new-entry cohort (50.8 versus 60.1 percent in the senior cohort) reflects, probably in large part, the phenomenon of younger faculty still at work on their doctoral or master's degrees. Another factor contributing to the disparity (though surely accounting for less of the difference between the cohorts than degrees-still-in-progress) is the higher incidence of professional degrees as the highest degrees among the junior faculty (10.9 percent) compared with their senior colleagues (8.5 percent).

When we examine the institutional type of the new hires' current affiliations (Table A-13), we find, not surprisingly, that at doctorate-granting institutions master's and baccalaureate degree holders are only minimally represented (15.0 percent at the research universities and 18.9 percent at the other doctoral institutions). We see also that far more new faculty in the natural sciences and social sciences currently hold doctorates (including professional doctorates: 76.1 percent of natural scientists and 74.7 percent of social scientists) than in the humanities (55.4 percent); this gap likely reflects large numbers of nondoctorate faculty specialists hired to teach basic English language courses, such as writing and introductory foreign language courses. In the fine arts, the proportion slips to barely one-third, an indicator that the master's of fine arts degree very often suffices as the "terminal degree" for these faculty members.

However, a cautionary note is in order: as noted, a considerable number of faculty members whose highest degrees are shown as master's or bachelor's undoubtedly are pursuing a higher degree at this relatively early stage of their careers; accordingly, the degree distributions for the new and senior cohorts are not strictly comparable. Even so, it is

Table 13 ⇒ Level of Highest Degree

	Number[a]	Percent	Highest degree			
			Professional	Doctoral	Master's	Bachelor's or less
All faculty	512,113	100.0	9.3	57.0	28.9	4.8
New faculty	170,922	100.0	10.9	50.8	31.3	7.0
Senior faculty	341,191	100.0	8.5	60.1	27.7	3.8

Note: Details may not add to total because of rounding.
a. Missing: 1,397 (0.8 percent) new faculty and 1,466 (0.4 percent) senior faculty.

noteworthy that women faculty in the new cohort are almost as likely to hold a master's as their highest degree (44.2 percent) as a doctorate (48.4 percent). This is in sharp contrast to the highest degrees earned by new-cohort men: 71.0 percent doctorates but only 22.4 percent master's. To some extent this finding surely reflects the larger number of women hired at two-year institutions and also the number of women whose appointments are in fields for which the doctorate is less crucial. Presumably, too, many of these women are currently pursuing doctorates. Nevertheless, the contrast between new-cohort women and men in this regard is striking and appears to follow roughly the highest-degree experience of their senior counterparts, for among them three-fourths of the men (75.0 percent) but barely more than half of the women (52.5 percent) hold doctorates.

Source of Highest Degree

Again, an overview of recent decades provides a useful point of departure. In 1957, well before the rapid expansion in the number of doctorate-granting institutions, nearly three-fourths of the doctorates in the traditional arts and sciences were awarded by the top twelve research universities; thus most aspirants to academic careers who found their way into the faculty ranks at four-year institutions bore exalted academic pedigrees (Berelson 1960). However, that remarkable concentration in so few universities soon began to unravel. By 1969, Trow (1975) reported that about 35 percent of the doctorates earned by faculty were from "major research universities." Today, nearly three-fifths of the doctorates of American academics were awarded by the fifty-one universities classified by the Carnegie Foundation for the Advancement of Teaching as Research University I's (National Center for Education Statistics 1994).[4] This expansion reflects the continuing trend toward increasing democratization in graduate study associated with the dramatic growth in the number of institutions offering doctoral degrees in the post–World War II period.

Our study's more recent comparison of sources for Ph.D.'s is revealing. Here we see what appears to be a somewhat greater variety in the source of doctoral degrees (including Ph.D.'s and other doctorates) as well as a modest shift downward through the hierarchy of institutional categories, as the percentage of faculty who earned their doctorates from Research University I's declined from 70.2 percent in the senior cohort to 66.4 percent among their junior colleagues. Put another way, this new cohort entered academic careers from a somewhat more diversified set of graduate institutions than did their predecessors (Table 14).

Table 14 ⇌ **Doctorate Source**

	Total	Research I	Research II	Doctoral I	Doctoral II	Compre-hensive I	Compre-hensive II	Other	Missing
New faculty	100.0	66.4	9.1	5.6	2.8	1.5	0.2	4.3	10.0
Male	100.0	66.0	8.8	4.9	2.9	1.0	0.1	5.0	11.2
Female	100.0	66.9	9.7	7.2	2.7	2.7	0.4	2.9	7.4
Senior faculty	100.0	70.2	10.0	6.7	2.4	1.4	0.0	2.8	6.5
Male	100.0	71.1	9.9	5.9	2.1	1.1	0.0	2.8	7.0
Female	100.0	66.9	10.5	9.4	3.3	2.4	0.0	2.9	4.6

Note: Includes only professional and doctoral degrees. Percents represent percentage of professional and doctoral degrees in cohort. Data represent 1994 Carnegie classifications, and this classification is not necessarily representative of an institution's classification when an individual received his or her first professional or doctoral degree from that institution. Details may not add to total because of rounding.

Once more, however, the cohorts are not strictly comparable. This is in part because some institutions are reclassified over time[5] and also because degrees from non-U.S. institutions are not categorized.[6] Among women, the proportion of highest degrees earned from research universities has not changed from the senior to the new-entrant cohort: slightly more than 76 percent in both cases. However, by focusing on the Research University I category, it is worth noting that women faculty in the new cohort have gained ground compared to their male colleagues in the share of the most prestigious doctorates. Whereas men in the senior cohort had earned a higher proportion of their doctorates (71.1 percent) from those institutions than had their female colleagues (66.9 percent), the reverse applies, albeit by a narrow margin, in the new cohort: the same 66.9 percent of women and 66.0 percent of the men.[7]

Undergraduate Honors

Has the tighter academic labor market yielded new faculty members whose academic records indicate that they were better qualified than their predecessors? One indicator would be whether the new-entry faculty had more impressive undergraduate records than their senior colleagues. Although it would be difficult to make meaningful comparisons between the two cohorts, both cohorts do look very much alike in the academic prizes they have garnered (Table 15). A higher percentage of new faculty (23.4 percent) graduated with high or highest honors (magna or summa cum laude) than did the senior faculty (19.9 percent), but this finding might in part reflect grade inflation. Evidence that the new cohort is superior to their seniors in this regard is thus inconclusive.

Table 15 ⇒ **Undergraduate Honors**

	National academic honor society	Cum laude or honors	Magna cum laude or high honors	Summa cum laude or highest honors	Other undergraduate honor
All faculty	30.3	19.2	12.6	8.5	25.8
New faculty	30.5	19.0	13.7	9.7	27.2
Senior faculty	30.2	19.3	12.0	7.9	25.2

Note: Percents represent affirmative responses by cohort.

Graduate School Support

New career entrants differ from earlier generations not only in the type of institution from which they earned their highest degrees but also in how they paid for their graduate education. This situation reflects, for the most part, recent changes in the mechanisms of financing graduate education (Table 16). For one thing, as one indicator of higher education's greater emphasis on research (see Chapter 5), a considerably larger percentage of new-entry faculty received research assistantships than had their senior colleagues (33.0 versus 27.6 percent). Meanwhile, the incidence of teaching assistantships, the largest category of graduate student support, declined slightly (46.5 versus 48.3 percent).

As a group, the new faculty are less likely to have received fellowships and veterans' aid but are somewhat more likely to have received scholarship support or another grant. They are much more likely than their senior colleagues to have borrowed their way through graduate school. Since the survey generated no data on the amount of money borrowed (which is frequently large, especially to attend some types of professional schools), it is not clear what sorts of loan repayment pressures the new-entry faculty bring into their early career years, but as other studies show, indebtedness is surely a significantly greater burden among these recent career entrants. And so the new entrants, whose compensation already tends to be constrained by the hard economic realities that impinge on higher education, also must absorb the financial pressures of repaying debt accumulated as undergraduates and as graduate or professional students.

Differences are also evident by gender. Women in both cohorts are far less likely than men to have received teaching or research assistantships or some other form of fellowship. However, larger proportions of women than men in both cohorts received another form of scholarship or grant. For the senior cohort, twice as many women as men appear to have

Table 16 ⇥ Graduate School Support

	Teaching assistantship	Research assistantship	Program / Residence hall assistantship	Fellowship	Scholarship	Grant	G.I. Bill, veterans' aid	Federal or state loan	Other loan	None
All faculty	47.7	29.4	2.2	29.1	18.0	11.0	8.5	17.9	5.6	15.8
New faculty	46.5	33.0	1.9	26.5	20.6	12.0	4.3	24.4	6.3	16.5
Male	49.4	39.0	1.9	29.2	19.1	11.3	6.6	23.3	6.3	13.3
Female	42.3	24.2	2.1	22.5	22.8	12.9	1.1	25.9	6.3	21.1
Senior faculty	48.3	27.6	2.4	30.4	16.6	10.5	10.6	14.7	5.3	15.4
Male	51.9	31.3	2.3	33.3	15.5	10.1	14.3	14.4	5.2	12.1
Female	39.1	18.3	2.6	23.2	19.6	11.6	1.3	15.5	5.3	23.8

Note: Percents represent percent of cohort.

received no outside financial assistance (23.8 versus 12.1 percent). This gender gap narrows only slightly within the new-faculty cohort (21.1 versus 13.3 percent).

Career Experience

Age at Award of Highest Degree and at Appointment to Current Position

Contrary to what might be predicted based on evidence of the increasing length of doctoral study in some fields (Bowen and Rudenstine 1992), new career entrants are receiving their highest degrees, be they at the doctoral or the master's level, at almost precisely the same age, on average, as their senior colleagues, namely in their early thirties (Table 17). But the full situation is more complex: although new entrants are receiving their highest degrees in their early thirties, they are being hired into their *current positions* at a considerably later age than their senior colleagues had been (median age of 37 versus 34). Or consider another way of viewing these data. Senior faculty members on average are hired into their current positions about four years after completing their highest degrees whereas for the new generation the interval is about eight years.

This development raises a number of questions:

Table 17 〜 **Age at Award of Highest Degree and at Appointment to Current Position**

	Age when granted highest degree			Age when hired in current position		
	Mean	Median	Mode	Mean	Median	Mode
New faculty	31.6	29	30	38.7	37	37
Doctorate[a]	32.0	30	31	38.6	36	37
Males	31.1	30	28	38.6	36	34
Females	34.1	32	28	38.6	37	38
Master's	31.5	29	29	38.1	38	39
Males	30.8	28	25	39.6	38	30
Females	32.1	30	26	38.6	38	43
Senior faculty	31.8	30	30	35.8	34	34
Doctorate	32.3	30	30	36.1	34	35
Males	31.4	30	28	35.9	34	31
Females	35.2	34	30	36.8	36	33
Master's	31.2	29	29	35.1	33	34
Males	30.3	29	27	34.3	33	29
Females	32.3	30	24	36.0	35	29

a. Doctorate refers to professional (M.D., D.D.S., LL.B.) and doctoral (Ph.D., Ed.D.) degrees.

- Have new entrants, after earning their highest degrees, simply bounced around among a number of short-term academic positions prior to assuming their current positions?
- Were they more likely than their senior colleagues to have held term appointments that were not renewed, to have held one or more post-doctoral positions, or to have been denied tenure?
- Have they simply taken much longer to find a full-time academic position in a difficult job market?

These questions led us to look more closely into the previous work history of new career entrants, especially their employment experiences following receipt of their highest degrees, in order to understand better the transition from graduate study to a full-time faculty appointment in the contemporary academy.

Previous Employment History

New career entrants are more likely than their predecessors to have had previous work experience prior to their current appointments. That holds for 78.6 percent of the new faculty, but for only 60.3 percent of the senior faculty (Table 18).[8] Although the new hires are much less likely to have had previous employment experience in either a four-year or a two-year post-secondary institution (43.8 versus 47.5 percent), they are much more likely to have worked in an employment sector outside postsecondary education. This shows up most dramatically in the significantly larger percentages of new-entry faculty members who had worked previously in consulting (4.3 versus 1.9 percent), hospital settings (8.4 versus 2.0 percent), foundations or other nonprofit organizations (2.4 versus 0.7 percent), for-profit businesses (8.7 versus 2.8 percent), and the federal government (2.9 versus 1.4 percent).

Viewed by function (primary responsibility) rather than by employment sector, new entrants are seen to have had a greater diversity of previous work responsibilities (Table 19). Compared with their predecessors, considerably larger proportions of the new entrants report having had previous experience in research, technical activities, clinical services, and administration—in each instance more than double the senior cohort's incidence of such work experience. One indicator of the gravitation of emphasis from teaching to research in recent years is discernible in the extent to which each cohort had held teaching or research-related jobs. Tellingly, the senior-faculty cohort was considerably more likely to have had a previous full-time teaching position (45.5 percent) than the new-faculty cohort

Table 18   Previous Employment Sector

	Any previous employment	Previous job by sector							
		Four-year college or university	Two-year college or university	Elementary or secondary	Consulting	Hospital	Foundation or other nonprofit	For-profit business	Federal government	Other
All faculty	66.8	40.7	5.9	4.4	2.7	4.2	1.3	4.8	1.9	0.9
New faculty	78.6	38.5	5.3	6.5	4.3	8.4	2.4	8.7	2.9	1.7
Senior faculty	60.3	41.4	6.1	3.3	1.9	2.0	0.7	2.8	1.4	0.6

Note: Percents shown for "Any previous employment" represent the percentage of the faculty, by cohort, who listed up to three full-time positions during the past fifteen years. Percents shown for each sector represent the percent breakdown within each cohort. Thus the sector percents are row percents that add to the "Any previous employment" values for new and senior faculty. Details may not add to total due to rounding.

Table 19 ⇒ **Previous Employment Primary Responsibility**

	Any previous employment	Teaching	Research	Technical services	Clinical services	Public service	Administration	Other
		Previous job by primary responsibility						
All faculty	66.8	41.0	9.5	4.1	3.5	0.8	4.3	3.5
New faculty	78.6	31.3	18.5	7.3	7.2	1.6	6.7	6.0
Senior faculty	60.3	45.5	4.9	2.5	1.6	0.5	3.0	2.3

Note: Percents shown for "Any previous employment" represent the percentage of the faculty, by cohort, who listed up to three full-time positions during the past fifteen years. Percents shown for primary responsibility represent the percent breakdown within each cohort. Thus the primary responsibility percents are row percents that add to the "Any previous employment" values for new and senior faculty. Details may not add to total due to rounding.

(31.3 percent). But the opposite tendency obtained for research: the junior cohort, as noted, was much more likely to have held a research-oriented job (18.5 versus 4.9 percent).

How are we to interpret these patterns of previous work experience? To what extent do they represent intentionally temporary employment undertaken while completing graduate study or forays into the long-term, full-time job market after finishing a graduate degree? To clarify these questions, the dates reported under previous employment history were used to identify those previous positions that were first assumed *after* the date of receipt of the highest degree but *before* the current position. That is to say, we probed the patterns of employment that transpired post–highest degree but pre–current position of new and senior faculty (Table 20). Though only a minority of faculty members in both cohorts reported having a full-time job following receipt of their highest degrees but preceding appointment to their current positions, the new cohort was more likely to have held such an intervening full-time position: roughly one-fifth of the senior cohort (18.2 percent) but nearly one-third of the new cohort (30.6 percent). Moreover, the substances of the cohort experiences are very different. For senior faculty the overwhelming majority of these post–highest degree/pre–current employment experiences were teaching positions. But for the new entrants with doctorates, teaching accounted for only about one-fourth of their employment positions immediately following the award of their highest degrees. We see, too, that new doctorally trained faculty held a wider variety of nonteaching positions before assuming their current teaching positions; research positions were far more commonplace. Moreover, the new entrants' post–highest degree/pre–current employment positions were more likely to have been located outside higher education than the positions of their senior colleagues, illustrating the more varied early career paths followed by the newer faculty members.

Table 20 ⇌ **Previous Employment History: Post–Highest Degree and Pre–Current Position**

| | Doctorate | | | | | | | |
	Total	Teaching	Research	Technical services	Clinical services	Public service	Administration	Other
All faculty	15.4	8.6	4.0	0.4	1.0	0.2	0.9	0.5
Within academe	14.2	8.5	3.7	0.2	0.7	0.1	0.7	0.3
Outside academe	1.2	0.1	0.3	0.2	0.3	0.1	0.2	0.2
New faculty	19.8	4.8	8.8	0.8	2.3	0.3	1.9	0.9
Within academe	16.6	4.5	8.1	0.5	1.3	0.2	1.5	0.5
Outside academe	3.2	0.3	0.7	0.3	1.0	0.1	0.4	0.4
Senior faculty	13.2	10.5	1.5	0.2	0.3	0.1	0.4	0.2
Within academe	12.7	10.4	1.5	0.1	0.3	0.0	0.3	0.1
Outside academe	0.5	0.1	0.0	0.1	0.0	0.1	0.1	0.1

Note: Faculty represented in this table are only those who held a position after receiving their highest degree and before attaining their current position. Details may not add to total because of rounding.

Tenure Status

The prototypical faculty position through most of the twentieth century was a full-time probationary appointment in the tenure-earning stream. This arrangement was in a sense codified by the principles incorporated in the American Association of University Professors' 1940 statement of principles on academic freedom and tenure (1995), and indeed the early conferral of tenure was commonplace in some fields in the hiring rush of the 1960s. During the 1970s, in response to the building job market glut and declining enrollments in some fields, institutions developed a variety of more flexible staffing responses. They increased the use of part-time appointments, especially in certain fields such as English composition, foreign languages, remedial mathematics, and business. Between 1969 and 1992, the proportion of total instructional staff who were part time soared from 22 percent to around 40 percent (Finkelstein and Schuster 1992; National Center for Education Statistics 1994). Current estimates vary, but a best guess is 42 or 43 percent. More recently, full-time faculty term appointments that entail no probationary period and do not lead to tenure have become increasingly common. In the early 1980s, about 12 percent of all faculty held such appointments (American Association of University Professors 1992). By 1992, about one-fifth of all full-time faculty in American

			Master's				
Total	Teaching	Research	Technical services	Clinical services	Public service	Administration	Other
7.0	4.9	0.2	0.4	0.4	0.1	0.6	0.4
5.9	4.5	0.1	0.2	0.2	0.1	0.5	0.3
1.1	0.4	0.1	0.2	0.2	0.0	0.1	0.1
10.8	6.1	0.5	1.0	0.9	0.2	1.3	0.8
8.1	5.1	0.4	0.5	0.4	0.1	1.0	0.6
2.7	1.0	0.1	0.5	0.5	0.1	0.3	0.2
5.0	4.3	0.0	0.1	0.2	0.0	0.3	0.1
4.7	4.1	0.0	0.1	0.1	0.0	0.3	0.1
0.3	0.2	0.0	0.0	0.1	0.0	0.0	0.0

colleges and universities worked in a non–tenure track position (Chronister, Baldwin, and Bailey 1992; National Education Association 1996), and that percentage is probably still rising.

Indeed a crucial difference between the two cohorts in our analysis shows up in the respective kinds of academic appointments they hold, particularly in regard to whether or not they occupy tenurable positions. Table 21 and Figure 7 show the tenure status of new entrants compared with their more senior colleagues.[9] The new-generation faculty are, of course, much less likely to be tenured: 23.9 percent compared with 73.0 percent of the more experienced cohort. An additional 42.9 percent of the new

Table 21 ⇌ Tenure Status

				Tenure status			
	Number	Percent	Tenured	On tenure track	Not on tenure track	No tenure for faculty status	No tenure system at institution
All faculty	514,976	100.0	56.6	21.4	9.7	4.4	8.0
New faculty	172,319	100.0	23.9	42.9	17.0	7.0	9.2
Senior faculty	342,657	100.0	73.0	10.5	6.0	3.2	7.3

Note: Details may not add to total because of rounding.

FIGURE 7. Cohort differences in types of appointments, full-time faculty

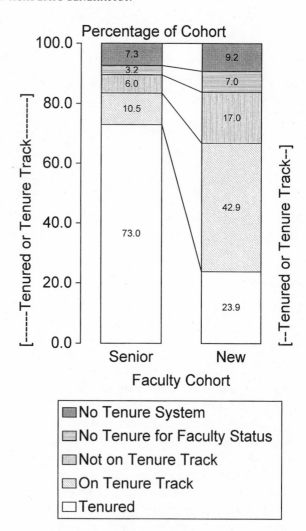

faculty and 10.5 percent of the senior faculty are "on tenure track but not tenured." The combination of the tenured plus tenure-eligible categories demonstrates the "tenure gap": 83.5 percent of the senior cohort but only 66.8 percent of the new-entry cohort. That finding represents a very substantial difference in the way faculty positions are being created and filled. Put in other terms, the new entrants are more than twice as likely not to be in the tenure stream: fully one-third (33.2 percent) are not in tenure-eligible positions compared with 16.5 percent of their more senior colleagues.

There is an alternative way of measuring the gap between the two cohorts in the proportions of appointments that are made off the tenure track, namely by removing from consideration the number of appointments made at institutions that simply do not have a tenure system. At those institutions a tenured or tenure-track appointment is not an option; accordingly, by stipulating such positions out of the denominator, one could argue that the resulting fraction better captures the extent to which the proportion of off-track appointments appears to be changing. Applying this logic, the intercohort gap remains palpable: the proportion of all senior-cohort faculty holding either tenured or tenure-track appointments is 90.1 percent compared with 73.6 percent for the new-entry cohort.[10]

When we control for gender, we find that females (both new and senior) are far more likely to be employed in non–tenure track positions than males (Table A-21). Some background will be useful. Since at least the 1930s, and perhaps forever, being female has been negatively associated with attainment of higher academic rank and the award of tenure. While the proportion of women who are full professors (and tenured) increased from one in eight in 1969 to one in four in 1988, the proportion of males who are full professors (and tenured) increased from one in three to one in two; proportionately, women remained at about 10 percent of all full professors during this period (Blackburn and Lawrence 1995). Extending these data to include all tenured faculty irrespective of rank, in 1979 women represented about one-tenth of the tenured faculty at universities, two-tenths at other four-year colleges, and three-tenths at two-year community colleges (Finkelstein 1984).

By 1992, however, the pace of change was clearly quickening. Most pronounced in our analysis is the fact that the new generation of male faculty is nearly twice as likely as their female colleagues to have already been awarded tenure (29.1 versus 16.5 percent). What more can we learn about this marked disparity in the paths toward achieving tenure? It is illuminating to examine this gender gap by institutional type and by program area.

Among institutional types (Table A-21), we find relatively higher percentages of tenure or tenure-track appointments for new entrants at research, doctoral, and comprehensive universities but, conversely, lesser proportions of such appointments at liberal arts and public two-year colleges (the latter typically resort to part-time adjunct rather than full-time nonladder appointments). New-generation full-time faculty at two-year colleges (28.8 percent) and at research universities (29.3 percent) are much more likely to have already obtained tenure than their counterparts at the other categories of institutions.[11]

When the data are reviewed by program area, we find that new faculty members in each area are much more likely to hold non–tenure track appointments than their senior colleagues. However, among new career entrants, natural scientists (25.5 percent) and social scientists (24.5 percent) are much less likely to be off ladder than faculty in the humanities (36.1 percent) and the professions (34.7 percent).

By isolating those new-cohort faculty members who have already been awarded tenure, several interesting findings emerge (Table A-21A). First, men have progressed to tenure (or in some instances presumably have been appointed initially with tenure) more readily than women at all institutional types and in all of the program area clusters. The differences are most pronounced in research, other doctoral, and comprehensive institutions; in those settings the ratio of tenured men to tenured women is 2:1. It is notable that more than one-third (35.2 percent) of the new-cohort men at research universities have already attained tenure. The highest incidence of tenure in the new cohort is found in the public two-year institutions, where 28.8 percent of men and women combined are tenured; this finding presumably reflects the shorter probationary period often used for faculty at community colleges.

Among program areas the differences by gender are persistently large. A notable exception is the fine arts; here the proportion of new-cohort women with tenure nearly equals that of men. The biggest difference is seen in the humanities, where, despite the fact that the majority of new-cohort humanists are women (see Table A-5), the proportion of tenured men is slightly more than twice that of women. Yet one more indicator of a gender gap is seen in the breakout by rank: among new-cohort full professors, many more men (80.6 percent) than women (66.8 percent) have attained tenure.

Some of the difference between the genders' respective "success rates" might be attributable to the difference in their median ages: 48 for the tenured new cohort of males and 46 for their female counterparts. This observation implies that this subset of men has had more experience than the women and that, plausibly, more of them have entered academic positions from careers in nonacademic sectors.

Job Satisfaction

How do new entrants compare with the previous generation on several dimensions of career and job satisfaction?

Since the early 1970s, American faculty members have expressed considerable pessimism about matters such as the decline in the professoriate's status, their compensation, and their career opportunities (Bowen and Schuster 1986). Yet, individually speaking, most by far continue to report satisfaction with their careers and their fit with their employing institutions; indeed, they display a remarkable durability in their positive sense of their personal career situation (Austin and Gamson 1983; Carnegie Foundation for the Advancement of Teaching 1986, 1989). In the 1970s, nine of ten reported that their institutions were a "good place for me." More than four-fifths expressed overall satisfaction with their academic careers, approximating levels reported in the 1960s (Parsons and Platt 1968; Eckert and Williams 1972) and in the early 1970s (Bayer 1973). By the mid-1980s, more than three-fourths reported that they would select an academic career again and nearly half were more enthusiastic "now" about their careers than when they had started (Carnegie Foundation for the Advancement of Teaching 1989, 91). As for compensation, about half rated salary as "good" or "excellent," comparable to 1969 results and slightly higher than those in the 1970s and early 1980s (Carnegie Foundation for the Advancement of Teaching 1989, 91), but, conversely, the other half were less sanguine.

Turning to our own analysis, satisfaction levels with the various dimensions of work are, on the whole, moderately high for both cohorts in our study (Table 22). However, compared to their senior counterparts, new entrants report being somewhat less satisfied with their current jobs in a number of respects. The biggest intercohort gap is seen in satisfaction with job security (2.9 mean score on a 4-point scale; 70.5 percent very or somewhat satisfied for the new cohort versus 3.4 and 86.5 percent for their senior colleagues). But, after all, few new-generation faculty, as previously noted, have already obtained tenure and fully one-third hold nontenurable appointments, so concerns about job security are readily understandable. Apart from job security, the two cohorts' patterns of responses are on the whole more similar than dissimilar. Some intercohort differences in satisfaction ratings can be seen regarding opportunities for advancement in rank at their institutions (65.8 percent of the new faculty saying that they are somewhat or very satisfied versus 71.2 percent for senior faculty), freedom to do outside consulting (76.4 versus 81.0 percent), spouse or partner employment opportunities in the geographic area (68.5 versus 75.8 percent), and time available for keeping current in one's field (44.9 versus 50.3 percent). Perhaps most surprisingly, the difference in satisfaction levels regarding "my workload" is not at all large: 66.7 percent of the new cohort and 70.1 percent of the senior cohort say that they are satisfied or very satisfied. Virtually no differences appear

Table 22 ⇒⊢ Job Satisfaction

	Work load		Job security		Advancement opportunities		Keeping current in field	
	Mean	Percent somewhat/ very satisfied	Mean	Percent somewhat/ very satisfied	Mean	Percent somewhat/ very satisfied	Mean	Percent somewhat/ very satisfied
All faculty	2.9	69.0	3.2	81.1	2.9	69.4	2.5	48.5
New faculty	2.8	66.7	2.9	70.5	2.8	65.8	2.4	44.9
Senior faculty	2.9	70.1	3.4	86.5	3.0	71.2	2.5	50.3

	Freedom for outside consulting		Salary		Benefits		Spouse employment opportunities	
	Mean	Percent somewhat/ very satisfied	Mean	Percent somewhat/ very satisfied	Mean	Percent somewhat/ very satisfied	Mean	Percent somewhat/ very satisfied
All faculty	3.1	79.5	2.5	54.8	3.0	75.2	3.0	73.4
New faculty	3.0	76.4	2.5	53.4	3.0	75.4	2.9	68.5
Senior faculty	3.2	81.0	2.5	55.6	3.0	75.1	3.0	75.8

Note: The item read as follows: "How satisfied or dissatisfied are you with the following aspects of your job at this institution? 1 = very dissatisfied; 2 = somewhat dissatisfied; 3 = somewhat satisfied; 4 = very satisfied." Percent somewhat/very satisfied represents cumulative percent of those who responded "somewhat satisfied" or "very satisfied."

between the two cohorts' satisfaction ratings for "my benefits" and for "my salary."

Salary and the time available to keep current in one's field are the two job dimensions that both cohorts rank the lowest in satisfaction. This is not surprising; salary is persistently a sore point for faculty members, as reported in study after study. As for not being able to stay abreast of one's field, such frustration is an inevitable consequence of the so-called knowledge explosion, reinforced by everyday job pressures.

Taking gender into account (Table A-22A), we find that women in both cohorts report being less satisfied than their male colleagues on all scales (except benefits and spousal employment). In both cohorts, women are considerably less satisfied with their salaries than are their male colleagues. Interestingly, the biggest gap between the genders is seen in the criterion "keeping current in the field." Here women in both cohorts register levels of satisfaction far lower than those of their men colleagues. Thus for the senior faculty 54.7 percent of the men, but only 39.3 percent of the women, say they are very or somewhat satisfied with their ability to keep current. And for the new cohort of faculty, 37.3 percent of the women, in contrast to 50.2 percent of the men, report being either very or somewhat satisfied. This veritable gulf for faculty who are presumably experiencing roughly the same kinds of pressures may reflect (as indicated in other parts of the survey) the finding that women are more seriously committed than their male colleagues to teaching and advising (Table A-24C), thus subjecting themselves to an even greater time crunch. There is undoubtedly a further factor: the disproportionate share of household responsibilities that many women surely continue to shoulder.

When differences among types of institutions are examined, new-generation faculty tend to be somewhat less satisfied than their seniors for most of the indicators across all institutional types (Table A-22B). New faculty at the public two-year institutions tend to be somewhat more satisfied on the criteria variables, whereas new faculty at the liberal arts colleges tend to express the least amount of satisfaction. This is a result that some will find surprising, for over time (at least until recent years) faculty members at the community colleges have tended to report relatively low levels of satisfaction while faculty at the liberal arts colleges (especially at the more selective Liberal Arts I campuses) have tended to be the most satisfied.

Viewed by academic program area, the natural scientists report marginally higher levels of satisfaction in both cohorts while the humanists tend to be the least satisfied (Table A-22C). An interesting point here is that the natural scientists also report spending more time at their work than their colleagues (see Table A-25); this result suggests that they derive more pleasure from their work, have been conditioned to accept very heavy work schedules, or both. Among other measures of job satisfaction, the humanists rather consistently lag behind their colleagues, most notably in trying to keep current in one's field.

Career Satisfaction: The Global Measures

The NSOPF-93 survey contains two global measures, often used in similar surveys, that attempt to assess faculty members' overall attitude about their work and chosen career. The first item reads, "If I had to do it over again, I would still choose an academic career." The substantial majority of male and female faculty in both cohorts agreed either somewhat or strongly: 88.7 percent of the new cohort and 89.2 percent of the senior cohort (Table 23). On a four-point scale with 4 representing "agree strongly" and 1 representing "disagree strongly," each cohort registers an impressive 3.5 mean score.

Table 23 ⇒ **Global Career Satisfaction**

| | "I would do it again" | | Job overall | |
	Mean	Percent somewhat/strongly agree	Mean	Percent somewhat/very satisfied
All faculty	3.5	89.1	3.2	84.2
New faculty	3.5	88.7	3.1	82.2
Senior faculty	3.5	89.2	3.2	85.2

Note: The first of the two global measures reads, "If I had to do it over again, I would still choose an academic career: 1 = disagree strongly; 2 = disagree somewhat; 3 = agree somewhat; 4 = agree strongly." Percent somewhat/very satisfied represents cumulative percent of those who responded "agree somewhat" or "agree strongly." The second asks about satisfaction with "my job here, overall: 1 = very dissatisfied; 2 = somewhat dissatisfied; 3 = somewhat satisfied; 4 = very satisfied." Percent somewhat/strongly agree represents cumulative percent of those who responded "somewhat satisfied" or "very satisfied."

The second global measure asks about satisfaction with "my job here, overall." Again, the responses are very positive, albeit not as emphatic as for the "If I had to do it over again" item. The mean scores are 3.1 for new faculty and 3.2 for senior faculty. Expressed in percentages, the substantial majority of faculty report satisfaction (either "somewhat satisfied" or "very satisfied") with their job overall: 82.2 percent of the new generation and 85.2 percent of their senior colleagues. Given that scores for faculty satisfaction with various components of their work all range downward from the high scores accorded overall job satisfaction, it would appear that the whole is indeed greater than the sum of the parts![12] Perhaps the most unexpected finding is that for the new-cohort faculty, levels of satisfaction, despite the pressures and insecurities with which many must contend, are in the same neighborhood as those registered by their established colleagues. One can speculate that the fact of having "won" a full-time appointment in such a highly competitive labor market itself contributed to their sense of satisfaction.

Taking gender, institutional type, and program areas into account, it is clear that levels of satisfaction on both global measures are consistently high across all categories (Table A-23). The mean scores on the 4-point scale for "I would still choose an academic career" are consistent—an impressive 3.5 (plus or minus 0.1) across the board.

Despite their concerns about particular features of their jobs, as previously described, women essentially pull even with men in overall job satisfaction among new-generation faculty (81.2 versus 82.9 percent for the men); the mean score for each is 3.1 (Table A-23). Among their senior colleagues, the mean score for men is 3.2 (85.9 percent somewhat or very satisfied) compared with 3.1 for women (83.5 percent somewhat or very satisfied).

Turning to institutional variations, overall job satisfaction appears again to run highest at the public two-year institutions (3.3 mean for both cohorts; 89.2 percent of the new faculty declaring themselves either very or somewhat satisfied). At the other institutions, the level of overall job satisfaction among the new faculty lags somewhat behind that of their senior colleagues.

Differences by program area vary only slightly. One notable departure, however, is the difference between new and senior natural scientists: the senior natural scientists express the highest satisfaction levels (91.7 percent report that they would again choose an academic career), but their junior colleagues, on the same measure, express the least satisfaction (86.6 percent). By contrast, the new-cohort humanists, social scientists, and faculty in the professions, when compared with their senior colleagues, report essentially the same, or even slightly higher, convictions that they would again embark on an academic career. On the measure of overall job satisfaction the differences are more attenuated, but the gap between the two cohorts of natural scientists remains the greatest. Perhaps not too much should be made of these differences, however, in view of the fact that the vast majority of the natural scientists in both cohorts indicate satisfaction.

The overriding message is this: on the whole the similarities between the cohorts—examined by gender, institutional type, or program area—are more significant than their differences. And the profession, viewed through any of these lenses, appears to be largely satisfied with its lot—both their choice of career and overall assessment of the components that make up the vocation.

In Summary

Compared with their senior colleagues, the new generation entered their academic careers from a more diverse educational background (as seen in the sources of their highest degrees) and with a more varied work history both within and outside higher education. Most significant is the finding that a large segment (about one-third) of the new generation is more likely than their seniors to have entered into "temporary" or "term" positions that do not offer a foothold on the traditional academic career ladder.

Turning to indicators of satisfaction, the new-entry cohort reports being less satisfied with their job security and prospects for advancement. But on the whole, both cohorts report at least moderate levels of satisfaction on most of the measures that make up job satisfaction. Although the new cohort's degree of satisfaction tends to trail slightly that of their senior colleagues on most measures, their responses are much more similar than dissimilar. Levels of satisfaction on two global measures are impressively high for both cohorts—indeed, considerably higher than those reported for the disaggregated dimensions of work. Again, the overall levels of satisfaction do not reveal much difference between the senior- and new-faculty cohorts.

FIVE

THE NEW ACADEMIC
GENERATION AT WORK

How is the new academic generation going about its work responsibilities? How do the new entrants into faculties of higher education compare with their senior colleagues in the ways in which they perform their tasks? Based on the NSOPF-93 survey, we can examine a number of dimensions of their work experience. These include both the actual and preferred distributions of their effort (that is, the percentage of work time devoted to teaching, research, service, and other activities), their office hours and the amount of contact with undergraduate students, instructional methods employed in the classroom, their involvement in research and publication, and the extent and nature of their outside employment (that is, their concurrent employment).

Distribution of Faculty Effort

To what extent do differences show up between the new entrants and their senior counterparts in the actual and preferred allocations of their time? Available data indicate that a generation ago (in the 1970s), faculty across all types of institutions were spending about 60–66 percent of their time teaching, about 14 percent in research, and about 18 percent in administration; in the university sector teaching time declined to 50–55 percent while research time increased to about 25 percent (Baldridge et al. 1978). By the early 1990s, as the data in Table 24 suggest, faculty involvement in teaching (53.8 percent) and in administration (12.8 percent) had both *declined* as time devoted to research increased to 20.1 percent. This shift is also reflected in the slippage between 1969 and 1989 in the proportion of faculty who indicated that their interests lay primarily in teaching (falling from 76 to 72 percent) and, even more steeply, in those who agreed that teaching effectiveness should be the primary criterion for promotion (from 77 to 69 percent) (Carnegie Foundation for the Advancement of Teaching 1989, 63–64; Russell 1992). The data spanning the past quarter-century thus tend to support the common impression: a broadening diffusion of the research university model into the collegiate sector.

These generational differences are also discernible in our data. New career entrants report spending 51.3 percent of their time teaching (less than the 55.1 percent reported by their senior colleagues), 22.5 percent of their time engaged in research (compared with the 18.9 percent reported by the senior faculty), a sizable 13.2 percent committed to administration, and 5.8 percent of their time performing service or other nonteaching activities (Table 24). In contrast to how they actually distribute their time, the new-cohort faculty would prefer to allocate less of their time to teaching (45.5 percent) and significantly more time to research (29.5 percent). This finding reveals a greater preference for research than that reported by their senior colleagues, who likewise would prefer to increase their time devoted to research—but only to a 25.1 percent commitment.

Table 24 🖚 **Actual and Preferred Distribution of Effort**

	Actual					
	Teaching	Research	Service	Professional growth	Administration	Consulting
All faculty	53.8	20.1	5.7	4.7	12.8	2.6
New faculty	51.3	22.5	5.8	4.9	13.2	2.2
Senior faculty	55.1	18.9	5.6	4.7	12.6	2.9
	Preferred					
	Teaching	Research	Service	Professional growth	Administration	Consulting
All faculty	48.6	26.6	5.4	8.0	7.9	3.3
New faculty	45.5	29.5	5.3	8.3	8.2	2.8
Senior faculty	50.1	25.1	5.4	7.8	7.8	3.5

Note: Percents represent percentage of total time (100 percent). Details may not add to total because of rounding.

Expressed another way, the new entrants would prefer to reallocate about 11–12 percent of their current commitments. This would entail, roughly, shifting a 6–7 percent block of their work time from teaching to research, transferring another 4–5 percent from administration to professional growth activities, and moving a fraction of 1 percent from service to consulting. Thus the new generation, given its druthers, yearns for a more *individualized* professional agenda (expanding their research, professional development, and consulting) but less communal involvement in teaching, administration, and service responsibilities.

Although their hoped-for reprioritizing would not constitute a huge shift in effort—perhaps on the order of six hours during the course of a fifty-hour work week (or roughly an hour a day)—the new look would nevertheless amount to a significant change. The desired reordering of priorities among the new entrants is not very different from what their more experienced colleagues seek: less teaching (by 5.0 percent of their total effort) but more research (by 6.2 percent), less administration (by 4.8 percent) but more professional growth (by 3.1 percent). The pattern for the two cohorts is the same, but for the senior cohort, given a magic wand, the degree of change would be milder.

These differences between new-entrant and senior-faculty cohorts did not just emerge in very recent years; they reflect well-established concomitants of academic career stages. Thus a generation ago new entrants to the American professoriate were found to rank research as a higher priority than their senior colleagues and to spend more time doing research—although, interestingly, they were discovered to have been no more productive in terms of publications (Hesseldenz and Rodgers 1976; Baldwin and Blackburn 1981).[1]

In examining differences among types of institutions (Table A-24A), we find the expected pattern: a progression that runs from low teaching and high research activity at research universities to high teaching and low research activity at public two-year colleges. Probably reflecting substantial pressures to publish, the new cohort in the research universities, which already reports spending more time in research (41.1 percent) than in teaching (32.9 percent), would prefer to extend the "teaching deficit" by further reducing teaching (to 30.6 percent) and escalating research (to 46.9 percent). A contrasting picture is seen among faculty at other doctoral institutions; in that venue the new-cohort faculty spend considerably more time teaching (43.0 percent of their effort) than in research (29.9 percent). Given a choice, they would devote roughly the same amount of their time to both pursuits—about 37 percent.

One finding stands out: the preference to shift time from teaching into research holds for both cohorts at all institutional types, as do preferences for less administrative work and more time for professional development.

The same pattern applies across fields: less time in the classroom, more in the lab, the stacks, the studio, and, very likely, at home at the word processor (Table A-24B). New faculty in the humanities report teaching the greatest percentage of time (62.7 percent of their total work effort) by a considerable margin, presumably reflecting in part the appreciable number of humanists whose appointments are non–tenure track (see Table A-21) and whose responsibilities are heavily teaching oriented. By contrast, new-cohort natural scientists spend by far the most time conducting research (31.6 percent); this commitment stands in sharp contrast to those of social scientists (23.4 percent), faculty in the professions (20.6 percent), humanists (14.9 percent), and faculty in the fine arts (11.5 percent). (For the senior cohort, natural and social scientists report the greatest amount of research involvement at over 22 percent.) Only the new-cohort humanists and fine arts faculty report spending less time conducting research than their senior colleagues. This anomaly can probably be explained in part, once again, by the considerable number of new-cohort humanists appointed to positions set aside for the teaching of writing and foreign languages.

Differences by gender are substantial among the new faculty (Table A-24C) and have historically always been so (Finkelstein 1984; Blackburn and Lawrence 1995). Compared with their male colleagues, new-cohort women spend significantly more of their time teaching (58.0 versus 46.6 percent) and much less time doing research (16.2 versus 26.8 percent). Like their male colleagues, the new-entry women would elect to allocate less time to teaching and more to research. Even so, their preferred pattern would still have them teaching significantly more than the men (by about 10 percentage points) while spending substantially less time conducting research (22.9 versus 34.1 percent).

Although the pattern of preferring to allocate more time for research holds for men and women in both new and senior cohorts, the differences are more emphatic between new and senior *male* faculty (a 7-point difference: 34.1 versus 27.0 percent) than between female new entrants and their senior female colleagues (a mere 3-point difference: 22.9% versus 20.3 percent).

How can the "research gap" between the sexes be explained? The data have established the clear preference among women faculty (as previously noted) to be more involved than their male colleagues in teaching and advising. But other factors come into play. For instance, the very strong research orientation of the natural scientists skews the overall numbers, and because the male natural scientists so outnumber the female natural scientists in both cohorts (Table A-5), the gap between the sexes is consequently somewhat more exaggerated. The results are also affected by the disproportionate representation of women at institutions in which research is not a high priority and, correspondingly, their underrepresentation in research-oriented venues; thus, as seen in Table A-5, women constitute 44.2 percent of all faculty at the public two-year colleges but only 24.6 percent at the research universities.

Given the substantial differences between the men and the women in both cohorts in how they allocate their time between research and teaching, as well as how they would prefer to balance those responsibilities, it will be useful to focus on a subset of faculty: those who are either tenured or on the tenure track. This approach cordons off those faculty members (disproportionately women, as shown previously) who occupy nontenurable, presumably teaching-intensive, positions. Zooming in on those tenured or tenure-track faculty (Table A-24D), we see that the patterns are very similar. That is, when gender comparisons are restricted to tenured or tenurable faculty, the women in both cohorts *still* teach considerably more than men. The gender gap is most apparent in the new cohort of faculty: the women say they spend 57.1 percent of their time teaching, substantially more than the 46.4 percent reported by their male colleagues. And although the women, like the men, would prefer to be teaching less, if both genders were to get their wishes, the women would still be teaching considerably more than their male counterparts. That difference holds for both cohorts. Thus restricting the sample to tenured or tenurable faculty does not make the two genders look more similar.

Because women are disproportionately found, as noted, in those institutions that pay more attention to teaching than to research, further insight into the apparent gender gap becomes possible by isolating the men and women who are at research universities, where the institutional commitment to research is unequivocal (Table A-24E). Focusing on this subset of faculty, the gender gap narrows. True, the women in both cohorts once again report spending a greater percentage of their time engaged in teaching (37.3 percent in the new cohort; 41.5 percent among the senior cohort) compared with the men (33.6 percent for the new cohort; 38.4 percent in the senior cohort). And true, too, that the women in both cohorts would prefer to be teaching more than the men. But the differences in all of these instances are quite small and might well disappear altogether once academic program area is taken into account. The converse seems to be true when examining research activity; that is, these women report spending less of their time than men doing research and would also prefer to spend less time than men conducting research. But again the differences are not great. Thus the oft-reported gender gap in teaching versus research narrows substantially when we zero in on the tenured or tenurable faculty at the most heavily research-oriented institutions.

That observation aside, two differences between men and women at the research universities merit comment. For reasons that are not clear, new women faculty report spending about twice as much of their time engaged in service activities compared with the men. Moreover the women *prefer* spending more of their time than men performing service activities. Curiously, this heavier service orientation, in terms of both involvement and preference, largely disappears within the senior cohort. A second curiosity is found in the effort associated with administrative activity. Here the new cohort of men say that they spend 15.0 percent of their time engaged in administration compared with 11.5 percent for the women. These gender differences, however, vanish for the senior cohort.

In summary, for all institutional types, for all fields, for both men and women, and for both new-generation faculty and their senior colleagues, the same general pattern of preferences holds. They *all* prefer to spend less time in teaching and more time engaged in research; they *all* desire more time for their own professional growth and for consulting but would like to spend less time engaged in administrative tasks. Overall, this pattern suggests that although cohort differences are not inconsequential— and are hardly surprising given the pressures to produce to which many early-career, probationary faculty are subjected—the shaping influences of institutional context, of discipline, and possibly of gender socialization are the more powerful determinants of how one's work effort is allocated among competing demands. The reality is that these connections appear to be more influential by far than how long ago faculty members entered upon their careers (see also Clark 1987; Blackburn and Lawrence 1995).

The Work Week

Paid and Unpaid Activities

Over the years, faculty workload, that is, the amount of time that faculty devote to their professional responsibilities, appears to have remained remarkably stable at about fifty hours per week (Yuker 1984; Russell 1992). Our own analysis shows that the new generation of faculty lead busy lives. As Table 25 shows, they report spending an average of 43.4 hours

Table 25 ⇌ **Weekly Hours Spent on Paid and Unpaid Activities**

	Institutional activities		Outside activities		
	Paid	Unpaid	Paid	Unpaid	Total hours
All faculty	42.3	5.1	2.7	2.0	52.1
New faculty	43.4	5.3	2.6	1.7	53.0
Senior faculty	41.7	5.1	2.8	2.1	51.7

Note: Institutional paid activities are defined as "all paid activities at this institution (teaching, research, administration, etc.)." Institutional unpaid activities are defined as "all unpaid activities at this institution." Outside paid activities are defined as "any other paid activities outside this institution (e.g., consulting, working on other jobs)." Outside unpaid activities are defined as "unpaid (pro bono) professional service activities outside this institution." Details may not add to total because of rounding.

per week in "paid activities at this institution" (defined in the questionnaire as "teaching, research, administration, etc.").[2] They spend an additional 5.3 hours weekly on "unpaid activities at this institution." (This category is not defined in the survey instrument, and accordingly it is unclear what activities respondents might have had in mind in calculating these "unpaid activities.") The new faculty's 49-hour institutional work week slightly exceeds the 47 hours reported by their seniors.

Apart from faculty members' on-campus activities, the survey asks about their activities "outside this institution," both paid and unpaid. Faculty report an average of 2.7 hours per week in outside paid activities, defined as "e.g., consulting, working on other jobs"; there is little difference between the cohorts. Faculty also report 2.0 weekly hours of "unpaid (pro bono) professional service activities outside this institution." Again, differences between the two cohorts are modest. On average, the senior faculty spend about a half hour per week more than their junior colleagues in combined paid and unpaid activities outside their campuses (4.9 versus 4.3 hours).

Differences between the sexes (Table A-25) show that new-cohort males report spending about 4 hours a week more than their female colleagues in institutional paid activities (45.1 versus 41.0 hours) and roughly the same amount of time in unpaid activities within the institution. Among senior faculty, interestingly, the women report spending about an hour more than the men engaged in unpaid institutional activities but an hour less than the men pursuing outside paid activities.

Reflecting historical patterns, substantial differences are evident among types of institutions in the number of hours committed each week to paid institutional activities (Russell 1992). The range extends from research universities, where new-cohort faculty report 49.3 weekly hours (about 3 hours a week more than their senior colleagues) to public two-year institutions, where the corresponding figures are substantially less: 36.6 hours for the new faculty and 35.4 hours for the senior cohort. Comparing cohorts, few differences are evident; the biggest intercohort gap is seen at the research universities, as noted.

There is relatively little variation by institutional type in the amount of unpaid institutional activities. It is notable that faculty at the two types of doctorate-granting institutions, having reported the greatest time spent in paid activities, indicate that they spend marginally less time involved in unpaid institutional activities than their counterparts at other types of institutions.

Differences among program areas are less pronounced than those among institutional types. Even so, natural scientists (46.6 hours for the new cohort and 44.3 hours among their seniors), followed closely by social scientists, report spending more time in institutional paid activities than their colleagues in other program areas.

Office Hours and Student Contact

The new academic generation spends 8.4 hours per week holding office hours and 4.8 hours per week in informal student contact. Both numbers are roughly equivalent to the time spent by their more seasoned colleagues, although the new faculty do spend about an hour more per week holding office hours than their senior colleagues (Table 26).

When the data are examined by institutional type, it appears that research university faculty spend less time holding office hours than faculty in other settings; presumably this is due in part to the role that teaching assistants play (Table A-26). Variation by institution in informal contact hours is slight.

Viewed by program area, both cohorts of faculty in the professions report holding the most office hours: 10.0 hours for the new faculty and 8.3 for the senior cohort. Few differences are evident in the category of informal contact hours.

Table 26 ⇒+ Weekly Office Hours and Student Contact Hours

	Office hours	Informal contact hours
All faculty	7.8	4.9
New faculty	8.4	4.8
Senior faculty	7.5	4.9

To put these results in perspective, it is worth noting that the amount of out-of-class faculty-student contact has always been minimal and typically targeted on a small percentage of students who take the initiative in seeking it out (Gaff and Wilson 1975).[3]

Teaching Strategies

Primary Instructional Methods

The pedagogical approaches of the two cohorts are strikingly similar in the extent to which each relies primarily on lectures, seminars, "discussion group or class presentations," or "lab, clinic or problem solving" (Table 27). That is to say, the new academic career entrants remain quite traditional in the kind of teaching they do. In the 1970s, a generation ago, the best available estimates suggested that 80–85 percent of university courses employed the lecture (Thielens 1987).[4] Much like earlier generations, the members of the new academic generation continue to rely heavily on lectures or lecture-discussion as the dominant mode of instruction; in fact, slightly more than three-fourths of the faculty rely primarily on lectures with virtually no difference between the cohorts in that regard.

The similarities between the cohorts hold when their primary instructional methods are examined by institutional type as well as by program area (Table A-27). However, the differences *between* the genders, *among* institutional types, and *among* program areas are plain and largely reflect familiar historical patterns (Gaff and Wilson 1975; Finkelstein 1995). For instance, males in both cohorts use the lecture method much more than do their female colleagues, whereas, in contrast, the female faculty are almost twice as likely to employ discussion as a primary instructional method. They are more likely, too, to use labs, clinics, or problem-solving exercises.

Table 27 ⇌ **Primary Instructional Methods Used**

	Lecture	Seminar	Discussion	Lab
All faculty	76.2	5.3	7.7	10.7
New faculty	76.7	5.1	7.3	11.0
Senior faculty	76.0	5.4	8.0	10.6

Note: Results refer to all for-credit courses offered. The questionnaire item read, "In how many of the undergraduate courses that you taught for credit did you use. . . ." Discussion is defined as discussion or class presentations. Lab is defined as laboratory, internship, role play, or cooperative learning groups. Details may not add to total because of rounding.

The liberal arts colleges stand out for their distinctive pedagogical approach. The faculty there are much less likely to rely primarily on lecturing and much more likely to utilize discussion groups or class presentations. Indeed, among the new-cohort faculty this propensity to use discussions and class presentations is especially evident; these new liberal arts college faculty members are more than twice as likely to use this mode of instruction as their counterparts at research, other doctoral, and two-year campuses.

Sharp differences are found among the academic program areas. For instance, lectures are far more commonplace in both cohorts among the social scientists but especially among the natural scientists. Discussion is the strategy of choice far more often among the humanists than among the others; however, discussion appears to be practically invisible in the natural sciences and fares only marginally better in the social sciences.

Other Instructional Methods

Turning to other pedagogical techniques, it is again clear that the practices of the two cohorts are much more congruent than divergent (Table 28). Indeed, the incidence of usage for all eleven instructional techniques or strategies is almost the same for both cohorts—within 5 percentage points in all eleven instances and most often within 3 percentage points. In the two examples in which the differences are greater than 4 percent, the inter-cohort differences are still very modest.

The extent to which computing is used for instructional purposes shows that the senior cohort is marginally more inclined than their junior colleagues (32.1 versus 27.8 percent) to make use of computational tools and software in their teaching. It is also not clear what to make of the responses indicating that about one-fourth of all faculty, new and old alike, are employing computer-aided instruction; this finding is at odds with other sources on the topic (Green and Gilbert 1995). A cautionary note is in order here because technology-linked pedagogical practices may well be changing rapidly, and the NSOPF-93 data are several years old at this writing (Green 1996). On the whole, however, the data demonstrate that the new generation has not strayed far from the methods modeled by their mentors.

As for differences by gender, women appear to draw on a greater repertoire of instructional methods than men (Table A-28). Overall, women in both cohorts report using each of the instructional methods examined more than men. The single exception is grading on a curve, a practice that men in both cohorts employ more often. The largest gender differences are in

Table 28 ⫘ Other Instructional Methods Used

	Computational tools/ software	Computer-aided instruction	Student presentations	Student evaluations	Multiple-choice exams	Essay exams	Short-answer exams	Term/research papers	Multiple drafts of written work	Grading on a curve	Competency-based grading
All faculty	30.7	24.7	44.7	25.6	38.4	42.6	39.0	40.3	23.8	23.5	38.7
New faculty	27.8	23.7	42.2	25.3	36.0	39.6	38.0	37.7	22.7	22.8	36.8
Senior faculty	32.1	25.2	45.9	25.8	39.6	44.1	39.4	41.6	24.3	23.9	39.6

Note: Percent represents faculty who responded "some" or "all." The questionnaire item read, "In how many of the undergraduate courses that you taught for credit did you use. . . ."

the use of student presentations and evaluations and multiple drafts of written work—both student-centered practices more favored by women faculty. The smallest differences are reported in examination practices and the use of instructional software.

A mix of instructional practices is seen among the types of institutions. Among the more evident variations are these: Substantially greater use by both cohorts of computational tools and software, computer-aided instruction, and multiple-choice exams is found in the public two-year sector. Far less use by both cohorts of student presentations and student evaluations of student work is seen at the doctorate-granting institutions, especially at the research universities. Compared with other sectors, the liberal arts faculty stand out for making considerably greater use of student presentations, essay exams, term and research papers, and multiple drafts of written work.

When the data are viewed by program area, a number of differences are predictable: greater use of computational tools and software among natural scientists and professional program faculty and of term and research papers among social scientists and humanists. The latter are much more likely to make use of multiple drafts of written work. Interestingly, it is the new-cohort fine arts faculty that report the most utilization of computer-aided instruction.

Involvement in Research and Publication

A generation ago, research and publication activity in American higher education was concentrated mostly at the top of the system: in the university sector and especially in the research universities, where the majority of faculty published. The majority of faculty in other sectors do not publish—and never have. As Ladd (1979) put it so succinctly, about 10 percent of the faculty produce 90 percent of the publications.

In the ensuing decades, we would expect that the university's research culture, which to varying degrees has penetrated the rest of the system, would have brought with it increasing rates of research involvement and publication. The available data suggest, however, that it has not. Ladd (1979) reported that 43 percent of the faculty in 1969 were not engaged in publishing; by 1992, that figure was about 40 percent (National Center for Education Statistics 1994).[5] What is clear is that, institutional type aside, discipline and career stage have always shaped—and still contribute heavily to shaping—faculty research and publication activity (Creswell 1985; Blackburn and Lawrence 1995).

In our analysis, new career entrants are shown to be slightly more likely than their more experienced colleagues to be engaged in research and writing (70.4 percent versus 69.4 percent) and, by a sizable margin, in funded research (33.2 versus 27.2 percent).[6] Having had much briefer careers, they are less likely to have published journal articles (refereed or nonrefereed), chapters, textbooks, books, or monographs (Table 29), but the differences between the cohorts are not great. Nearly 70 percent of both groups have presented papers at professional conferences, reflecting the rough equivalence of research involvement in both groups.

Comparing genders, new-generation academic men and women both are more likely to be engaged in research than their respective senior colleagues (Table A-29A). In all, males are appreciably more likely than females to be engaged in research and publication among both the new and senior faculty cohorts. Thus 75.5 percent of new-cohort males report that during the current academic term (fall 1992) they were "engaged in professional research, writing, or creative works." This total compares with 63.1 percent of their women colleagues. An almost identical gap separates the men and women in the senior cohort. Similarly, the new-cohort men are far more likely to be "engaged in any funded research or funded creative endeavors" (38.9 versus 25.0 percent of the women) and, within the two previous years, to have published in a refereed journal (62.9 versus 41.9 percent of the women). Women in the new cohort draw nearly even with men in the proportion who present at conferences and slightly surpass men in "exhibitions or performances in the fine or applied arts."

A number of factors, discussed previously in other contexts, undoubtedly contribute to this apparent gender gap in research and publication. They include institutional type (e.g., women are disproportionately located in the community colleges) and program area (e.g., women are less likely to be appointed in the publication-rich natural sciences and more likely to hold non–tenure track appointments, for instance in teaching composition or introductory foreign languages, for which there are few if any research expectations).

To scrutinize gender differences more closely, it is instructive to isolate men and women at the research universities who hold either tenured or tenure-track appointments (Table A-29B). This is revealing because the gender gap in research and writing, seemingly so pronounced in Table A-29A, largely disappears! Two points are immediately evident: (1) Almost all (more than nine of ten) are engaged in research and writing (especially in the pressured new-faculty cohort). (2) The gender gap narrows to 2 or

Table 29 ╪ Involvement in Research and Publication

	Engaged in research/ writing	Engaged in funded research	Published in refereed journals	Published in nonrefereed journals	Created work in juried media	Created work in nonjuried media	Published book reviews	Published chapters
All faculty	69.7	29.2	58.0	36.1	6.4	13.3	28.6	30.9
New faculty	70.4	33.2	54.3	31.3	5.8	12.5	20.6	27.4
Senior faculty	69.4	27.2	59.8	38.5	6.7	13.7	32.6	32.7

	Published textbooks	Published books	Published monographs	Published technical reports	Presented at conferences	Gave exhibitions or performances	Held patents or copyrights	Published computer software
All faculty	11.1	14.6	11.6	29.2	68.5	8.8	8.0	6.0
New faculty	5.6	10.2	7.9	27.2	67.1	8.2	6.1	5.7
Senior faculty	13.9	16.9	13.5	30.2	69.2	9.1	9.0	6.2

Note: Percents represent percentage of all faculty.

3 percentage points (compared with a dozen or so points if we do not control for institutional type and for type of appointment, as was seen in Table A-29A).

Other pronounced differences remain even when keeping the microscope focused on this select contingent, but they appear to reflect differences among fields in the kinds of scholarly activity that are rewarded and in extramural funding opportunities. To illustrate, many more new-cohort men (72.1 percent) than women (61.4 percent) report that they are engaged in funded research. This result is probably a function of the disproportionate number of men in the natural sciences (where funded research is often a prerequisite for the survival of probationary faculty), as well as the much greater presence of women in the humanities (where extramural support is very hard to come by). In addition, whereas more men than women publish in refereed journals (89.1 versus 77.4 percent among new-cohort faculty), more women produce works in juried and nonjuried media. Note, too, that the gender gap virtually vanishes among new-cohort faculty in such categories as published books (17.7 percent of the men versus 16.6 percent of the women) and conference presentation rates.

In fact, in a demonstration of staying focused on what counts most for promotion and tenure, these tenured or tenure-track new-cohort faculty members at research universities, both men and women, are more likely than their senior colleagues to be engaged in two critical activities: research and writing and conducting funded research. (Conversely, senior-cohort women report publishing in refereed journals more than their junior colleagues.) In those categories that are usually less vital to the survival of probationary faculty, an opposite pattern emerges: the research university new-cohort faculty (again both men and women) are *less* likely than their senior counterparts to publish in *non*refereed journals, to create works in juried and in nonjuried media, or to publish book reviews, textbooks, or books (to cite key examples). In this subset of faculty, the men are far more likely than the women to have published computer software products.

When we control for institutional type, we find, to no one's surprise, that research and writing are substantially more prevalent in doctorate-granting universities (Table A-29C). Liberal arts colleges are intermediate on this measure, and public two-year colleges fall at the low end.

Differences by program area array along the lines historically associated with favored publishing outlets: natural scientists publish in refereed journals; humanists and social scientists engage in writing books (Biglan 1973; Braxton and Hargens 1996) (Table A-29D).

Several cohort differences are notable among program areas. For instance, considerably more new-entry natural scientists are engaged in funded research (49.8 percent) compared with senior natural scientists (37.7 percent)—one indicator that the pressure is on. In addition, whereas the new-entry social scientists and humanists lag behind their senior colleagues in journal publication, the new-entry natural scientists, in sharp contrast, are publishing in refereed journals at about the same rate as their senior colleagues.

Concurrent Employment

To what extent do members of each faculty cohort in each type of institution and each program area engage in full-time or part-time employment outside their employing institutions? Roughly one-fourth of faculty members in both the new and senior cohorts report some concurrent outside employment: 23.6 percent of the new cohort and 24.7 percent of the senior cohort (Table 30). For the vast majority, such outside employment is part time. It is worth noting, however, that 1.9 percent of the full-time faculty (2.4 percent of the new-cohort faculty and 1.7 percent of the senior faculty) report that their "main other job" was full time (Table 30). One is left to ponder the ethical and legal implications of this phenomenon.

Men in both cohorts are more likely than their women colleagues to hold concurrent jobs, whether full or part time (Table A-30). This difference is more prominent within the senior cohort.

Among faculty at different types of institutions, there are minimal differences in concurrent employment frequency—with one intriguing exception. Among new-cohort faculty, those at the research and doctoral universities are least likely to report outside employment (18.8 and 19.7 percent, respectively, compared with 24.0–27.2 percent among faculty at other institutional types). Presumably it is at these institutions that the

Table 30 ⇌ Concurrent Employment

	Total	Full-time	Part-time
All faculty	24.3	1.9	22.4
New faculty	23.6	2.4	21.2
Senior faculty	24.7	1.7	23.0

Note: Percents represent percentage of total number of faculty within cohort. The questionnaire item read, "During the 1992 Fall term did you have other employment including any outside consulting or other self-owned business, or private practice?" Details may not add to total because of rounding.

demands on new faculty are greatest (and compensation highest), militating against extramural activity.

Among program areas, faculty in the fine arts and the professions are by far the most likely to be employed outside their institutions. In the fine arts, 39.7 percent of the new cohort and 42.2 percent of the senior cohort were so employed; in the professions, the figures were 29.1 and 29.8 percent, respectively. This finding contrasts sharply with the experience of the humanists (16.4 and 15.6 percent, respectively) and the natural scientists (14.6 and 18.8 percent, respectively). The social scientists report levels of concurrent employment midway between the fine arts and professions on the one hand and the humanities and natural sciences on the other.

Turning now to the employment sectors in which faculty members pursue their concurrent work (and restricting the responses to one "main" concurrent job per faculty member), some interesting findings emerge (Table 31). The biggest area by far is the sector-spanning category of "consulting, freelance work, self-founded business, or private practice." Concurrent work of this type (reported by 12.6 percent of all faculty members) accounts for over half of the concurrent employment engaged in by the faculty members in both cohorts for all program areas and institutional types. None of the other sectors approaches that cluster of employment roles in popularity among faculty. Among the other sectors, higher education (3.5 percent) accounts for the next largest incidence of concurrent employment of all faculty (2.7 percent at a "4-year college or university, graduate or professional school" and 0.8 percent at a "2-year or other postsecondary institution").

The two cohorts are distributed roughly evenly among the employment sectors. However, the new faculty members are slightly more likely than their senior colleagues to be employed in the health care sector, whereas senior faculty are somewhat more likely to be involved in consulting and freelance work and in foundations and nonprofits, as well as federal, state, and local government work.

Taking gender into account, the prevalence of men in the sector consisting of consulting and freelance work is seen again (Table A-31). New-cohort women are more likely than men to hold concurrent jobs in "hospital or other health care or clinical settings." Men are more likely than women, albeit slightly, to work concurrently for a higher education or government employer, whereas women are more likely to be employed in elementary or secondary schools.

Viewing the findings by institutional type, it is interesting to note that faculty at two-year institutions, in both cohorts, are more likely than

Table 31 ⚑ Concurrent Employment Sector

	Four-year college or university	Two-year college	Elementary or secondary school	Consulting, freelance, private business, or private practice	Hospital, health care, or clinical practice	Foundation or nonprofit	For-profit business or industry	Federal, state, local government or military	Other
All faculty	2.7	0.8	0.4	12.6	2.5	0.9	1.6	1.0	1.9
New faculty	2.7	1.0	0.4	11.4	3.3	0.7	1.5	0.9	1.7
Senior faculty	2.7	0.7	0.4	13.2	2.1	1.0	1.6	1.1	2.0

Note: Percents represent percentage of total number of faculty within cohort. The questionnaire item read, "Not counting any employment at this institution, what was the employment sector of the main other job you held during Fall 1992?" Details may not add to total because of rounding.

faculty at other types of institutions to work concurrently in a higher education or health care setting. Faculty at liberal arts colleges, although still engaged in extramural employment to an extent roughly on a par with their colleagues at other types of institutions, especially in the foundation or nonprofit and government sectors, are least likely to be engaged in free-lance work or private practice. This finding no doubt reflects the relative dearth of professional faculty vis-à-vis other institutional types.

In Summary

Although the new generation of career entrants are more diverse than their more experienced colleagues in gender and race/ethnicity, in educational background, and in their work histories, those differences are not reflected in major ways in the nature and distribution of their current work activities. In terms of their teaching strategies, the data show them to be much like their more experienced colleagues in their basic pedagogical approaches (lecturing, for example, still dominates). And like faculty throughout the post–World War II period, both cohorts currently spend far more time teaching and less time in research and publishing. But—reflecting the shift in recent years to a greater emphasis on research that extends well beyond the traditionally research-intensive institutions—our analysis shows that faculty of both genders and in all institution types and program areas would prefer a mix of responsibilities that would enable them to teach less in order to have more time for conducting research. Time spent with students does not vary much between the two cohorts.

Yet there is one pronounced difference: the new-entry faculty are considerably more research oriented than their senior counterparts. This involvement in research may reflect their "career age" rather than purely generational differences; that is, the junior faculty, most of them still in a probationary status, presumably are engaged more heavily in research as a strategy for securing their careers.

As for differences between the genders, it is clear on the one hand that women, in fact, spend a greater proportion of their time engaged in teaching than do men. Furthermore, whereas women would prefer (as do men) to shift a portion of their time from teaching to research, the women's preferred pattern would nevertheless result in more time devoted to teaching than would be the preference of their male associates. Viewed only in that way, a gender gap—women inclined more than men to teach, men gravitating more than women to conducting research—is palpable. It is notable, however, that if the comparison is limited to tenured or tenure-track faculty at research universities, the putative gender gap narrows very substantially in terms of both the extent of involvement in research and the preference to shift work effort from teaching into research. The same patterns are discernible in the tables that report involvement in various types of research and publication.

The data on instructional methods demonstrate that, despite differences between genders, among institution types, and among program areas, there are not many variations between the two cohorts. If significant changes in pedagogical behavior are under way, they surely are not captured by our data, which demonstrate much more continuity than reform.

An important conclusion is inescapable: the two cohorts differ much more in terms of *who* they are than in *what* they do.

SIX

THE ATTITUDES AND VALUES OF THE NEW ACADEMIC GENERATION

To what extent and in what ways are the demographic characteristics, career structure, and on-the-job experiences of this new academic generation of American higher education faculty reflected in the values and attitudes they bring to their work? NSOPF-93 allows us to examine attitudes toward faculty roles and rewards, opinions about their instructional duties, and perceptions of their campuses' environments and facilities. These perceptual measures supplement in important ways the faculty members' descriptions of how they behave in their work; in this chapter we probe their views about various dimensions of academic life as they live it.

Faculty Roles and Rewards

As noted earlier, a progressive spread of the research university culture throughout most of American higher education took place between 1969 and 1989 (Carnegie Foundation for the Advancement of Teaching 1989). During that two-decade span (Russell 1992)

- The proportion of faculty reporting that their "interests lie primarily in (or are leaning toward) teaching" declined from 76 percent to 72 percent.

- The proportion of faculty agreeing that "teaching effectiveness should be the primary criterion for promotion" declined sharply from 77 percent to 69 percent.
- The percentage of faculty reporting that "it is difficult for a person to receive tenure if he/she does not publish" rose steeply from 41 percent to 54 percent.

The more recent NSOPF-93 data enable us to examine what current faculty members think about the relative importance of teaching and research. This inquiry reveals that the new and senior generations agree that teaching effectiveness still ought to be the primary criterion for promotion and tenure (3.1 mean on a 4-point scale) (Table 32). Indeed, the responses of both cohorts are essentially identical: 77.4 percent of the new faculty and 77.7 percent of the senior faculty agree somewhat or strongly that teaching should be the salient standard for promotion. Despite the fact that each cohort would prefer to trade off some teaching in order to be doing more research (as established in Chapter 5), only about one-third of each cohort agrees (either somewhat or strongly) that research and publication *should* be the primary criterion for promotion (34.2 percent of the new-entry faculty; 32.7 percent of the senior cohort). This may represent a slight reversal in the steady momentum over the previous two decades toward establishing research as the primary criterion for promotion (as

Table 32 ⇒ Perceptions of Faculty Roles and Rewards

	Teaching should be promotion criterion		Research should be promotion criterion		Research rewarded more than teaching		Assessment will improve quality of education	
	Mean	Percent somewhat/ strongly agree	Mean	Percent somewhat/ strongly agree	Mean	Percent somewhat/ strongly agree	Mean	Percent somewhat/ strongly agree
All faculty	3.1	77.6	2.1	33.2	2.5	49.9	2.0	32.9
New faculty	3.1	77.4	2.1	34.2	2.4	48.5	2.1	36.1
Senior faculty	3.2	77.7	2.1	32.7	2.5	50.6	2.0	31.3

Note: The questionnaire items read, "Indicate the extent to which you agree or disagree with these statements: 1 = disagree strongly; 2 = disagree somewhat; 3 = agree somewhat; 4 = agree strongly." Teaching as promotion criterion: "Teaching effectiveness should be the primary criterion for promotion of college teachers at this institution." Research as promotion criterion: "Research/publications should be the primary criterion for promotion of college teachers at this institution." Research rewarded more than teaching: "At this institution, research is rewarded more than teaching." Assessment will improve quality of education: "State or federally mandated assessment requirements will improve the quality of undergraduate education." Percent somewhat/strongly agree represents cumulative percentage of those who responded "somewhat agree" or "strongly agree." Means and percents were calculated using only those faculty who had responded in each category; thus the number of valid responses is different for each category.

evident in the Carnegie data), but it is difficult to tell. As a contrary indicator, the new cohort, as noted, is marginally more supportive of the primacy of the research and publication criterion than are their senior colleagues.

Naturally the importance that faculty attach to the practice of rewarding teaching is increasingly prevalent as one moves from the university sector to the two-year colleges (Table A-32A). A certain amount of ambivalence is evident among research university faculty. In these bastions of research, the faculty are evenly divided concerning whether teaching or research should serve as the primary criterion for reward: 54.2 percent of the new faculty prefer teaching as the standard, but 54.1 percent advocate research. Among their senior colleagues, somewhat more support for the rule of research is evident: 52.1 percent cast their votes for teaching compared with 57.5 percent for research.[1]

A further vantage point is afforded by the questionnaire item that shifts from the prescriptive to the descriptive by asking whether faculty members agree that at their institutions "research is rewarded more than teaching." In contrast to mixed views regarding what ought to be, few signs of ambivalence are evident in faculty members' depiction of prevailing realities. Again, as would be expected, the proportion of faculty members who report that research *is* the dominant criterion declines steeply from the research universities to the community colleges: whereas about nine-tenths of all faculty at research universities believe that research in actuality is rewarded more than teaching, the proportion plummets to less than 10 percent of the community college faculty.

An interesting split is seen by institutional type. At the research and other doctoral institutions and at the comprehensives, the proportion of faculty members—especially at the first two institutional types—who say that research in fact *is* rewarded more is far larger than the proportion of their colleagues who prefer research as the primary criterion. Thus among research university faculty, whereas 54.1 percent of the new cohort and 57.5 percent of the senior cohort would choose research as the primary promotion criterion, overwhelming majorities of each cohort (86.9 percent of the new-entry cohort and 90.0 percent of their senior counterparts) declare that research is rewarded more than teaching. The gap between "is" and "ought to be" is more attenuated among the faculty at the comprehensive institutions. But at the liberal arts institutions the reverse holds: about 20 percent of the faculty in both cohorts would prefer research primacy compared with a modest 15 percent or so who report that research in actuality counts for more. The differences at the two-year institutions are slight.

Several items suggest that the importance attached to teaching may indeed represent a real normative departure of this generation from its predecessors—providing flickers of hope for those who urge a reemphasis on teaching.

First, new entrants are less likely (albeit marginally so) than their senior colleagues to perceive that "research is rewarded more than teaching." The most striking contrast is evident in the comprehensive institutions, where only 35.6 percent of the new cohort (2.2 mean on a 4-point scale), but 44.7 percent of the senior cohort (2.4 mean), perceive that research is in fact rewarded more than teaching. This result may represent an important shift in values at the comprehensive institutions, perhaps a return, at least part way, to their formerly less ambiguous commitments to teaching. This shift suggests that, at least from the new faculty's perspective, teaching's star may be on the rise. Alternatively, they may simply be more naive or more idealistic, possibly misreading their environment—at their own peril!

Second, the new entrants are more likely to believe that "state or federally mandated assessment requirements will improve the quality of undergraduate education." This result implies a greater willingness on the part of newer faculty members to bolster undergraduate education even if to do so would entail government involvement via mandated assessment requirements. Interestingly, these cohort differences regarding assessment hold across institutional types, even at the research and doctoral universities.

When the data are viewed by program area, the natural and social scientists in both cohorts are relatively more research oriented, both in terms of the value they attach to research and publication and in their perceptions of how the reward system actually works. The contrast is most vivid in comparison with the humanities faculty.

Echoing data reported earlier about the stronger receptivity to teaching among women faculty, a decidedly greater preference for teaching among women than among men is again seen. Both cohorts of female faculty advocate that teaching should be the primary criterion for promotion: among the new entrants (81.9 percent of women [3.2 mean] versus 74.2 percent of men [3.0 mean]) and likewise among their senior colleagues (83.2 percent [3.3 mean] versus 75.5 percent [3.1 mean]). Interestingly, the men in both cohorts tend to perceive more than the women that research is in fact rewarded more than teaching; this finding perhaps reflects in part the greater proportion of men in the natural and social sciences, where research is accorded a relatively greater priority, and is probably also a function of the large number of women in the community colleges, where teaching is emphasized so strongly.

But do these differences hold up when comparing men and women situated in roughly the same career circumstances? Once more, zooming in on the tenured or tenure-track faculty at the research-oriented institutions (as was done in Chapter 5) provides a different vantage point (Table A-32B). This time the analysis shows that differences between the genders remain emphatic. At the research and other doctoral universities the tenured or tenurable male faculty are much more likely than their female colleagues to hold that research rather than teaching should be the primary criterion for promotion. There are substantial differences within the senior-faculty cohort (56.2 percent of the men but only 47.1 percent of the women endorse research as the primary criterion). The intergender differences are also wide among new-entry faculty: 57.0 percent of the men but only 50.1 percent of the women. That is to say, the substantial gap between "is" and "ought to be" holds for both faculty cohorts.

However, shifting from the prescriptive to the descriptive, the gender gap closes almost completely. That is, when responding to the statement, "At this institution, research is rewarded more than teaching," the differences between male and female faculty at the research-oriented campuses almost disappear. In fact, in both cohorts the women more than the men believe that research is the primary criterion used on their campuses. Thus the disjunction, as perceived by women, between "is" and "ought to be" is very large compared with the men's perceptions, and this holds true for both cohorts. This gap can be expressed as follows:

	Research should be primary criterion	Research is rewarded more	Difference
New-faculty males	57.0	80.9	23.9
New-faculty females	50.1	83.4	33.3
Senior-faculty males	56.2	84.0	27.8
Senior-faculty females	47.1	84.3	37.2

Seen in this light, women faculty within the cadre that is on the tenure track at the doctoral institutions look out over a gulf between what they think the system *should* reward and what they see as in fact getting rewarded. Although there are also prescriptive-descriptive differences as seen by the men, the chasm narrows substantially.

A summary comment may be useful to contrast the descriptive and prescriptive views about the proper role of research in the academy. The faculty's perception of the extent to which research *is* rewarded more than teaching consistently exceeds their beliefs about the extent to which research *should* serve as the primary criterion for promotion and tenure; this disparity exists for both genders, for institutional types (with exceptions), and for program areas. The gap is most obvious in the doctorate-granting sector (research and doctoral institutions combined). On the other hand, at the liberal arts colleges only about 17 percent of the senior cohort and even fewer of the junior cohort (about 15 percent) believe that research *is* rewarded more than teaching, and somewhat more faculty in each cohort (roughly 20 percent) appear to favor a research "upgrade."

Instructional Duties

Overall, new career entrants, as well as their more experienced faculty colleagues, are in very high proportions satisfied with various aspects of their instructional responsibilities (Table 33). This is especially so regarding the autonomy they have in making curricular and scheduling decisions about their courses (both content and method); in this regard, academic freedom appears to be alive and well. Although the new entrants tend to be very slightly less satisfied than their seniors on this measure of autonomy, this small deficit in satisfaction levels among the new faculty becomes somewhat more pronounced concerning their teaching assignment prerogatives and the time available to them to work with students as advisors. Somewhat less satisfaction is also evident regarding their authority to make decisions about the "other (non-instructional) aspects" of their jobs.[2]

Table 33 ⇒ Perceptions of Instructional Duties

	Course content and methods		Noninstructional aspects		Course choice		Time for students	
	Mean	Percent somewhat/ strongly satisfied	Mean	Percent somewhat/ strongly satisfied	Mean	Percent somewhat/ strongly satisfied	Mean	Percent somewhat/ strongly satisfied
All faculty	3.7	94.5	3.0	75.2	3.3	85.7	3.1	79.7
New faculty	3.7	94.0	3.0	76.0	3.2	83.1	3.0	77.1
Senior faculty	3.7	94.8	3.0	74.9	3.4	86.9	3.1	80.9

Note: The questionnaire items read, "How satisfied are you with each of these aspects of your instructional duties: 1 = very dissatisfied; 2 = somewhat dissatisfied; 3 = somewhat satisfied; 4 = very satisfied." Content and methods: "Authority I have to make decisions about content and methods in the courses I teach." Noninstructional aspects: "Authority I have to make decisions about other (non-instructional) aspects of my job." Courses: "Authority I have to make decisions about what courses I teach." Time for students: "Time available for working with students as an advisor, mentor, etc." Percent somewhat/very satisifed represents cumulative percentage of those who responded "somewhat satisfied" or "very satisfied." Means and percents were calculated using only those faculty who had responded in each category; thus the number of valid responses is different for each category.

Even so, three-quarters of each cohort say they are either somewhat or very satisfied in that regard.

The same patterns obtain across institutional types and across program areas (Table A-33). The degree of faculty satisfaction regarding their autonomy—their ability to influence course content and methods, what they teach, and the noninstructional dimensions of their jobs—does not vary much either by type of institution or by program area. Taking gender into account, men in the senior cohort consistently report higher levels of satisfaction on the autonomy measures. However, the differences by gender among the new entrants tends to narrow, suggesting that the new-generation women are perhaps being treated more equitably than their veteran counterparts. For instance, senior men are more likely than senior women to be somewhat or very satisfied about their authority to decide what courses they will teach (88.1 percent versus 83.9 percent). But that difference shrinks slightly in the junior cohort. The gender gap is more pronounced in regard to the time available for working with students as an advisor or mentor, suggesting that women would prefer more time for that purpose, that they experience more demands on themselves to function as advisors or mentors, or both.

The Campus Environment

Undergraduate Education

About two-thirds of new entrants and senior faculty report that they are somewhat satisfied or very satisfied with the quality of students on their campuses (Table 34). Some optimism is visible in both cohorts about their campuses' success in meeting their students' educational needs. That is, more faculty members in both cohorts express the opinion that their institutions' ability "to meet the educational needs of entering students" has improved rather than worsened. For both cohorts combined, 38.4 percent report that the situation has improved, 22.3 percent say that it has worsened, and 33.7 percent indicate that it has stayed the same. (Another 5.6 percent [10.8 percent among the new faculty] say that they do not know.)

Faculty at the research and other doctoral universities and especially at the liberal arts colleges (75.9 percent of the senior faculty and 74.1 percent of the new cohort) are the most pleased with the quality of their undergraduate students (Table A-34), whereas faculty at the comprehensive and community college campuses are least satisfied. Faculty at most types of institutions report seeing some improvement in their institution's ability "to meet the educational needs of entering students." This is most evident

Table 34 ⇌ **Perceptions of Campus Environment:**
Undergraduate Education

| | Quality of undergraduates | | Institution is meeting the educational needs of students | | | |
	Mean	Percent somewhat/very satisfied	Worsened	Stayed the same	Improved	Don't know
All faculty	2.8	67.7	22.3	33.7	38.4	5.6
New faculty	2.8	68.4	19.7	33.3	36.2	10.8
Senior faculty	2.8	67.4	23.6	33.9	39.6	2.9

Note: The first questionnaire item read, "How satisfied are you with each of the following aspects of your instructional duties at this institution? 1 = very dissatisfied; 2 = somewhat dissatisfied; 3 = somewhat satisfied; 4 = very satisfied." For "Quality of undergraduate students whom I have taught here," percent somewhat/very satisfied represents cumulative percentage of those who responded "somewhat satisfied" or "very satisfied." Means and percents were calculated using only those faculty who responded. The second questionnaire item read, "Please indicate your opinion regarding whether each of the following has worsened, stayed the same, or improved in recent years at this institution." Item: "Ability of this institution to meet the educational needs of entering students." Percents represent row percentage totaling 100%.

at the liberal arts colleges and public two-year colleges. But faculty perceptions of progress at the research universities lag considerably behind those in the other sectors: in both cohorts more faculty think that their campuses are losing ground in meeting students' educational needs than discern progress. Interestingly, for each institutional type (and also for each program area) the senior cohort, more than the junior cohort, perceives that their institutions have improved in their ability to meet their students' educational needs, albeit by narrow margins. This result is perhaps attributable to the fact that the junior faculty members, whose experience on campus by definition has been abbreviated, simply cannot detect their campuses' real progress. (Note, too, the larger proportion of "don't know" responses among these new faculty.) Or perhaps their senior colleagues tend to be too willing to accept as improvements modest advances that fail to impress their younger (and more idealistic?) colleagues.

Turning to the academic program areas, faculty in the professions are more inclined than their liberal arts colleagues to be pleased with the quality of their students and to think that their institutions have improved in their ability to meet their students' educational needs. Among them, faculty in the natural sciences (both cohorts) and fine arts (new cohort) are the least satisfied with the quality of undergraduate students.

The women in both cohorts report greater satisfaction than their male colleagues with the quality of undergraduates. They also discern greater progress in meeting the educational needs of their students; among senior faculty, 45.1 percent of the women but only 37.3 percent of the men perceive improvement. This result may be attributable, in part, to the underrepresentation of women in the research university, where perceived improvements, as already noted, are scarce.

Equity Issues

Both cohorts report satisfaction with the extent to which women and racial/ethnic minority faculty members are treated equitably (Table 35). However, an obvious caveat is in order: most of the respondents to these survey items are white males (rather than either women or minority faculty members), and they are arguably less disposed to perceive issues of inequitable treatment than are the groups that historically have been subjected to inequities within the academy. In any event, the degree of satisfaction reported by new entrants about equitable treatment is somewhat less than that expressed by their more senior colleagues. Thus 76.7 percent of the senior faculty and 74.0 percent of the new faculty agree somewhat or strongly that "female faculty members are treated fairly at this institution." Correspondingly, about 82.6 percent of the senior cohort and 79.1 percent of the junior cohort agree somewhat or strongly that "faculty who are members of racial or ethnic minorities are treated fairly at this institution." This finding suggests either that inequities have increased, at least as perceived by junior faculty members, or perhaps that sensitivities on these issues have heightened.

Perceptions about the fair treatment of faculty who are women or are members of racial or ethnic minorities vary by race. Table A-35A focuses on the perceptions, broken out by racial group, of the equitable treatment

Table 35 ⇒ Perceptions of Campus Environment: Equity Issues

	Female faculty		Minority faculty	
	Mean	Percent somewhat/strongly agree	Mean	Percent somewhat/strongly agree
All faculty	3.1	75.8	3.2	81.4
New faculty	3.0	74.0	3.1	79.1
Senior faculty	3.1	76.7	3.2	82.6

Note: The questionnaire items read, "Please indicate the extent to which you agree or disagree with each of the following statements: 1 = disagree strongly; 2 = disagree somewhat; 3 = agree somewhat; 4 = agree strongly." Female faculty: "Female faculty members are treated fairly at this institution." Minority faculty: "Faculty who are members of racial or ethnic minorities are treated fairly at this institution." Percent somewhat/strongly agree represents cumulative percentage of those who responded "somewhat agree" or "strongly agree." Means and percents were calculated using only those faculty who had responded in each category; thus the number of valid responses is different for each category.

of female and minority faculty. Here it emerges that Black faculty are the least likely, and Asian / Pacific Islander faculty the most likely, to report that women faculty are treated fairly—with white faculty at the midpoint among the five racial groups. The wide differences in perceptions by Black and Asian / Pacific Islander faculty may be largely a function of the much higher percentage of women among the Black faculty (about 47 percent) than among the Asian / Pacific Islander faculty (only 25 percent).[3]

Minority faculty are much less likely than their white colleagues to discern equitable treatment on campus for racial/ethnic minority groups. Whereas 83.5 percent of whites agree either somewhat or strongly that minority faculty are treated fairly, the percentages among the four other major racial groups range well below that level of approbation: from 65.6 to 73.6 percent, with Black and Hispanic faculty members being the least persuaded that minority faculty receive equitable treatment. It is not surprising to find that white faculty members in both cohorts are substantially more inclined than their minority colleagues to report that minority faculty are treated equitably.

Along with faculty at the public two-year colleges, the liberal arts faculty are the most satisfied with the treatment accorded female and minority faculty (Table A-35B). Differences by program area do emerge in perceptions of equity. Natural scientists across both cohorts are considerably more sanguine regarding both of the equity issues examined here; they view their institutions as being more successful in addressing issues of fairness for women and for minority faculty.

Viewing the data by gender, women faculty in both cohorts report less equity for women and for minority faculty by substantial margins. In fact, women in both cohorts are less satisfied by far in this regard than are men. The gap is more pronounced among the senior faculty than among the new entrants—but it is emphatic nevertheless. Thus only 57.2 percent of senior women agree somewhat or strongly that female faculty are treated fairly— in stark contrast to 84.4 percent of the senior men. This 27-point chasm narrows among new-generation faculty, but the divide is still substantial: 63.2 percent of the new-cohort women report perceptions of fair treatment compared with 81.5 percent of their male colleagues. The same patterns hold in perceptions of the treatment of minority faculty, although the differences between the genders are not as extreme—in part because women faculty in both cohorts are much more likely to report that women are treated unfairly than they are to report that minorities are treated unfairly. It is perhaps noteworthy that whereas new-entry women are more likely than their senior counterparts to perceive equitable treatment of women and minority faculty, the reverse holds for the men in both cohorts. That is, the new-entry men are less persuaded than their senior colleagues that both women and minority faculty are accorded equitable treatment.

Work Pressures

Faculty in both cohorts express deep concern about mounting pressures to increase faculty workload and about diminished external funding opportunities (Table 36). Views about "pressure to increase faculty workload at this institution" are uniformly bleak. Roughly half the faculty in all categories report that the pressures have "worsened" while fewer than 10 percent perceive that the situation has improved.

Looking at the institutional variations, faculty in all institutional categories report that the pressure to increase faculty workload has worsened, as has "the ability of faculty to obtain external funding" (Table A-36). These perceptions are felt most keenly at the two types of doctorate-granting universities; at these institutions more than half of the faculty report increased workload pressures compared with a mere handful (5–9 percent) who report decreased pressures. At the liberal arts colleges, the outlook is more sanguine: a roughly even split between those who think the situation has deteriorated and those who believe it has stayed the same. Even so, small proportions indicate that workload pressures have lessened. There are relatively few variations by program area regarding trends in work pressure.

In response to the question about obtaining external funding, larger proportions of research university faculty, as might be expected, report growing difficulties. When the findings are viewed by program, the natural scientists, by a wide margin in both cohorts, observe that their ability to obtain external funding has worsened.

Table 36 ⇌ Perceptions of Campus Environment: Work Pressures

	Pressure to increase faculty workload				Ability of faculty to obtain external funding			
	Worsened	Stayed the same	Improved	Don't know	Worsened	Stayed the same	Improved	Don't know
All faculty	51.0	34.7	8.3	6.0	37.7	27.4	18.4	16.5
New faculty	49.8	31.9	7.5	10.8	36.6	24.9	16.5	22.0
Senior faculty	51.6	36.1	8.7	3.6	38.3	28.7	19.3	13.7

Note: The questionnaire items read, "Please indicate your opinion regarding whether each of the following has worsened, stayed the same, or improved in recent years at this institution." Item: "Pressure to increase faculty workload at this institution." Item: "The ability of faculty to obtain external funding." Percents represent row percentage totaling 100%.

Differences between male and female faculty are evident. More women than men in both cohorts report that faculty workload pressures have worsened—by a substantial margin in the senior cohort, wherein 56.1 percent of the women but only 49.9 percent of the men indicate greater workload pressures. The opposite holds regarding sponsored research: the men in both cohorts perceive declining opportunities for research support. This gender difference is especially marked among new-cohort faculty (39.9 percent of the men and 31.7 percent of the women).

Campus Facilities and Resources

The majority of both cohorts are generally satisfied with campus facilities and resources. There are some exceptions, particularly concerning the inadequacy of research equipment, laboratory space, research assistants, and interinstitutional computer networks. New career entrants are somewhat less satisfied than are their senior colleagues in some areas: mainframe computer facilities, library holdings, and office space. There are few instances of a wide gap between the two cohorts.

We turn now to the various components that make up facilities and resources. For our purposes the issues relating to facilities and resources can be divided into three groups: space-related issues, computing, and other support.

Space issues encompass laboratory space (and supplies), classroom space, office space, and studio or performance space (Table 37). The consistency across these four categories is remarkable; mean scores (on a 4-point

Table 37 ⇒ Perceptions of Campus Facilities: Space Issues

	Laboratory space and supplies		Classroom space		Office space		Studio/ performance space	
	Mean	Percent good/ very good	Mean	Percent good/ very good	Mean	Percent good/ very good	Mean	Percent good/ very good
All faculty	2.8	65.7	2.8	70.8	2.9	70.8	2.7	63.3
New faculty	2.8	65.4	2.8	70.6	2.8	67.4	2.7	61.9
Senior faculty	2.8	65.8	2.8	71.0	2.9	72.6	2.7	64.1

Note: The questionnaire items read, "How would you rate each of the following facilities or resources at this institution that were available for your own use during the 1992 Fall term? 1 = very poor; 2 = poor; 3 = good; 4 = very good." Percent good/very good represents cumulative percentage of those who responded "good" or "very good." Means and percents were calculated using only those faculty who responded in each category; thus the number of valid responses is different for each category.

scale) are all at 2.8 plus or minus 0.1 (3.0 is "good" and 4.0 is "very good").

Men in both cohorts consistently report somewhat higher levels of satisfaction with space availability than do women, across all space-related categories (Table A-37). Big differences do not appear among institutional types, but there are exceptions: for instance, faculty in comprehensive institutions in both cohorts are considerably less satisfied with laboratory space and supplies than are their counterparts at other institutions.

Either office space is getting more cramped or the new faculty came to their jobs with unrealistic expectations regarding the kinds of office accommodations they would find: in every category (gender, institutional type, and program area) the new cohort is less approving of their office space than are their seniors.

Satisfaction levels with computing—spanning personal computing, centralized (mainframe) computer facilities, and computer networks with other institutions—are mainly positive: roughly three-fourths of the faculty judge personal and mainframe computing to be good or very good and two-thirds feel similarly about the adequacy of computer networking (Table 38). The biggest intercohort difference occurs regarding campus mainframe computing; here the new-cohort faculty are considerably less satisfied than the senior cohort: 73.6 percent of the new faculty say that centralized or mainframe computing facilities are good or very good compared with 80.1 percent of their senior colleagues. This finding probably reflects the numbers of new faculty who trained in relatively computing-rich graduate programs but who now find themselves at

Table 38 ⇒ Perceptions of Campus Facilities: Computing Resources

	Personal computers		Centralized computer facilities		Computer networks with other institutions		Audiovisual equipment	
	Mean	Percent good/ very good	Mean	Percent good/ very good	Mean	Percent good/ very good	Mean	Percent good/ very good
All faculty	3.1	77.3	3.0	77.9	2.8	68.1	3.0	77.6
New faculty	3.0	76.8	2.9	73.6	2.8	65.5	2.9	77.1
Senior faculty	3.1	77.5	3.1	80.1	2.8	69.5	3.0	77.9

Note: The questionnaire items read, "How would you rate each of the following facilities or resources at this institution that were available for your own use during the 1992 Fall term? 1 = very poor; 2 = poor; 3 = good; 4 = very good." Percent good/very good represents cumulative percentage of those who responded "good" or "very good." Means and percents were calculated using only those faculty who responded in each category; thus the number of valid responses is different for each category.

institutions with fewer computing resources. There is less satisfaction among both cohorts with computer networking.

The men are more likely than the women to find computing adequate (Table A-38). The satisfaction gap reaches nearly 10 percentage points for personal computers. Seen by institutional type, a clear relationship is evident: the more research-oriented the type of institution, the more likely it is that faculty members are satisfied with computing capabilities. Differences among academic program areas are not great.

"Other support" covers a mélange of issues: basic research equipment and instruments, availability of research assistants, secretarial support, and library holdings (Table 39).[4] The ratings on audiovisual equipment rank the highest among these categories, trailed somewhat by research equipment, library holdings, and then secretarial support. The availability of research assistants lags much farther behind. Interestingly, new-cohort faculty are more satisfied than their senior colleagues with the availability of research assistants but less pleased with library holdings. The latter phenomenon may again be a function of new faculty having earlier become accustomed to the extensive collections at research universities, where so many of them trained but do not now teach.

Gender differences show up again in all of these "other support" categories except audiovisual equipment (Table A-39). The gap is most pronounced in the male faculty members' higher levels of satisfaction, in both cohorts, regarding basic research equipment and research assistants. This

Table 39 ⇒ Perceptions of Campus Facilities: Other Support

	Basic research equipment/ instruments		Availability of research assistants		Secretarial support		Library holdings	
	Mean	Percent good/ very good	Mean	Percent good/ very good	Mean	Percent good/ very good	Mean	Percent good/ very good
All faculty	2.8	68.1	2.3	42.8	2.7	64.2	2.8	66.7
New faculty	2.8	68.6	2.3	45.0	2.7	64.3	2.7	63.3
Senior faculty	2.8	67.9	2.3	41.7	2.7	64.1	2.8	68.3

Note: The questionnaire items read, "How would you rate each of the following facilities or resources at this institution that were available for your own use during the 1992 Fall term? 1 = very poor; 2 = poor; 3 = good; 4 = very good." Percent good/very good represents cumulative percentage of those who responded "good" or "very good." Means and percents were calculated using only those faculty who responded in each category; thus the number of valid responses is different for each category.

result can presumably be partially explained by the larger proportion of males in the natural sciences, where equipment and assistants are more commonplace. But the differences persist in the men's greater satisfaction with secretarial support and library holdings, for which the same kind of explanation would not seem to hold.

To summarize, cutting across the twelve categories in this series of six tables, we find that when we control for *institutional type*, faculty at research and doctoral universities are seen as being the most satisfied with research equipment and supplies, computer facilities, and library holdings. This level of satisfaction tends to diminish for both cohorts from the universities to the two-year colleges. Comparing the new entrants with their more experienced colleagues, the biggest gap in satisfaction, perhaps unexpectedly, is seen among faculty at liberal arts colleges; less satisfaction among their new faculty is visible in almost every category. A pattern of more moderate differences between the two cohorts is evident at the research, other doctoral, and comprehensive campuses in most of the satisfaction categories. In two areas (library holdings and centralized [mainframe] computers) the new-entry faculty report less satisfaction at every institutional type; for centralized computing the margins consistently exceed 5 percent (that is, the percentage of faculty members who rate a category as either good or very good).

In comparing the two cohorts across categories by *program area*, not much change is evident on most items. Natural scientists are most satisfied with research facilities and laboratory space, and they tend to be more satisfied regarding other facilities than are their counterparts in the other three program areas. The humanists, on the other hand, are consistently less satisfied with campus facilities and resources than are the faculty in the other program areas.

A comparison of *men's and women's perceptions* of campus facilities and resources shows that the women consistently are more critical. This result applies in both cohorts and is seen across all of the categories (although in some instances the differences are very small). In fact, of the twenty-four points of comparison (twelve categories times two cohorts), men's satisfaction levels (as measured by ratings of "very good" or "good") are higher in twenty-two instances. The two exceptions, by narrow margins, pertain to audiovisual equipment.

Finally, both male and female new faculty tend to be marginally less satisfied with campus facilities than are their counterparts among the senior faculty.

In Summary

Although more diverse in a variety of background characteristics than earlier academic generations, new career entrants appear to resemble roughly their more experienced colleagues in the relative importance they ascribe to research and teaching, the autonomy they experience in their work, and their perceptions of the adequacy of the facilities and resources available in their campus work environments. One important difference is that new-cohort women are decidedly less likely than men to perceive that women and minorities are treated equitably on their campuses. Another difference is that women in both cohorts are less likely than men to report satisfaction with the work environment.

SEVEN

THE NEW ACADEMIC GENERATION AND THE FUTURE OF AMERICAN HIGHER EDUCATION

Our comparison of those faculty members that have recently entered institutions of higher education and their predecessors, the established generation, has demonstrated both similarities and dissimilarities between them. The ways in which the new entrants are like and unlike their predecessors have important implications for who the future faculty will be and what priorities they will bring with them to their academic tasks. Their competencies and interests will influence strongly for years to come how higher education will be conducted in the United States.

Perhaps the most striking characteristic of the new faculty cohort is its sheer size. Contrary to what many observers would have expected, there has been considerable movement into faculty ranks in recent years. Although general perceptions have been of a quiescent, almost impermeable, academic labor market, in fact the marketplace has been much more porous—more dynamic—at least in some very important respects. Though the size of the academic enterprise may have been, roughly speaking, in a steady state in recent years, that condition masks the underlying movement of many thousands of faculty members departing and being replaced (albeit not one for one). By our calculation, fully one-third (33.5 percent) of all full-time faculty have seven years or less of full-time faculty experience. In fact, a formidable 41.4 percent of all full-time faculty at private research universities fall into the new-faculty cohort, suggesting a huge rate of turnover in that sector.

This is not to say that the academic labor market has in general been accommodating to job seekers, for it decidedly has not. Supply far outstrips demand virtually across the board. It is to say that quietly, almost invisibly, a large number of new members have nonetheless been infused into the ranks of the full-time faculty in recent years (for our purposes, between 1986 and 1992), a development that is examined further in the following pages. Moreover, there is no indication that this steady rate of infusion has changed in the several years since the 1992–93 national survey took place, meaning that higher education continues to renew itself even during periods in which marketplace conditions are not good. Much change has taken place—and it presumably continues apace. A summary comparing the two cohorts' characteristics follows.

Summary of Intercohort Comparisons

The new generation of academic career entrants is much more diverse demographically than the previous generation, most dramatically in terms of the numerical ascendance of women, but also in the increased representation of faculty of color (particularly Asian males) and of foreign nationals. Taking just these factors of gender, race, and nativity into account, a sizable shift in the characteristics of the American faculty is evident in the distinctive backgrounds of the new generation of academics. For the senior cohort of faculty, 58.6 percent are native-born white males. But within the new-faculty cohort—numbering, as noted, fully one-third of the current faculty—the majority status of native-born white males disappears, shrinking to 43.2 percent. The goal of diversifying a once-homogeneous faculty has been at least partially realized (highlights are displayed in Appendix B).

The new entrants differ from their senior colleagues in terms of both their institutional and their disciplinary homes. Proportionately more hiring of new faculty appears to have taken place at the two types of doctorate-granting institutions; indeed, almost 36 percent of all full-time faculty in the research university category qualify as new compared with 30.4 percent at the comprehensive and 32.2 percent at the public two-year institutions. A more dramatic shift is evident in the distribution of new faculty members among program areas: their programmatic venues are considerably more likely than those of their predecessors to fall outside the traditional liberal arts. Whereas about 55 percent of the senior cohort hold appointments in liberal arts academic units, fewer than half (49.0 percent) of their newer colleagues are so positioned. The new generation of college faculty continues to be drawn from the higher socioeconomic strata of American society, and this is evident even when controlling for their age and gender.

The new entrants are embarking on their academic careers with a richer variety of experiences: a more diverse educational background in terms of the distribution of their academic degrees, as well as a considerably more varied work history. A large segment of the new generation—one-third of them—hold temporary or term appointments, rather than starting out on the traditional, tenure-bearing academic career ladder. Thus whereas 83.5 percent of the senior cohort hold tenure-track appointments, only 66.8 percent of their junior colleagues have comparable positions. Not surprisingly, the new-cohort faculty are significantly less satisfied with their job security and also less sanguine about their prospects for advancement.

Whereas the new generation of career entrants are much more balanced than their more senior colleagues in terms of gender and considerably more diverse in their race and nativity, educational background, work history, and career experiences, those differences in the main are not reflected in the nature and scope of their work activities. The new cohort, like their senior counterparts, spend most of their time teaching and less time engaged in research and publishing. However, faculty in all categories in both cohorts—each institutional type, each program area, and both genders—express a preference for doing less teaching and for engaging in more research. In terms of their teaching techniques, the new faculty are similar to their more experienced colleagues in their basic pedagogical approaches: lecturing still dominates, and the new cohort does not appear to be employing classroom strategies that differ much from traditional approaches.

In their respective attitudes about various aspects of their work, including satisfaction with their jobs and careers, the similarities between the two cohorts are more obvious than the dissimilarities that separate them. In that regard, it would appear that the new entrants, despite some significant differences in their background characteristics, were well socialized by their mentors into the "old ways."

To repeat an observation that threads its way through the preceding chapters, the two cohorts differ more in who they are than in what they do. This then is our study's central thesis. And from this finding flow important consequences about the future of the faculty and the nature of academic work.

Implications for the Future Faculty and Their Work

In considering the implications of the changing characteristics of the new generation of academics, the starting point must be the large size of this cohort. Because the new-entrant cohort is so large—we measure it at 172,000 out of the total of 515,000 full-time faculty members (or one of every three)—it is likely to have a much more pervasive influence in shaping academic values and practices in the years ahead. What then are the implications that can be drawn from this sizable cohort's identity for the future direction of higher education?

The first point to consider is that the new cohort is so demographically different from the senior cohort. White males, as noted, are the dominant presence in the older cohort. With the increasing presence of women and minority faculty, the white males' share of the new faculty has shrunk. They compose a distinct minority of the new cohort (at 43.2 percent, as noted, if U.S. nativity is also factored in). The steady rate of change has cumulatively shrunk the modal faculty type (white, male, U.S. born) to a slim majority—52.6 percent of all full-time faculty members—and that majority status may already have disappeared. One can imagine that the momentum toward further diversification by gender and race will continue, given diversity's presumably expanded faculty constituency. So the first likely downstream effect will be a still richer diversification of the faculty.

To be sure, the resistance to affirmative action programs—in the larger society and more specifically in higher education settings—has not yet played itself out at this writing. Thus it is not readily predictable whether the kind of message sent by California voters in November 1996 in passing Proposition 209 (the so-called California Civil Rights Initiative [CCRI]) will prove to be a forerunner of similar measures adopted in other venues. Or will the CCRI and similar initiatives, while reflecting popular frustrations with color- (and gender-) sensitive admissions policies, fail to constitute an effective rejection of decades-old practices favoring diversity? The resolution of these complex issues will heavily influence who gets to enter the graduate school pipeline—the gateway, ultimately, to faculty appointments.

And so a widening political base in opposition to affirmative action *could* impede or even reverse the trends toward the diversification of faculty that are so evident in our own analyses. The outcomes will depend to no small degree on how the state and federal courts assess the legality of such measures. Meanwhile, a significant broadening of the diversity of the faculty has already taken place, and the presence of this cohort, although not yet entrenched in secure senior ranks, suggests an increasingly favorable climate for continuing diversification. Consider, too, that in the always murky domain of personnel decisions, where subjective judgments ultimately hold sway, the power to exclude—practiced with chilling effectiveness over the years by academic traditionalists—is also the power to be more inclusive.

A second implication: this diversification of the faculty is likely to accelerate movement toward greater multiculturalism in the curriculum. Such movement presumably would draw additional support from the increasing number of faculty members who are not native U.S. citizens. Thus the struggles over curriculum content, sometimes waged with ferocity in recent years, are more likely to tilt in the direction of a more culturally diverse curriculum. Although this anticipated development would be in part a function of a more diverse faculty constituency, further momentum is likely to flow from the increasingly diverse student population. The caveats described in discussing the future of faculty diversification are no less applicable regarding shifts in the curriculum, but a more multiculturally oriented curriculum would appear to be on its way.

A third, related, trend is the internationalization of the American faculty, which is proceeding at a remarkable pace. The sharply increased presence of foreign-born faculty in the new cohort compared with the senior cohort has been documented in Chapter 3.

Of course, U.S. colleges and universities have always drawn scholars from abroad. The well-chronicled exodus from Europe earlier in this century, as Jewish scholars in particular fled Nazi persecution, was an era that yielded incalculable benefits to American higher learning and to the larger society (Steinberg 1974). But the parade of immigrants has stretched well beyond that era. Indeed there has been much fretting about "brain drain" from other nations as their talented scholars (and other professionals), attracted to resource-rich American colleges and universities, followed the well-worn paths to these shores (Bouvier and Simcox 1995). For decades scholars have been drawn from severely resource-poor higher learning settings throughout the world: the Indian subcontinent, Africa, and East and Southeast Asia are leading examples. Even in relatively affluent Western European settings, where higher education has come under mounting political pressure to be more responsive to market conditions, the United States becomes more alluring. The political forces acting on universities in the United Kingdom are a striking example, as substantial proportions of faculty members, even those at the most prestigious British universities, indicate an interest in relocating to more supportive environments, particularly in the United States (Schuster 1994). The almost half a million students from other countries studying in the United States—both as undergraduates and especially as graduate and professional students—further accelerate the internationalization of American higher education.

The relocation of scholars to the United States may recently have accelerated as a function of two roughly concurrent developments (Schuster 1994). First is the dissolution of the Soviet Union. The struggles in the emergent independent republics and in the nations formerly within the Soviet orbit to move from a command economy to a market economy have resulted, at least in the short run, in their universities and research institutes faring very poorly in the intensified competition for adequate appropriations; academic salaries and research funds have typically shriveled. Under these conditions, emigration becomes much more enticing. Thus the instability of prospects for higher education in that part of the world has boosted the movement of academics to the United States.

A second development is of a very different nature. The Immigration Act of 1990 (P.L. 101-649), a sweeping reform of U.S. immigration policies, contains one extraordinary feature aimed unambiguously at attracting the most talented scholars from other nations. Section 121(b)(1) of Part 2 (Employment-Based Immigrants) establishes a "preference system" for several categories of "priority workers"—including "outstanding professors and researchers" (see Schuster 1994).

These two developments must be viewed in the larger context of a rapidly changing environment, spanning such factors as the accelerating movement in recent decades toward international political and economic interdependence; the ascendancy of English as the undisputed first language of international higher learning; and the explosion of globe-shrinking technologies and the heightened planetwide consciousness of the "global village." All these factors, both contextual and specific to higher education, have accentuated the porous nature of national boundaries in the world of higher learning and in particular have contributed to the internationalization of U.S. higher education.

A further observation is pertinent here. This influx of nationals from other countries to the U.S. academy has been taking place at a time when the academic labor market has been relatively tight. Yes, a steady stream of new hires has been occurring (thus the robust size of the new cohort of faculty). But the anticipated increase in demand for new faculty, spurred particularly by replacement needs and expanding enrollments, will probably lead to many further job openings and accordingly to a mounting interest among academics abroad in relocating to the United States. In the not-distant future it is reasonable to anticipate that the American academy will have become ever more cosmopolitan in who its faculty are and in what they teach.

A fourth implication of the changes that are now under way is that support among faculty for the traditional liberal arts may come under increasing pressure. Environmental pressures, including student preferences, always exert a powerful effect on the curriculum (Rudolph 1977),[1] but the internal faculty stakeholders are influential as well. The inescapable fact is that the liberal arts core of higher education has atrophied in recent years in response to an array of market-driven pressures (Riesman 1980; Stadtman 1980). Now the influence of in-house faculty advocates of the liberal arts tradition may be dwindling as their proportion erodes. This is not to say that faculty members who are not based in the liberal arts are likely to be hostile to liberal learning. It is to say that as hard curricular choices are made, in an era of scarce resources, the proportion of faculty outside the liberal arts appears to be expanding and, conversely, the traditional liberal arts faculty now constitute an ever smaller minority among the new-cohort faculty. Thus the base of potential support for general education or liberal studies arguably has been, and will continue to be, diminished.

Fifth is another crucial dimension of the traditional academy under pressure: the shrinking proportion of faculty who are tenurable (either tenured or on the tenure track). This powerful trend can be seen in two parallel developments. One is the large and growing number of faculty who are part time. The proportion of such appointments now appears to be at least 42 or 43 percent (by headcount)—roughly double the proportion of such appointments a generation ago in the early 1970s.[2]

The second development is the contraction in the proportion of tenure-track positions as increasing numbers of faculty appointments are made in other categories—some short-term, others longer-term, but all less closely coupled with the host institution and its particular future. It is as though the concentric circles that have always represented the differing degrees of mutual commitment (both faculty to campus and campus to faculty) have been altered: the core inner circle (depicting the tenure-track appointments) has been squeezed mightily while the diameters of the circles that represent the more transient appointments have expanded. Loyalty dissipates in both directions—that is, institution to faculty and, in consequence, vice versa (Gappa and Leslie 1993, 1997; Stetar and Finkelstein 1997).[3] This means that the core faculty is diminished in some basic sense. Fewer faculty now carry a heavier responsibility, and they are on notice

that their position in the old order is giving way to new staffing impera-
tives. This development alone—quite apart from the other changes that have
been noted—can, and no doubt will, transform what it means to embark
on a faculty career. As the nature of the academic profession undergoes
momentous changes, every aspect of how higher education is conducted
is inevitably affected.

Some would argue not only that this transformation of faculty careers
is reasonable (even unavoidable given the realities that are reconfiguring
virtually all other sectors of contemporary American society) but also
that these changes are highly desirable. Without the flexibility—the nim-
bleness allowed by short-term commitments (the very antithesis of a
tenured-in faculty)—higher education's ability to respond to ever-shifting
(and ever more rapidly shifting) conditions would be undermined. Society,
so the argument goes, would be the ultimate loser.

Others, however, are much more apprehensive about the net result
of the trade-offs envisioned in the passion to achieve organizational flexibility. The redirection of academic careers into less stable, more contingent career pathways strikes a cautionary note for those who might
otherwise be attracted to the academic profession. It is likely that a considerable number of highly able persons, weighing the relative merits of
academic careers, would find the prospects unappealing—given the
arduous pledgeships that so often characterize graduate training and probationary faculty status—and would opt for other careers. This presumed
caution or aversion would be heightened by the continuing replacement
of core faculty positions with appointments that are even more subject to
ever-fluctuating environmental conditions. More generally, one must ponder the subtle consequences over time of an academic profession sheared
of its relatively secure—and, yes, privileged—status, however difficult it
may be to measure those consequences.

The present study is not the forum for teasing out all the ramifications,
for weighing all the trade-offs, attendant to reconfiguring staffing patterns.
But the accelerating shrinkage of the core faculty incontestably has significance far beyond what may be scornfully dismissed by critics as the faculty's special pleading, its penchant for protecting its own interests. The
hugely important central issue is whether, in the longer run, society will
be better served by institutions of higher learning populated by faculty members whose status, however dressed-up are their titles, is likely to be
much more transient, and who find themselves working in environments
characterized by the diminution of mutual loyalties (Schuster 1998).

Sixth, it is apparent that the new-faculty cohort is even more oriented toward research than their senior colleagues, and this discovery has important implications for the ongoing efforts throughout higher education to promote more effective teaching. One might have thought that pressures in recent years to improve the quality of undergraduate education, with an emphasis on upgrading teaching, might have been reflected in the work of recently hired faculty members—in terms of both their current distribution of effort and their performances. After all, the assessment movement, which began to accelerate in the mid-1980s, seems not yet to have lost any momentum.

Colleges and universities whose missions have included or emphasized research have been persistently exhorted (by, among others, accrediting associations and state policymakers) to pay more attention to teaching. Yet the NSOPF-93 survey quite clearly establishes that this large cohort of new faculty, even more than their predecessors, is desirous of trading teaching time for research time. The extent of the preferred reallocation varies among institutional types, by program area, and by gender, but the direction is uniform: more research, less teaching.

It is important to take into account concurrently the indicators that teaching, despite the evidence just cited, may be experiencing a resurgence. Several indicators militating in that direction were described in Chapter 5. Chief among these signs is the pattern of responses among faculty, most notably in the research universities, concerning the role of teaching in guiding promotion decisions. Although teaching, to no one's surprise, is the preferred primary criterion for promotion in the other types of institutions, in the research universities—where the research culture is broad and deep—about as many faculty vote for teaching as for research as the appropriate primary standard for promotion. Their ambivalence about how much weight *should* be accorded to research is all the more remarkable because seven of every eight research university faculty members indicate that research *is* the de facto primary criterion (Table A-32A). Lest this expression by research university faculty be hailed too enthusiastically by advocates of undergraduate education, it should be recalled that research university faculty in both cohorts indicated that they would nevertheless prefer to be spending more of their time doing research and less time teaching (Table A-24A).

A second development should give more cause for hope to the partisans of more effective teaching: the rapid rate at which women are winning full-time academic appointments. Time and again, consistent with previous research, our data show that women faculty seem to place more value on teaching than their male colleagues. The demographic trend toward greater gender balance in the faculty would appear to bode well for enhanced attention to teaching.

Just what this mix of developments suggests is not entirely clear. To be sure, advocates of improved teaching, from both within and outside the academy, may be discouraged if they perceive a stiffening faculty resistance to calls from administrators and external critics to be more attentive to their teaching responsibilities. But other factors surely come into play, including the conflicting pressures that squeeze the faculty, especially the newer faculty: teaching loads often thought to be onerous combined with the relentless urgency of publishing and/or perishing. (The desire to exchange teaching for research time, after all, surely must be motivated in no small part by basic survival instincts [see, for example, Fairweather 1996].) Whatever the factors that shape the current work of faculty and provide a window onto the future, one conclusion is inescapable: the challenge of improving teaching at the undergraduate level is not likely to dissipate in the near future.

Seventh, it appears that various sectors within higher education are being affected differently by prevailing conditions. The survey suggests that faculty in some types of institutions may be faring better—or in any event that they are more satisfied—than their counterparts in other types of institutions. Two threads are particularly visible. Each represents what might be regarded as a corrective in the sense that each runs counter to findings drawn from faculty surveys over the past two decades: (1) The community college faculty respondents to NSOPF-93 consistently report higher levels of satisfaction with their work than faculty at the other types of institutions. (2) Faculty at liberal arts colleges, conversely, report relatively less satisfaction. The former case appears to represent a continuation of a trend evident in several recent surveys; thus the era of community college faculty being counted among the least satisfied with their lot may now have come to an end (Cohen and Brawer 1977; Seidman 1985). In the case of liberal arts colleges, the era of relatively good times may be giving way to the crunch of financial realities (Breneman 1994). However, sizable differences probably still persist between the more affluent, more selective subset of liberal arts colleges and their less affluent, less selective cousins—although the NSOPF-93 data do not address that issue. In all, it may be that a measure of leavening among types of institutions— a kind of regression toward the mean as measured by faculty satisfaction— has been taking place within higher education.

In Conclusion

The responses to the 1993 National Study of Postsecondary Faculty provide a lens through which the future of the academic profession, and indeed of higher education, can be glimpsed. The lens may be more translucent than transparent; unpredictable events undoubtedly will intervene to recast higher education's future. But the view afforded by this survey is of a faculty more richly diverse in their origins yet, at this stage, still closely allied with the traditional ways of conducting higher education. The academic profession is also revealed as being in the midst of drastic organizational change as the core of the profession—the full-time faculty in tenure-eligible appointments—is compressed into a fraction of its former size. Certainly the consequences of these developments, for faculty members as well as society as a whole, will be of more than merely academic interest.

EXTENDED TABLES

A-2   Program area, disaggregated

A-3   Age by gender, institutional type, and program area

A-4   Academic rank by gender, institutional type, and program area

A-4A   Full professors in the new-faculty cohort by gender, institutional
       type, program area, and age

A-5   Gender by institutional type and program area

A-5A   New-cohort female faculty by program area

A-6   Race/ethnicity by gender, institutional type, and program area

A-6A   Representation of Black, Hispanic, and Asian / Pacific Islander
       faculty: Top five program areas

A-7   Citizenship by gender, institutional type, and program area

A-7A   Citizenship: Program area for selected, nonnative Asian / Pacific
       Islander new faculty

A-8   Father's educational level by gender and age

A-9   Mother's educational level by gender and age

A-10   Marital status by gender and age

A-11   Native-born white males by institutional type and program area

A-13   Level of highest degree by gender, institutional type, and
       program area

A-21   Tenure status by gender, institutional type, and program area

A-21A Tenured new faculty by institutional type, program area, rank, and age

A-22A Job satisfaction by gender

A-22B Job satisfaction by institutional type

A-22C Job satisfaction by program area

A-23 Global career satisfaction by gender, institutional type, and program area

A-24A Actual and preferred distribution of effort by institutional type

A-24B Actual and preferred distribution of effort by program area

A-24C Actual and preferred distribution of effort by gender

A-24D Actual and preferred distribution of effort between teaching and research: Tenured and tenure-track faculty by gender

A-24E Actual and preferred distribution of effort: Tenured and tenure-track faculty at research universities by gender

A-25 Weekly hours spent on paid and unpaid activities by gender, institutional type, and program area

A-26 Weekly office hours and student contact hours by gender, institutional type, and program area

A-27 Primary instructional methods used by gender, institutional type, and program area

A-28 Other instructional methods used by gender, institutional type, and program area

A-29A Involvement in research and publication by gender

A-29B Involvement in research and publication: Tenured and tenure-track faculty at research universities by gender

A-29C Involvement in research and publication by institutional type

A-29D Involvement in research and publication by program area

A-30 Concurrent employment by gender, institutional type, and program area

A-31 Concurrent employment sector by gender, institutional type, and program area

A-32A Perceptions of faculty roles and rewards by gender, institutional type, and program area

A-32B Perceptions of faculty roles and rewards: Tenured and tenure-track faculty at research and doctoral universities by gender

A-33 Perceptions of instructional duties by gender, institutional type, and program area

A-34 Perceptions of campus environment: Undergraduate education by gender, institutional type, and program area

A-35A Perceptions of campus environment: Equity issues by race

A-35B Perceptions of campus environment: Equity issues by gender, institutional type, and program area

A-36   Perceptions of campus environment: Work pressures by gender, institutional type, and program area

A-37   Perceptions of campus facilities: Space issues by gender, institutional type, and program area

A-38   Perceptions of campus facilities: Computing resources by gender, institutional type, and program area

A-39   Perceptions of campus facilities: Other support by gender, institutional type, and program area

Table A-2 ⇒ Program Area, Disaggregated

	All faculty	New faculty Number[a]	New faculty Percent[b]	New faculty as percent of all faculty
Agriculture and home economics	12,319	3,745	2.3	30.4
Business	39,442	13,293	7.3	33.7
Communications	9,527	4,003	2.4+	42.0
Education	35,151	11,326	6.9	32.2
Teacher education	12,351	3,728	2.3	30.2
Other education	22,800	7,598	4.6	33.3
Engineering	25,116	9,278	5.7	36.9
General engineering	855	351	0.2	41.1
Civil engineering	3,343	1,104	0.7	33.0
Electrical engineering	7,329	2,577	1.6	35.2
Mechanical engineering	4,332	1,341	0.8	31.0
Chemical engineering	1,765	933	0.6	52.9
Other engineering	4,457	2,043	1.2	45.8
Engineering related	3,036	930	0.6	30.6
Health-related	65,672	26,070	15.9	39.7
First professional health	26,812	11,621	7.1+	43.3
Nursing	20,436	7,570	4.6	37.0
Other health sciences	18,424	6,879	4.2	37.3
Law	8,148	2,327	1.4	28.6
Liberal arts and sciences	266,944	81,289	49.2	30.5
Fine arts	31,045	8,394	5.1–	27.0
English	37,981	11,466	7.0	30.2
Foreign language	13,969	4,292	2.6	30.7
History	14,522	3,049	1.9–	21.0
Philosophy	8,307	2,697	1.6	32.5
Biological science	35,437	12,938	7.9	36.5
Physical science	28,565	7,909	4.8–	27.7
Mathematics	25,983	7,353	4.1–	28.3
Computer science	13,397	4,932	3.0	36.8
Economics	9,742	2,699	1.6–	27.7
Political science	9,389	3,071	1.9	32.7
Psychology	17,141	5,955	3.6	34.7
Sociology	9,719	2,878	1.8	29.6
Other social sciences	11,747	3,656	2.2	31.1
Occupational programs	14,751	4,822	2.9	32.7
All other programs	26,071	9,885	6.0+	37.9

Note: Details may not add to total because of rounding.
a. Missing: 8,147 (4.7 percent) new faculty and 5,585 (1.6 percent) senior faculty.
b. Positive (+) or negative (–) signs in this column represent a change in market share of at least 20 percentage points from senior to new faculty.

116

	Senior faculty	
Number[a]	Percent	Senior faculty as percent of of all faculty
8,547	2.5	69.4
26,149	7.8	66.3
5,524	1.6	58.0
23,826	7.1	67.8
8,623	2.6	69.8
15,203	4.5	66.7
15,838	4.7	63.1
504	1.0	58.9
2,239	0.7	67.0
4,752	1.4	64.8
2,991	0.9	69.0
832	0.2	47.1
2,414	0.7	54.2
2,106	0.6	69.4
39,604	11.7	60.3
15,192	4.5	56.7
12,867	3.8	63.0
11,545	3.4	62.7
5,821	1.7	71.4
185,648	56.1	69.5
22,651	6.7	73.0
26,515	7.9	69.8
9,678	2.9	69.3
11,473	3.4	79.0
5,609	1.7	67.5
22,500	6.7	63.5
20,657	6.1	72.3
18,619	5.5	71.7
8,465	2.5	63.2
7,044	2.1	72.3
6,318	1.9	67.3
11,186	3.3	65.3
6,842	2.0	70.4
8,091	2.4	68.9
9,929	2.9	67.3
16,186 .	4.8	62.1

Table A-3 ⇌ Age by Gender, Institutional Type, and Program Area

	Number	Percent	Mean	<30	30–34
By cohort					
New faculty	172,318	100.0	42.1	3.7	16.9
Senior faculty	342,657	100.0	51.2	0.1	1.3
By gender					
New faculty					
Males	101,974	100.0	42.3	3.1	17.5
Females	70,345	100.0	41.8	4.8	16.1
Senior faculty					
Males	244,860	100.0	52.0	0.1	1.1
Females	97,797	100.0	49.3	0.3	1.9
By institutional type					
New faculty					
Research universities	50,886	100.0	40.6	3.4	19.6
Other doctorate-granting institutions[a]	26,361	100.0	41.3	2.7	20.8
Comprehensive institutions	39,929	100.0	42.8	3.7	16.6
Private liberal arts institutions	12,662	100.0	41.3	4.8	17.4
Public two-year institutions	33,283	100.0	43.6	4.5	11.9
All other[b]	9,217	100.0	45.4	4.5	10.0
Senior faculty					
Research universities	90,727	100.0	51.8	0.0	1.1
Other doctorate-granting institutions	48,945	100.0	51.2	0.1	2.2
Comprehensive institutions	91,490	100.0	51.4	0.3	0.9
Private liberal arts institutions	24,764	100.0	50.8	0.1	1.1
Public two-year institutions	70,246	100.0	50.6	0.2	1.6
All other	15,586	100.0	51.1	0.0	1.8
By program area					
New faculty					
Professions	59,966	100.0	42.6	2.4	17.1
Liberal arts and sciences	81,297	100.0	41.4	4.1	17.4
Fine arts	8,394	100.0	41.9	3.7	17.3
Humanities	21,504	100.0	42.2	4.4	13.5
Natural sciences	33,141	100.0	41.2	4.0	17.6
Social sciences	18,258	100.0	40.6	4.5	21.4
All other program areas	24,782	100.0	43.5	4.9	14.8
Senior faculty					
Professions	105,416	100.0	50.9	0.2	1.7
Liberal arts and sciences	185,647	100.0	51.5	0.1	1.1
Fine arts	22,651	100.0	50.8	0.5	1.6
Humanities	53,275	100.0	52.4	0.1	0.6
Natural sciences	70,241	100.0	51.2	0.1	1.5
Social sciences	39,480	100.0	51.3	0.1	0.6
All other program areas	46,033	100.0	51.1	0.0	1.6

Note: Details may not add to total because of rounding.
a. Includes medical schools.
b. Includes public liberal arts, private two-year, and other specialized institutions except medical schools.

	Age						
35–39	40–44	45–49	50–54	55–59	60–64	65–69	>69
24.3	20.6	13.9	10.0	5.8	3.2	1.1	0.5
6.0	15.0	20.8	22.4	17.0	11.6	4.6	1.4
25.3	19.7	12.4	10.0	6.4	3.9	1.5	0.4
22.8	22.0	16.0	10.0	4.9	2.3	0.6	0.6
4.9	13.4	19.7	22.8	18.4	13.0	5.1	1.6
8.7	19.0	23.5	21.4	13.3	7.9	3.2	0.9
30.5	20.9	10.0	6.6	4.6	3.1	1.2	0.1
26.8	21.4	12.3	6.9	5.5	1.7	1.1	0.9
20.8	20.5	15.2	11.8	6.0	3.9	1.0	0.4
26.9	20.0	14.8	6.8	5.5	1.9	1.6	0.3
17.9	20.3	18.8	15.2	6.9	3.5	0.5	0.5
16.9	19.4	15.0	15.2	8.9	6.2	2.6	1.5
5.9	16.0	19.9	19.6	16.9	13.1	5.6	1.8
5.6	16.1	20.0	22.0	15.5	11.8	4.7	2.1
5.8	13.0	20.8	24.2	17.7	11.8	4.5	1.1
7.1	17.0	22.1	18.4	16.2	12.8	4.7	0.7
5.8	14.7	22.3	25.3	17.3	9.1	2.9	0.8
7.5	14.7	18.6	22.2	17.8	9.9	5.8	1.6
21.0	23.7	13.7	10.7	6.0	4.1	1.0	0.3
27.1	19.6	14.0	8.8	5.1	2.5	1.0	0.4
25.0	19.2	15.4	10.3	6.0	1.4	1.1	0.7
24.4	19.6	18.8	11.2	5.5	1.8	0.7	0.1
29.7	19.8	11.1	8.2	5.8	2.1	1.3	0.3
26.7	19.3	13.1	6.4	3.1	4.3	0.6	0.6
22.2	16.9	13.8	12.4	8.0	3.9	1.9	1.2
6.9	16.0	21.7	19.5	15.9	12.2	4.7	1.4
5.7	14.1	20.2	24.1	17.8	11.2	4.6	1.3
7.1	16.8	19.3	20.1	19.1	10.8	4.3	0.5
4.2	11.1	20.3	25.5	18.7	13.2	4.8	1.5
6.1	14.9	20.4	24.0	17.0	10.0	4.6	1.4
6.0	15.0	20.1	24.9	17.1	11.0	4.4	1.0
5.3	16.2	20.6	22.2	16.8	11.2	4.0	2.2

Table A-4 ⇒+ Academic Rank by Gender, Institutional Type, and Program Area

	Number	Percent
By gender		
New faculty		
Males	101,974	100.0
Females	70,345	100.0
Senior faculty		
Males	244,860	100.0
Females	97,797	100.0
By institutional type		
New faculty		
Research universities	50,865	100.0
Other doctorate-granting institutions[a]	26,362	100.0
Comprehensive institutions	39,928	100.0
Private liberal arts	12,661	100.0
Public two-year	33,282	100.0
All other[b]	9,218	100.0
Senior faculty		
Research universities	90,727	100.0
Other doctorate-granting institutions	49,844	100.0
Comprehensive institutions	91,488	100.0
Private liberal arts	24,765	100.0
Public two-year	70,245	100.0
All other	15,586	100.0
By program area		
New faculty		
Professions	59,966	100.0
Liberal arts and sciences	81,297	100.0
Fine arts	8,394	100.0
Humanities	21,504	100.0
Natural sciences	33,141	100.0
Social sciences	18,258	100.0
All other program areas	24,782	100.0
Senior faculty		
Professions	105,416	100.0
Liberal arts and sciences	185,647	100.0
Fine arts	22,651	100.0
Humanities	53,275	100.0
Natural sciences	70,241	100.0
Social sciences	39,480	100.0
All other program areas	46,033	100.0

Note: Details may not add to total because of rounding.
a. Includes medical schools.
b. Includes public liberal arts, private two-year, and other specialized institutions except medical schools.

| | Academic rank | | | | | |
Professor	Associate professor	Assistant professor	Instructor	Lecturer	Other	Not applicable
16.6	17.1	42.3	16.0	1.9	4.3	1.8
5.2	11.9	42.9	26.1	5.0	5.7	3.2
49.6	28.2	9.8	7.6	0.8	1.3	2.7
23.9	29.1	22.1	15.3	3.2	2.0	4.4
15.7	18.0	44.8	5.1	6.3	9.6	0.5
12.1	13.3	57.7	12.9	1.7	2.1	0.2
10.6	16.8	50.5	17.0	3.0	1.9	0.2
8.4	15.0	52.0	17.1	2.9	3.7	0.9
8.5	7.3	16.5	55.0	0.5	3.8	8.4
13.6	22.6	33.6	15.4	1.0	4.7	9.1
54.4	29.6	9.6	1.4	2.9	1.8	0.3
44.6	33.2	13.8	5.7	1.4	1.2	0.1
43.5	32.9	17.7	3.9	1.3	0.3	0.4
40.4	33.0	19.1	3.7	1.0	1.2	1.6
25.3	16.8	9.7	33.4	0.3	2.6	11.9
37.1	26.2	15.3	9.1	0.3	1.7	10.3
12.2	16.1	42.0	22.0	3.1	3.3	1.5
11.7	16.0	45.0	18.3	3.5	2.7	2.8
12.0	14.8	45.0	16.4	4.4	4.0	3.4
9.6	13.4	39.1	26.5	6.6	0.8	4.0
12.9	17.9	45.4	16.4	1.9	3.3	2.3
12.0	16.0	51.1	12.9	2.5	3.4	2.0
13.3	11.8	41.1	24.9	3.1	3.5	2.3
35.3	31.6	18.3	10.3	1.2	1.2	2.2
46.8	27.7	10.9	8.0	1.8	1.0	3.9
42.2	30.8	12.5	6.5	1.9	1.3	4.8
43.6	26.8	11.8	10.0	2.6	0.8	4.5
49.0	26.1	9.5	9.1	1.4	1.0	4.0
50.2	29.8	11.3	4.4	1.2	1.0	2.2
42.5	24.9	11.9	15.7	1.0	1.5	2.5

Table A-4A Full Professors in the New-Faculty Cohort by Gender, Institutional Type, Program Area, and Age

	Full professors	
	Number	Percent
By gender		
Males	16,927	82.3
Females	3,643	17.7
By institutional type		
Research universities	7,970	38.7
Other doctorate-granting institutions[a]	3,195	15.5
Comprehensive institutions	4,245	20.6
Private liberal arts institutions	1,063	5.2
Public two-year institutions	2,842	13.8
All other[b]	1,255	6.1
By program area		
Professions	9,634	46.9
Humanities	2,073	10.1
Natural sciences	4,273	20.8
Social sciences	2,189	10.6
All other	1,959	9.5
By age		
<30	70	0.3
30–34	596	2.9
35–39	567	2.8
40–44	2,518	12.2
45–49	3,950	19.2
50–54	5,692	27.7
55–59	3,608	17.5
60–64	2,333	11.3
65–69	1,106	5.4
>69	131	0.6

Note: Details may not add to total because of rounding.
a. Includes medical schools.
b. Includes public liberal arts, private two-year, and other specialized institutions except medical schools.

Table A-5 ⚮ Gender by Institutional Type and Program Area

	All faculty		New faculty		Senior faculty		New females as percent of all females
	Male	Female	Male	Female	Male	Female	
By institutional type							
All institutions	67.4	32.7	59.2	40.8	71.5	28.5	41.8
All research universities	75.4	24.6	67.2	32.8	80.0	20.0	47.9
Public	77.0	23.0	67.8	32.2	81.8	18.2	48.0
Private	70.0	30.0	65.5	34.5	73.1	26.9	47.5
All other doctorate-granting institutions[a]	72.3	27.7	67.1	33.0	75.0	25.0	41.1
Public	70.5	29.5	62.1	37.9	74.7	25.3	43.2
Private	75.9	24.2	76.0	24.0	75.7	24.3	36.0
All comprehensive institutions	66.2	33.8	56.3	43.7	70.5	29.5	39.3
Public	66.7	33.4	56.9	43.1	70.8	29.2	38.6
Private	65.1	34.9	55.0	45.0	69.8	30.2	40.9
Private liberal arts institutions	61.0	39.0	49.3	50.7	66.9	33.1	43.9
Public two-year institutions	55.8	44.2	46.8	53.2	60.1	39.9	38.7
All other institutions[b]	70.3	29.7	63.1	36.9	74.5	25.5	46.1
By program area							
All program areas	67.4	32.7	59.0	41.0	71.5	28.5	40.5
Professions	59.9	40.1	56.0	44.0	62.1	37.9	39.8
Liberal arts and sciences	70.8	29.2	60.2	39.8	75.5	24.6	41.5
Fine arts	67.0	33.0	49.0	51.0	73.6	26.4	41.7
Humanities	58.8	41.3	46.1	53.9	63.9	36.2	37.6
Natural sciences	79.5	20.5	71.4	28.7	83.3	16.7	44.8
Social sciences	72.9	27.1	61.6	38.4	78.1	21.9	44.9
All other program areas	71.8	28.2	62.6	37.4	76.8	23.3	48.6

Note: Details may not add to total because of rounding.
a. Includes medical schools.
b. Includes public liberal arts, private two-year, and other specialized institutions except medical schools.

123

Table A-5A ⇒ New-Cohort Female Faculty by Program Area

	All faculty[a]	New females (percent)	New females as percent of new faculty (males and females)	New females as percent of all females
All program areas	503,141	100.0	39.5	40.5
Agriculture and home economics	12,319	1.2	22.6	29.0
Business	39,442	6.2	36.1	36.3
Communication	9,527	2.8	48.8	59.1
Education	35,151	10.4	64.4	40.0
Teacher education	12,351	3.4	64.1	34.9
Other education	22,800	7.0	64.5	43.2
Engineering	25,116	1.6	12.0	73.9
General engineering	855	0.1	12.8	100.0
Civil engineering	3,343	0.1	5.3	49.2
Electrical engineering	7,329	0.5	12.7	89.6
Mechanical engineering	4,332	0.2	12.4	48.7
Chemical engineering	1,765	0.2	13.9	100.0
Other engineering	4,457	0.4	12.2	72.7
Engineering-related	3,036	0.2	14.8	84.7
Health-related	65,672	19.2	51.9	39.1
First professional health	26,812	3.4	20.5	44.3
Nursing	20,436	10.5	97.7	36.8
Other health sciences	18,424	5.3	54.6	41.1
Law	8,148	1.8	54.8	47.1
Liberal arts and sciences	266,944	46.0	40.1	41.5
English	37,981	10.3	86.0	37.7
Fine arts	31,045	6.1	37.3	41.7
Foreign language	13,969	3.7	60.9	36.3
History	14,522	1.7	40.3	36.4
Philosophy	8,307	0.7	19.3	46.4
Biological science	35,437	6.3	34.5	50.5
Physical science	28,565	2.0	17.4	42.1
Mathematics	25,983	3.5	36.8	39.4
Computer science	13,397	1.7	23.7	41.6
Economics	9,742	0.6	14.5	25.7
Political science	9,389	1.4	31.3	56.3
Psychology	17,141	4.4	51.7	47.6
Sociology	9,719	1.2	28.6	34.4
Other social sciences	11,747	2.5	48.2	49.6
Occupational programs	14,751	1.4	20.2	41.2
All other programs	26,071	6.0	42.8	48.6

Note: Details may not add to total because of rounding.
a. Missing: 6,274 (3.6 percent) new faculty and 5,561 (1.6 percent) senior faculty.

Table A-6 ⇌ Race/Ethnicity by Gender, Institutional Type, and Program Area

	Number	Percent	Race/ethnicity American Indian / Alaskan Native	Asian / Pacific Islander	Black not Hispanic	Hispanic	White not Hispanic
By gender							
New faculty							
Males	101,974	100.0	0.5	9.3	4.6	3.1	82.4
Females	70,345	100.0	0.5	5.3	7.2	3.0	84.1
Senior faculty							
Males	244,860	100.0	0.5	4.8	3.6	2.4	88.8
Females	97,797	100.0	0.4	3.4	7.0	2.0	87.3
By institutional type							
New faculty							
All research universities	50,867	100.0	0.1	11.5	3.6	3.0	81.9
All other doctorate-granting institutions[a]	26,361	100.0	0.8	9.8	4.5	3.3	81.6
All comprehensive institutions	39,928	100.0	0.5	6.2	9.2	2.8	81.3
Private liberal arts institutions	12,662	100.0	0.6	4.0	5.9	2.0	87.5
Public two-year institutions	33,283	100.0	1.0	4.0	6.0	4.0	85.0
All other institutions[b]	9,217	100.0	0.6	5.4	3.9	1.9	88.2
Senior faculty							
All research universities	90,728	100.0	0.1	5.9	2.3	1.8	89.9
All other doctorate-granting institutions	49,845	100.0	0.6	5.4	3.0	2.0	89.1
All comprehensive institutions	91,489	100.0	0.2	4.1	6.7	2.2	86.8
Private liberal arts institutions	24,765	100.0	0.4	2.4	4.9	1.2	91.1
Public two-year institutions	70,245	100.0	1.1	2.9	5.9	3.8	86.3
All other institutions	15,586	100.0	0.3	4.3	3.6	1.2	90.6
By program area							
New faculty							
Professions	59,966	100.0	0.6	8.0	6.6	2.7	82.1
Liberal arts and sciences	81,296	100.0	0.5	7.2	5.0	3.5	83.9
Fine arts	8,393	100.0	0.5	5.2	5.3	3.7	85.3
Humanities	21,504	100.0	0.4	6.0	4.3	4.5	84.8
Natural sciences	33,142	100.0	0.8	10.0	4.3	2.8	82.1
Social sciences	18,258	100.0	0.1	4.3	6.8	3.4	85.4
All other program areas	24,781	100.0	0.4	3.8	6.3	2.8	86.7
Senior faculty							
Professions	105,416	100.0	0.6	5.3	5.1	1.9	87.2
Liberal arts and sciences	185,646	100.0	0.4	4.3	4.0	2.5	88.8
Fine arts	22,651	100.0	0.5	2.1	5.6	1.9	89.9
Humanities	53,276	100.0	0.5	2.4	3.8	3.8	89.6
Natural sciences	70,242	100.0	0.1	7.1	3.0	1.9	87.8
Social sciences	39,480	100.0	0.5	3.1	5.3	2.3	88.7
All other program areas	46,033	100.0	0.4	2.6	5.4	2.2	89.4

Note: Details may not add to total because of rounding.

a. Includes medical schools.

b. Includes public liberal arts, private two-year, and other specialized institutions except medical schools.

Table A-6A Representation of Black, Hispanic, and Asian / Pacific Islander Faculty: Top Five Program Areas

Program	Percent of Black faculty	Program	Percent of Hispanic faculty	Program	Percent of Asian / Pacific Islander faculty
			All faculty		
Other education	9.3	Foreign language	12.5	Engineering	15.1
English	7.2	English	7.5	Mathematics	9.3
Business	7.1	Other education	7.0	Physical sciences	8.8
Fine arts	6.7	First professional health	6.5	First professional health	7.3
All other programs	6.6	Fine Arts	6.3	Business	6.6
			New faculty		
Other education	8.9	Foreign language	10.1	Engineering	12.4
All other programs	7.7	First professional health	8.3	First professional health	8.6
Business	7.6	Other education	7.9	Mathematics	8.5
First professional health	7.1	Fine arts	7.0	Business	7.5
English	6.9	Engineering	6.4	Biological science	6.5
			Senior faculty		
Other education	9.5	Foreign language	14.2	Engineering	17.4
Fine arts	8.3	English	9.1	Physical sciences	11.1
English/literature	7.4	Other education	6.4	Mathematics	9.9
Nursing	7.0	All other programs	5.9	Business	5.7
All other programs	5.9	Fine arts	5.8	First professional health	5.4

Table A-7 ⇌ Citizenship by Gender, Institutional Type, and Program Area

	Number	Percent	Native U.S. citizen	Naturalized U.S. citizen	Permanent resident	Temporary resident
By gender						
New faculty						
Males	101,974	100.0	79.3	5.9	11.9	3.0
Females	70,345	100.0	88.7	4.4	4.4	2.6
Senior faculty						
Males	244,860	100.0	87.3	8.2	4.0	0.5
Females	97,797	100.0	91.3	5.5	3.0	0.2
By institutional type						
New faculty						
Research universities	50,867	100.0	73.4	6.1	14.6	6.0
Other doctorate-granting institutions[a]	26,362	100.0	80.7	6.8	9.3	3.1
Comprehensive institutions	39,929	100.0	86.3	4.5	7.7	1.6
Private liberal arts institutions	12,662	100.0	89.5	4.0	5.6	0.9
Public two-year institutions	33,283	100.0	92.9	3.9	3.2	0.1
All other[b]	9,217	100.0	86.2	6.7	5.3	1.8
Senior faculty						
Research universities	90,727	100.0	83.0	10.5	5.9	0.6
Other doctorate-granting institutions	49,845	100.0	86.4	8.6	4.8	0.3
Comprehensive institutions	91,490	100.0	90.2	6.4	3.0	0.4
Private liberal arts institutions	24,764	100.0	91.4	5.8	2.8	0.1
Public two-year institutions	70,246	100.0	94.2	4.7	1.1	0.1
All other	15,586	100.0	86.7	6.9	5.4	1.0
By program area						
New faculty						
Professions	59,966	100.0	84.0	5.6	7.8	2.6
Liberal arts and sciences	81,297	100.0	81.5	5.4	10.6	2.5
Fine arts	8,394	100.0	88.6	5.9	4.8	0.8
Humanities	21,504	100.0	84.5	5.0	8.0	2.5
Natural sciences	33,141	100.0	75.3	6.3	14.6	3.8
Social sciences	18,258	100.0	85.9	3.8	9.3	1.1
All other program areas	24,782	100.0	90.8	3.0	4.6	1.7
Senior faculty						
Professions	105,416	100.0	88.1	8.1	3.5	0.3
Liberal arts and sciences	185,647	100.0	87.7	7.7	4.1	0.5
Fine arts	22,651	100.0	94.9	3.0	1.9	0.2
Humanities	53,275	100.0	87.2	9.0	3.3	0.5
Natural sciences	70,241	100.0	85.6	9.1	4.7	0.6
Social sciences	39,480	100.0	87.7	6.2	5.5	0.5
All other program areas	46,033	100.0	93.0	4.4	2.5	0.1

Note: Details may not add to total because of rounding.

a. Includes medical schools.

b. Includes public liberal arts, private two-year, and other specialized institutions except medical schools.

Table A-7A ⇌ Citizenship: Program Area for Selected, Nonnative Asian / Pacific Islander New Faculty

	All new faculty	Nonnative Asian / Pacific Islanders	Nonnative Asian / Pacific Islanders as percent of all new faculty
Biological sciences	12,938	355	2.7
Physical sciences	7,909	272	3.4
Mathematics	6,767	598	8.8
Engineering	9,278	584	6.3
Computer science	4,932	429	8.7

Note: Selected, nonnative Asian faculty refers to those faculty listing their birth country as China, Hong Kong, Japan, Korea, and Taiwan. Details may not add to total because of rounding.

Table A-8 ☩ Father's Educational Level by Gender and Age

	Number	Percent	Less than high school diploma	High school diploma	Some college	Associate degree	Bachelor's degree	Master's degree	Doctorate / professional degree	Other	Don't know
						Father's educational level					
By gender											
New faculty											
Males	101,974	100.0	21.1	24.0	10.9	1.7	17.1	10.0	13.6	1.1	0.5
Females	70,345	100.0	17.8	25.8	12.5	2.5	17.0	10.0	12.5	1.1	0.8
Senior faculty											
Males	244,860	100.0	29.9	24.9	11.5	1.9	12.9	7.0	10.6	0.6	0.7
Females	97,797	100.0	25.2	24.4	11.8	2.3	16.3	6.9	11.0	1.2	0.9
By age											
New faculty											
<35	35,609	100.0	10.8	25.0	9.8	3.4	18.6	13.1	17.9	0.9	0.6
35–44	77,361	100.0	15.8	24.9	10.9	2.0	19.6	11.7	14.0	0.8	0.3
45–54	41,095	100.0	27.8	24.9	13.9	1.4	14.0	6.4	9.5	1.5	0.6
55–64	15,553	100.0	35.7	23.4	13.7	0.7	10.8	5.8	7.2	1.4	1.3
65–70	2,060	100.0	43.3	21.9	4.5	0.0	8.6	2.5	15.2	4.0	0.0
>70	641	100.0	26.2	18.6	9.4	0.0	7.3	0.0	10.0	0.0	28.5
Senior faculty											
<35	5,028	100.0	24.3	22.5	14.3	3.4	17.7	5.2	11.6	0.0	1.1
35–44	71,746	100.0	16.5	27.7	13.3	2.5	17.0	10.6	11.1	0.8	0.5
45–54	147,800	100.0	26.4	26.2	11.4	1.9	14.2	7.0	11.6	0.7	0.5
55–64	97,771	100.0	38.6	21.1	11.6	1.8	11.8	4.8	8.2	0.9	1.2
65–70	17,317	100.0	39.0	23.2	7.4	1.1	9.5	4.5	13.1	0.3	2.0
>70	2,997	100.0	39.4	17.3	2.4	2.2	5.3	7.9	22.5	0.0	3.0

Note: Details may not add to total because of rounding.

Table A-9 ⚕ Mother's Educational Level by Gender and Age

	Number	Percent	Less than high school diploma	High school diploma	Some college	Associate degree	Bachelor's degree	Master's degree	Doctorate / professional degree	Other	Don't know
By gender											
New faculty											
Males	101,974	100.0	19.5	35.5	11.9	4.2	16.1	9.4	2.1	1.0	0.5
Females	70,345	100.0	16.3	33.5	13.9	5.0	17.5	8.8	2.9	2.0	0.2
Senior faculty											
Males	244,860	100.0	25.5	35.4	13.3	4.0	13.6	5.5	1.5	0.6	0.6
Females	97,797	100.0	20.7	32.7	14.9	4.3	15.7	7.5	1.7	2.1	0.2
By age											
New faculty											
<35	35,608	100.0	12.2	32.8	10.8	5.3	18.1	15.5	3.2	3.2	0.3
35–44	77,361	100.0	13.9	35.2	13.1	4.6	19.2	9.7	2.8	2.8	0.3
45–54	41,097	100.0	24.1	36.5	13.6	4.1	14.1	5.0	1.0	1.0	0.2
55–64	15,551	100.0	33.5	33.5	11.6	3.9	9.3	4.3	1.8	1.8	1.0
65–70	2,061	100.0	41.5	22.1	21.6	2.5	6.8	0.0	0.0	3.3	2.1
>70	640	100.0	46.3	36.3	7.2	3.0	0.0	7.3	0.0	0.0	0.0
Senior faculty											
<35	5,029	100.0	22.0	31.1	14.7	6.1	13.1	8.8	1.7	0.4	2.5
35–44	71,748	100.0	14.9	36.2	15.3	4.9	17.4	8.4	1.3	1.4	0.2
45–54	147,797	100.0	21.4	36.2	13.6	4.0	15.1	6.8	1.7	0.9	0.2
55–64	97,772	100.0	32.9	32.6	12.6	3.2	11.6	3.7	1.6	1.0	0.8
65–70	17,317	100.0	35.4	28.6	14.3	4.5	9.3	3.6	1.8	0.5	2.1
>70	2,997	100.0	28.1	30.1	14.3	10.9	10.6	3.0	1.2	0.0	1.9

Mother's educational level

Note: Details may not add to total because of rounding.

Table A-10 Marital Status by Gender and Age

	Number	Percent	Marital status					
			Never been married	Married	Living with someone	Separated	Divorced	Widowed
By gender								
New faculty								
Males	101,974	100.0	12.5	78.4	2.3	1.3	5.3	0.3
Females	70,345	100.0	18.5	62.2	4.1	1.6	12.1	1.6
Senior faculty								
Males	244,860	100.0	5.8	83.2	1.6	1.2	7.4	0.8
Females	97,797	100.0	17.1	61.5	3.0	1.3	14.1	3.1
By age								
New faculty								
<35	25,717	100.0	27.8	61.8	5.9	0.6	3.9	0.1
35–44	123,749	100.0	14.8	73.9	2.9	1.6	6.4	0.3
45–54	5,175	100.0	8.4	74.3	1.6	1.5	13.1	1.2
55–64	2,408	100.0	4.6	77.2	0.8	1.9	13.4	2.0
65–70	13,878	100.0	3.2	84.9	0.0	0.0	3.8	8.2
>70	1,391	100.0	16.3	46.0	0.0	5.0	4.2	28.5
Senior faculty								
<35	30,931	100.0	25.3	53.7	10.7	2.2	8.0	0.1
35–44	263,872	100.0	13.3	74.1	2.6	1.5	8.2	0.2
45–54	6,893	100.0	7.5	78.2	2.0	1.1	10.4	0.8
55–64	4,089	100.0	7.5	77.8	1.6	1.2	9.6	2.4
65–70	31,774	100.0	7.8	80.9	0.5	0.5	4.0	6.4
>70	5,097	100.0	10.4	78.2	0.0	0.0	4.7	6.7

Note: Details may not add to total because of rounding.

Table A-11 ⇒ Native-Born White Males by Institutional Type and Program Area

	All faculty	New faculty	Senior faculty
By institutional type			
All institutions	53.4	43.2	58.6
All research universities	56.7	44.9	63.3
Public	59.2	46.2	66.0
Private	48.5	41.4	53.4
All other doctorate-granting institutions[a]	56.1	47.2	60.9
Public	54.7	43.6	60.4
Private	58.9	53.8	61.9
All comprehensive institutions	53.3	42.0	58.2
Public	52.2	40.6	57.2
Private	56.0	45.4	61.0
Private liberal arts institutions	54.3	41.0	61.2
Public two-year institutions	44.8	38.1	50.8
All other institutions[b]	44.5	39.5	47.5
By program area			
All program areas	53.4	43.2	58.6
Professions	46.3	40.4	49.6
Business	58.8	52.3	62.0
Education	41.1	30.3	46.2
Engineering	58.0	52.9	61.0
Health sciences	37.1	34.3	39.0
Liberal arts and sciences	56.2	43.4	61.9
Fine arts	57.0	37.8	64.1
Humanities	48.6	36.8	53.4
Natural sciences	59.1	46.4	66.2
Social sciences	49.4	41.6	53.6
All other program areas	60.9	51.5	65.9

Note: Percentages represent percent of native-born white males within each category. Details may not add to total because of rounding.
a. Includes medical schools.
b. Includes public liberal arts, private two-year, and other specialized institutions except medical schools.

Table A-13 ≈+ Level of Highest Degree by Gender, Institutional Type, and Program Area

				Highest degree		
	Number[a]	Percent	Professional	Doctoral	Master's	Bachelor's or less
By gender						
New faculty						
Males	100,844	100.0	13.0	58.0	22.4	6.6
Females	70,078	100.0	7.9	40.5	44.2	7.5
Senior faculty						
Males	243,681	100.0	9.7	65.3	21.6	3.4
Females	97,510	100.0	5.5	47.0	43.1	4.5
By institutional type						
New faculty						
All research universities	50,274	100.0	17.0	68.0	12.5	2.5
All other doctorate-granting institutions[b]	26,262	100.0	23.3	57.8	16.6	2.3
All comprehensive institutions	39,812	100.0	5.0	58.2	34.3	2.4
Private liberal arts institutions	12,616	100.0	3.0	55.2	38.8	2.9
Public two-year institutions	32,781	100.0	2.4	12.7	60.9	24.1
All other institutions[c]	9,177	100.0	8.4	34.7	47.6	9.3
Senior faculty						
All research universities	90,496	100.0	14.3	76.1	8.7	0.9
All other doctorate-granting institutions	49,676	100.0	15.4	70.5	13.4	0.7
All comprehensive institutions	91,310	100.0	5.1	71.6	22.5	0.8
Private liberal arts institutions	24,703	100.0	3.5	62.8	31.4	2.3
Public two-year institutions	69,553	100.0	2.0	18.7	66.0	13.4
All other institutions	15,454	100.0	9.1	46.3	38.1	6.5
By program area						
New faculty						
Professions	59,532	100.0	19.8	40.5	31.9	7.8
Liberal arts and sciences	80,891	100.0	4.0	62.1	30.7	3.3
Fine arts	8,239	100.0	1.2	33.0	58.8	7.1
Humanities	21,504	100.0	2.3	53.1	42.0	2.5
Natural sciences	33,059	100.0	5.1	71.0	19.7	4.2
Social sciences	18,089	100.0	5.1	69.6	24.3	1.0
All other program areas	24,320	100.0	12.4	40.2	31.5	15.9
Senior faculty						
Professions	105,209	100.0	14.2	51.4	30.1	4.2
Liberal arts and sciences	185,098	100.0	3.4	69.0	26.0	1.6
Fine arts	22,340	100.0	5.4	36.0	54.1	4.4
Humanities	53,208	100.0	1.9	70.7	26.6	0.7
Natural sciences	70,123	100.0	4.2	71.6	22.4	1.9
Social sciences	39,427	100.0	3.1	80.6	15.6	0.8
All other program areas	45,345	100.0	16.2	44.7	28.6	10.5

Note: Details may not add to total because of rounding.
a. Missing: 1,397 (0.8 percent) new faculty and 1,466 (0.4 percent) senior faculty.
b. Includes medical schools.
c. Includes public liberal arts, private two-year, and other specialized institutions except medical schools.

Table A-21 ⇒ Tenure Status by Gender, Institutional Type, and Program Area

	Number	Percent	Tenured	On tenure track	Not on tenure track	No tenure for faculty status	No tenure system at institution
By gender							
New Faculty							
Males	101,974	100.0	29.1	42.8	14.7	5.6	7.8
Females	70,345	100.0	16.5	43.2	20.2	8.9	11.2
Senior faculty							
Males	244,860	100.0	78.4	8.7	4.4	2.5	6.0
Females	97,797	100.0	59.5	14.9	10.1	4.9	10.7
By institutional type							
New faculty							
All research universities	50,867	100.0	29.3	41.8	19.7	8.5	0.7
All other doctorate-granting institutions[a]	26,362	100.0	20.1	51.1	20.2	6.7	1.9
All comprehensive institutions	39,929	100.0	20.4	50.8	19.9	5.8	3.1
Private liberal arts institutions	12,662	100.0	17.2	46.3	19.7	5.2	11.6
Public two-year institutions	33,283	100.0	28.8	33.2	8.1	6.5	23.4
All other institutions[b]	9,217	100.0	12.2	22.1	7.8	9.0	48.9
Senior faculty							
All research universities	90,727	100.0	80.9	6.9	7.5	3.6	1.2
All other doctorate-granting institutions	49,845	100.0	72.0	13.7	9.2	3.7	1.5
All comprehensive institutions	91,490	100.0	77.7	13.6	5.4	2.1	1.2
Private liberal arts institutions	24,764	100.0	64.4	15.6	6.3	4.8	9.0
Public two-year institutions	70,246	100.0	67.6	7.2	2.7	2.6	20.0
All other institutions	15,586	100.0	40.7	10.0	5.4	5.7	38.1
By program area							
New faculty							
Professions	59,966	100.0	22.2	43.0	18.5	6.4	9.8
Liberal arts and sciences	81,297	100.0	25.9	45.2	15.3	5.3	8.4
Fine arts	8,394	100.0	21.8	44.3	14.3	4.3	15.3
Humanities	21,504	100.0	22.9	41.0	17.6	8.1	10.4
Natural sciences	33,141	100.0	29.1	45.4	13.9	5.1	6.5
Social sciences	18,258	100.0	25.4	50.1	15.5	2.7	6.3
All other program areas	24,782	100.0	25.5	42.3	13.4	7.4	11.4
Senior faculty							
Professions	105,416	100.0	67.2	13.4	8.5	2.7	8.2
Liberal arts and sciences	185,647	100.0	77.2	8.7	4.5	2.8	6.9
Fine arts	22,651	100.0	68.4	11.5	4.8	2.6	12.7
Humanities	53,275	100.0	75.9	8.2	5.0	3.4	7.4
Natural sciences	70,241	100.0	78.7	8.1	4.8	2.8	5.7
Social sciences	39,480	100.0	81.1	8.6	3.3	2.2	4.8
All other program areas	46,033	100.0	72.6	11.7	5.3	3.0	7.4

Note: Details may not add to total because of rounding.
a. Includes medical schools.
b. Includes public liberal arts, private two-year, and other specialized institutions except medical schools.

Table A-21A ⇌ Tenured New Faculty by Institutional Type, Program Area, Rank, and Age

	Percent tenured		
	All new faculty	New males	New females
By institutional type			
All research universities	23.6	35.2	17.3
All other doctorate-granting institutions[a]	20.1	24.6	11.1
All comprehensive institutions	20.4	25.7	13.6
Private liberal arts institutions	17.2	19.7	14.8
Public two-year institutions	28.8	34.7	23.6
All other institutions[b]	12.2	15.0	7.4
By program area			
Professions	22.2	27.0	16.2
Liberal arts and sciences	25.9	31.4	17.6
Fine arts	21.8	23.4	20.3
Humanities	22.9	32.0	15.1
Natural sciences	29.1	32.9	19.7
Social sciences	25.4	30.5	17.3
All other program areas	25.5	31.5	15.6
By rank			
Professor	78.1	80.6	66.8
Associate professor	60.5	60.9	59.7
Assistant professor	4.5	4.0	5.2
Instructor	11.7	15.8	8.1
Lecturer	2.8	1.3	3.6
Other	16.5	17.4	15.8
By age (median)		48.0	46.0

a. Includes medical schools.
b. Includes public liberal arts, private two-year, and other specialized institutions except medical schools.

Table A-22A ⇌ Job Satisfaction by Gender

| | Job satisfaction | | | |
| | Work load | | Job security | |
	Mean	Percent somewhat/ very satisfied	Mean	Percent somewhat/ very satisfied
New faculty				
Males	2.9	69.0	3.0	72.8
Females	2.7	63.3	2.8	67.1
Senior faculty				
Males	3.0	73.3	3.5	88.4
Females	2.7	62.2	3.2	81.5

| | Freedom for outside consulting | | Salary | |
	Mean	Percent somewhat/ very satisfied	Mean	Percent somewhat/ very satisfied
New faculty				
Males	3.1	78.4	2.6	56.4
Females	3.0	73.6	2.4	49.0
Senior faculty				
Males	3.2	83.0	2.6	57.9
Females	3.0	76.0	2.4	49.9

Note: The item read as follows: "How satisfied or dissatisfied are you with the following aspects of your job at this institution? 1 = very dissatisfied; 2 = somewhat dissatisfied; 3 = somewhat satisfied; 4 = very satisfied." Percent somewhat/very satisfied represents cumulative percentage of those who responded "somewhat satisfied" or "very satisfied."

	Advancement opportunities		Keeping current in field	
Mean	Percent somewhat/ very satisfied	Mean	Percent somewhat/ very satisfied
2.9	69.5	2.5	50.2
2.7	60.6	2.3	37.3
3.1	74.3	2.6	54.7
2.8	63.3	2.3	39.3

	Benefits		Spouse employment opportunities	
Mean	Percent somewhat/ very satisfied	Mean	Percent somewhat/ very satisfied
3.0	75.2	2.8	67.3
3.0	75.6	2.9	70.3
3.0	75.1	3.0	76.0
3.0	75.3	3.0	75.3

Table A-22B ⇌ Job Satisfaction by Institutional Type

	Work load	
	Mean	Percent somewhat/ very satisfied
New faculty		
All research universities	2.8	67.3
All other doctorate-granting institutions[a]	2.9	68.1
All comprehensive institutions	2.8	63.3
Private liberal arts institutions	2.7	61.8
Public two-year institutions	2.9	69.6
All other institutions[b]	2.9	70.5
Senior faculty		
All research universities	3.1	77.3
All other doctorate-granting institutions	3.0	73.0
All comprehensive institutions	2.8	62.6
Private liberal arts institutions	2.8	64.7
Public two-year institutions	2.9	70.6
All other institutions	2.9	69.8

	Freedom for outside consulting	
	Mean	Percent somewhat/ very satisfied
New faculty		
All research universities	3.1	79.0
All other doctorate-granting institutions	3.0	77.1
All comprehensive institutions	3.0	74.3
Private liberal arts institutions	2.9	74.1
Public two-year institutions	3.0	75.7
All other institutions	3.0	75.0
Senior faculty		
All research universities	3.3	86.3
All other doctorate granting institutions	3.2	82.3
All comprehensive institutions	3.1	80.3
Private liberal arts institutions	3.1	77.8
Public two-year institutions	3.1	76.6
All other institutions	3.0	74.3

Note: The item read as follows: "How satisfied or dissatisfied are you with the following aspects of your job at this institution? 1 = very dissatisfied; 2 = somewhat dissatisfied; 3 = somewhat satisfied; 4 = very satisfied." Percent somewhat/very satisfied represents cumulative percentage of those who responded "somewhat satisfied" or "very satisfied."
a. Includes medical schools.
b. Includes public liberal arts, private two-year, and other specialized institutions except medical schools.

Job satisfaction

Job security		Advancement opportunities		Keeping current in field	
Mean	Percent somewhat/ very satisfied	Mean	Percent somewhat/ very satisfied	Mean	Percent somewhat/ very satisfied
2.9	67.9	2.9	68.0	2.5	50.7
2.8	67.7	2.8	65.2	2.5	47.9
2.8	67.7	2.8	64.3	2.3	38.8
2.8	65.9	2.8	67.1	2.1	29.7
3.2	83.3	2.8	64.8	2.4	46.6
2.8	65.6	2.7	64.7	2.4	46.5
3.5	86.9	3.1	74.3	2.7	59.1
3.3	84.7	3.0	70.6	2.7	55.0
3.4	87.3	3.0	71.6	2.4	45.2
3.4	86.1	3.1	77.2	2.4	40.8
3.4	87.8	2.8	65.1	2.5	46.1
3.1	79.0	2.9	69.5	2.5	49.0

Salary		Benefits		Spouse employment opportunities	
Mean	Percent somewhat/ very satisfied	Mean	Percent somewhat/ very satisfied	Mean	Percent somewhat/ very satisfied
2.6	54.8	3.0	75.6	2.8	65.4
2.5	54.9	3.0	75.3	2.9	70.6
2.4	48.1	2.9	72.6	2.9	66.6
2.3	43.1	2.8	66.9	2.8	64.0
2.6	59.5	3.1	82.9	3.0	75.2
2.5	55.6	2.9	71.3	2.9	70.5
2.6	56.5	3.0	75.4	3.0	75.5
2.5	55.3	2.9	73.4	3.0	76.4
2.4	50.3	2.9	73.4	3.0	73.7
2.5	52.0	2.8	66.6	3.0	74.6
2.7	62.0	3.1	81.3	3.1	79.1
2.6	58.5	2.9	74.9	3.1	76.3

Table A-22C ⇒ Job Satisfaction by Program Area

	Work load	
		Percent somewhat/ very
	Mean	satisfied
New faculty		
Professions	2.9	67.7
Liberal arts and sciences	2.8	65.3
Fine arts	2.6	58.9
Humanities	2.7	60.3
Natural sciences	2.9	71.4
Social sciences	2.7	73.4
All other program areas	2.8	67.8
Senior faculty		
Professions	3.0	72.2
Liberal arts and sciences	2.9	68.6
Fine arts	2.8	64.5
Humanities	2.8	63.8
Natural sciences	3.0	72.7
Social sciences	2.9	69.9
All other program areas	2.9	71.1

	Freedom for outside consulting	
		Percent somewhat/ very
	Mean	satisfied
New faculty		
Professions	3.0	75.4
Liberal arts and sciences	3.0	77.2
Fine arts	3.0	71.3
Humanities	3.0	75.8
Natural sciences	3.1	78.9
Social sciences	3.0	78.7
All other program areas	3.0	76.4
Senior faculty		
Professions	3.1	80.4
Liberal arts and sciences	3.2	81.4
Fine arts	3.1	77.4
Humanities	3.1	78.0
Natural sciences	3.2	84.1
Social sciences	3.2	83.4
All other program areas	3.2	81.5

Note: The item read as follows: "How satisfied or dissatisfied are you with the following aspects of your job at this institution? 1 = very dissatisfied; 2 = somewhat dissatisfied; 3 = somewhat satisfied; 4 = very satisfied." Percent somewhat/very satisfied represents cumulative percentage of those who responded "somewhat satisfied" or "very satisfied."

Job satisfaction

Job security		Advancement opportunities		Keeping current in field	
Mean	Percent somewhat/ very satisfied	Mean	Percent somewhat/ very satisfied	Mean	Percent somewhat/ very satisfied
3.0	72.6	2.8	66.5	2.5	48.9
2.9	69.3	2.8	66.6	2.3	40.9
2.8	66.9	2.8	67.1	2.2	31.0
2.8	65.2	2.8	64.8	2.2	37.3
3.0	72.5	2.9	67.4	2.5	47.8
2.9	69.4	2.8	67.2	2.3	37.0
3.0	72.3	2.8	65.7	2.4	44.8
3.3	85.3	2.9	79.5	2.6	51.9
3.5	87.9	3.0	72.0	2.5	49.4
3.3	82.4	2.9	68.5	2.5	47.3
3.4	87.4	3.0	70.1	2.4	53.6
3.5	88.6	3.0	72.6	2.6	51.6
3.5	90.5	3.1	75.0	2.6	54.6
3.3	83.7	3.0	72.7	2.5	50.0

Salary		Benefits		Spouse employment opportunities	
Mean	Percent somewhat/ very satisfied	Mean	Percent somewhat/ very satisfied	Mean	Percent somewhat/ very satisfied
2.5	54.4	3.0	77.5	3.0	72.9
2.5	55.2	2.9	73.0	2.8	65.3
2.4	60.1	3.0	74.1	2.7	60.7
2.4	48.0	2.9	72.3	2.8	64.4
2.6	57.3	3.0	74.7	2.9	67.8
2.4	48.9	2.9	70.5	2.8	63.7
2.5	55.5	3.0	77.1	2.9	68.7
2.6	57.9	3.0	77.4	3.0	76.3
2.5	52.8	3.0	73.4	3.0	75.6
2.3	44.4	2.9	70.1	3.0	72.7
2.4	50.3	2.9	71.2	3.0	71.4
2.6	57.4	3.0	76.1	3.0	77.0
2.5	52.9	3.0	73.3	3.0	75.4
2.6	60.4	3.0	85.7	3.1	80.1

Table A-23 ⇌ Global Career Satisfaction by Gender, Institutional Type, and Program Area

	"I would do it again"		Job overall	
	Mean	Percent somewhat/strongly agree	Mean	Percent somewhat/very satisfied
By gender				
New faculty				
Males	3.5	88.7	3.1	82.9
Females	3.5	88.7	3.1	81.2
Senior faculty				
Males	3.5	89.6	3.2	85.9
Females	3.5	88.4	3.1	83.5
By institutional type				
New faculty				
All research universities	3.4	86.3	3.1	80.6
All other doctorate-granting institutions[a]	3.4	89.5	3.0	78.3
All comprehensive institutions	3.5	88.9	3.0	81.5
Private liberal arts institutions	3.5	89.2	3.1	82.2
Public two-year institutions	3.5	90.9	3.3	89.2
All other institutions[b]	3.5	89.8	3.1	79.8
Senior faculty				
All research universities	3.5	89.3	3.2	84.9
All other doctorate-granting institutions	3.5	88.2	3.2	84.5
All comprehensive institutions	3.5	89.3	3.1	83.3
Private liberal arts institutions	3.6	90.2	3.2	84.0
Public two-year institutions	3.5	89.5	3.3	89.5
All other institutions	3.5	89.0	3.2	83.1
By program area				
New faculty				
Professions	3.5	90.2	3.1	84.1
Liberal arts and sciences	3.5	88.2	3.1	80.7
Fine arts	3.4	87.0	3.0	78.1
Humanities	3.5	89.4	3.1	81.0
Natural sciences	3.4	86.6	3.1	80.7
Social sciences	3.5	90.3	3.1	81.7
All other program areas	3.4	87.3	3.2	83.5
Senior faculty				
Professions	3.5	88.7	3.2	87.6
Liberal arts and sciences	3.5	89.7	3.2	83.3
Fine arts	3.5	88.8	3.1	79.8
Humanities	3.5	87.4	3.1	81.0
Natural sciences	3.6	91.7	3.2	85.3
Social sciences	3.5	89.8	3.2	85.0
All other program areas	3.5	89.4	3.3	87.9

Note: The first of the two global measures reads, "If I had to do it over again, I would still choose an academic career: 1 = disagree strongly; 2 = disagree somewhat; 3 = agree somewhat; 4 = agree strongly." Percent somewhat/strongly agree represents cumulative percent of those who responded "agree somewhat" or "agree strongly." The second asks about satisfaction with "my job here, overall: 1 = very dissatisfied; 2 = somewhat dissatisfied; 3 = somewhat satisfied; 4 = very satisfied." Percent somewhat/very satisfied represents cumulative percent of those who responded "somewhat satisfied" or "very satisfied."

a. Includes medical schools.

b. Includes public liberal arts, private two-year, and other specialized institutions except medical schools.

142

Table A-24A ➤ Actual and Preferred Distribution of Effort by Institutional Type

	Teaching	Research	Service	Professional growth	Administration	Consulting
			Actual			
New faculty						
All research universities	32.9	41.1	6.5	4.0	13.3	1.7
All other doctorate-granting institutions[a]	43.0	29.9	7.2	4.3	13.9	1.8
All comprehensive institutions	59.4	14.8	5.2	5.0	13.2	2.3
Private liberal arts institutions	62.2	11.3	4.7	5.1	14.0	2.7
Public two-year institutions	69.2	4.7	4.8	6.1	12.0	2.9
All other institutions[b]	60.7	11.3	5.8	6.1	13.6	2.3
Senior faculty						
All research universities	38.6	34.8	6.0	3.4	13.4	3.3
All other doctorate-granting institutions	47.5	24.6	6.4	4.1	14.6	2.6
All comprehensive institutions	59.5	14.1	5.6	5.1	12.4	2.9
Private liberal arts institutions	63.1	11.7	4.0	5.4	13.1	2.1
Public two-year institutions	71.9	4.8	5.2	5.8	9.7	2.6
All other institutions	61.8	11.5	5.0	4.7	14.4	2.6
			Preferred			
New faculty						
All research universities	30.6	46.9	5.0	6.8	7.9	2.2
All other doctorate-granting institutions	37.6	37.2	7.0	7.0	8.4	2.8
All comprehensive institutions	50.4	23.9	5.0	9.0	8.4	3.2
Private liberal arts institutions	53.8	20.4	4.8	9.5	8.4	3.1
Public two-year institutions	63.5	9.9	4.6	10.1	7.9	3.3
All other institutions	52.3	19.6	6.1	10.0	9.0	3.1
Senior faculty						
All research universities	36.2	40.4	5.4	5.9	8.0	3.8
All other doctorate-granting institutions	42.7	31.2	6.5	6.8	8.9	3.7
All comprehensive institutions	52.8	21.6	5.2	8.4	7.8	3.7
Private liberal arts institutions	56.4	20.1	4.4	8.7	7.3	2.6
Public two-year institutions	66.4	9.0	5.1	9.5	6.6	3.1
All other institutions	55.8	17.0	5.6	8.8	9.2	3.7

Note: Percents represent percentage of total time (100 percent). Details may not add to total because of rounding.
a. Includes medical schools.
b. Includes public liberal arts, private two-year, and other specialized institutions except medical schools.

Table A-24B ⇌ Actual and Preferred Distribution of Effort by Program Area

| | Actual | | | | | |
	Teaching	Research	Service	Professional growth	Administration	Consulting
New faculty						
Professions	49.3	20.6	8.3	5.3	13.7	2.6
Liberal arts and sciences	54.7	23.3	3.9	4.7	11.3	1.8
Fine arts	59.2	11.5	3.7	7.3	14.2	4.1
Humanities	62.7	14.9	3.7	5.1	11.8	1.4
Natural sciences	50.0	31.6	3.2	3.8	9.8	1.4
Social sciences	52.0	23.4	5.6	4.7	12.4	1.9
All other program areas	55.3	16.0	6.5	4.6	14.7	2.9
Senior faculty						
Professions	54.1	16.3	7.0	5.0	13.8	3.5
Liberal arts and sciences	56.7	20.3	4.5	4.3	11.3	2.4
Fine arts	56.1	16.4	5.4	5.9	10.3	4.5
Humanities	61.3	17.4	4.1	4.1	11.3	1.5
Natural sciences	55.8	22.8	4.1	3.9	11.2	2.1
Social sciences	52.7	22.2	5.3	4.5	12.3	2.9
All other program areas	54.4	17.2	6.3	5.3	13.3	3.3

| | Preferred | | | | | |
	Teaching	Research	Service	Professional growth	Administration	Consulting
New faculty						
Professions	45.2	26.4	7.6	8.9	8.5	3.3
Liberal arts and sciences	47.1	32.1	3.7	8.1	6.5	2.3
Fine arts	49.8	21.1	3.4	12.3	8.1	4.9
Humanities	54.7	24.3	3.3	8.6	6.7	1.8
Natural sciences	43.1	39.6	3.1	6.6	5.4	1.9
Social sciences	43.9	32.6	5.3	8.0	7.7	2.5
All other program areas	49.2	23.0	5.4	8.5	9.6	3.8
Senior faculty						
Professions	49.9	21.5	6.7	8.2	9.3	4.2
Liberal arts and sciences	50.9	27.5	4.3	7.6	6.3	3.0
Fine arts	50.5	22.3	4.8	9.5	6.2	4.8
Humanities	54.7	24.8	4.0	7.7	6.2	2.2
Natural sciences	50.4	29.5	3.9	7.1	6.4	2.7
Social sciences	47.0	30.6	5.2	7.1	6.5	3.5
All other program areas	50.7	21.8	6.5	8.0	9.0	3.9

Note: Percents represent percentage of total time (100 percent). Details may not add to total because of rounding.

Table A-24C ⇌ **Actual and Preferred Distribution of Effort by Gender**

				Actual		
	Teaching	Research	Service	Professional growth	Administration	Consulting
New faculty						
Males	46.6	26.8	5.4	4.5	14.1	2.5
Females	58.0	16.2	6.4	5.4	11.9	1.7
Senior faculty						
Males	52.8	21.0	5.5	4.4	12.8	3.3
Females	61.0	13.8	5.8	5.2	12.0	1.9
				Preferred		
	Teaching	Research	Service	Professional growth	Administration	Consulting
New faculty						
Males	41.5	34.1	5.0	7.5	8.6	3.2
Females	51.2	22.9	5.7	9.6	7.7	2.4
Senior faculty						
Males	48.6	27.0	5.2	7.2	7.8	3.8
Females	54.0	20.3	5.8	9.1	7.8	2.7

Note: Percents represent percentage of total time (100 percent). Details may not add to total because of rounding.

Table A-24D ⇌ **Actual and Preferred Distribution of Effort between Teaching and Research: Tenured and Tenure-Track Faculty by Gender**

	Teaching			Research		
	Actual	Preferred	Difference	Actual	Preferred	Difference
New faculty						
Males	46.4	41.2	−5.2	27.4	35.6	8.2
Females	57.1	49.1	−8.0	18.2	26.3	8.1
Senior Faculty						
Males	52.3	48.1	−4.2	21.8	27.9	6.1
Females	59.3	52.5	−6.8	15.1	22.1	7.0

Note: Percents represent percentage of total time (100 percent). Details may not add to total because of rounding.

Table A-24E ⇌ **Actual and Preferred Distribution of Effort: Tenured and Tenure-Track Faculty at Research Universities by Gender**

	Teaching	Research	Service	Professional growth	Administration	Consulting
			Actual			
New faculty						
Males	33.6	41.0	4.8	3.2	15.0	2.1
Females	37.3	34.9	9.6	3.1	11.5	1.6
Senior faculty						
Males	38.4	35.3	5.7	3.4	13.1	3.6
Females	41.5	32.7	5.8	3.7	13.4	2.1
			Preferred			
New faculty						
Males	31.0	49.0	3.8	5.5	7.9	2.6
Females	32.3	42.4	7.3	6.8	6.8	2.1
Senior faculty						
Males	36.3	41.0	4.9	5.6	7.6	4.1
Females	37.9	38.8	6.3	6.9	7.3	2.7

Note: Percents represent percentage of total time (100 percent). Details may not add to total because of rounding.

Table A-25 ⇒ **Weekly Hours Spent on Paid and Unpaid Activities by Gender, Institutional Type, and Program Area**

	Institutional activities		Outside activities		
	Paid	Unpaid	Paid	Unpaid	Total hours
By gender					
New faculty					
Males	45.1	5.2	2.9	1.7	54.9
Females	41.0	5.4	2.2	1.7	50.3
Senior faculty					
Males	42.4	4.8	3.1	2.0	52.3
Females	40.2	5.6	2.0	2.3	50.1
By institutional type					
New faculty					
Research universities	49.3	4.2	1.7	1.5	56.7
Other doctorate-granting institutions[a]	46.2	4.7	2.6	1.7	55.2
Comprehensive institutions	41.1	6.0	2.8	1.9	51.8
Private liberal arts institutions	41.6	6.3	3.2	1.7	52.8
Public two-year institutions	36.6	6.3	3.3	1.9	48.1
All other institutions[b]	39.7	5.2	2.8	1.4	49.1
Senior faculty					
Research universities	46.4	4.1	2.8	2.0	55.3
Other doctorate-granting institutions	44.8	3.9	2.6	2.3	53.6
Comprehensive institutions	40.7	5.9	2.9	2.4	51.9
Private liberal arts institutions	41.6	5.4	2.5	1.7	51.2
Public two-year institutions	35.4	5.9	3.0	1.8	46.1
All other institutions	39.0	5.1	2.9	1.9	48.9
By program area					
New faculty					
Professions	43.3	5.4	3.0	1.9	53.6
Liberal arts and sciences	43.9	5.2	2.1	1.5	52.7
Fine arts	38.0	6.4	4.8	2.5	51.7
Humanities	40.7	5.9	1.7	1.3	49.6
Natural sciences	46.6	4.8	1.5	1.1	54.0
Social sciences	45.3	4.8	2.6	1.9	54.6
All other program areas	41.9	5.5	3.4	2.1	52.9
Senior faculty					
Professions	41.6	4.8	3.2	2.2	51.8
Liberal arts and sciences	42.0	5.2	2.5	1.9	51.6
Fine arts	35.1	7.4	4.5	2.5	49.5
Humanities	41.6	5.6	1.8	1.7	50.7
Natural sciences	44.3	4.3	2.2	1.7	52.5
Social sciences	42.2	5.1	3.0	2.3	52.6
All other program areas	41.0	5.1	3.1	2.7	51.9

Note: Institutional paid activities are defined as "all paid activities at this institution (teaching, research, administration, etc.)." Institutional unpaid activities are defined as "all unpaid activities at this institution." Outside paid activities are defined as "any other paid activities outside this institution (e.g., consulting, working on other jobs)." Outside unpaid activities are defined as "unpaid (pro bono) professional service activities outside this institution." Details may not add to total because of rounding.
a. Includes medical schools.
b. Includes public liberal arts, private two-year, and other specialized institutions except medical schools.

Table A-26 ⇒ **Weekly Office Hours and Student Contact Hours by Gender, Institutional Type, and Program Area**

	Office hours	Informal contact hours
By gender		
New faculty		
Males	8.8	4.9
Females	7.8	4.7
Senior faculty		
Males	7.6	4.9
Females	7.5	4.8
By institutional type		
New faculty		
Research universities	7.3	4.7
Other doctorate-granting institutions[a]	9.7	4.4
Comprehensive institutions	8.4	5.3
Private liberal arts institutions	8.6	5.5
Public two-year institutions	9.0	4.4
All other institutions[b]	8.3	4.6
Senior faculty		
Research universities	6.3	4.8
Other doctorate-granting institutions	8.0	4.5
Comprehensive institutions	8.0	5.1
Private liberal arts institutions	7.8	5.7
Public two-year institutions	8.2	4.7
All other institutions	7.3	5.0
By program area		
New faculty		
Professions	10.0	5.0
Liberal arts and sciences	6.8	4.6
Fine arts	6.5	5.2
Humanities	6.8	4.2
Natural sciences	7.0	4.9
Social sciences	6.7	4.2
All other program areas	8.5	5.1
Senior faculty		
Professions	8.3	4.9
Liberal arts and sciences	6.7	4.7
Fine arts	6.1	5.6
Humanities	7.0	4.2
Natural sciences	6.6	4.7
Social sciences	6.8	4.9
All other program areas	8.9	5.7

a. Includes medical schools.
b. Includes public liberal arts, private two-year, and other specialized institutions except medical schools.

Table A-27 ⇒⊢ Primary Instructional Methods Used by Gender, Institutional Type, and Program Area

	Lecture	Seminar	Discussion	Lab
By gender				
New faculty				
Males	81.6	4.1	5.5	8.9
Females	69.7	6.5	9.9	14.0
Senior faculty				
Males	78.8	5.0	6.7	9.5
Females	69.1	6.5	11.1	13.3
By institutional type				
New faculty				
All research universities	83.5	7.5	4.5	4.5
All other doctorate-granting institutions[a]	80.5	5.3	5.4	8.9
All comprehensive institutions	74.4	4.9	8.9	11.7
Private liberal arts institutions	61.5	8.2	15.9	14.4
Public two-year institutions	72.3	0.9	7.6	19.2
All other institutions[b]	74.9	2.3	8.0	14.9
Senior faculty				
All research universities	79.7	7.9	6.0	6.3
All other doctorate-granting institutions	77.8	7.0	6.4	8.9
All comprehensive institutions	75.2	4.7	8.8	11.3
Private liberal arts institutions	67.7	8.0	13.0	11.3
Public two-year institutions	74.9	0.8	9.1	15.2
All other institutions	72.2	6.6	6.5	14.8
By program area				
New faculty				
Professions	75.3	5.1	6.4	13.3
Liberal arts and sciences	77.7	5.4	7.9	9.1
Fine arts	47.4	4.4	6.0	42.2
Humanities	61.8	9.4	20.5	8.3
Natural sciences	90.0	2.8	2.1	5.0
Social sciences	87.8	5.6	4.3	2.3
All other program areas	73.0	4.6	8.7	13.6
Senior faculty				
Professions	73.7	5.8	7.9	12.7
Liberal arts and sciences	77.6	5.1	8.1	9.1
Fine arts	54.3	4.0	5.9	35.8
Humanities	66.0	8.2	19.0	6.9
Natural sciences	89.2	2.0	2.8	6.1
Social sciences	86.1	7.2	4.3	2.4
All other program areas	73.5	6.1	7.9	12.5

Note: Results refer to all for-credit courses offered. The questionnaire item read, "In how many of the undergraduate courses that you taught for credit did you use. . . ." Discussion is defined as discussion or class presentations. Lab is defined as laboratory, internship, role play, or cooperative learning groups. Details may not add to total because of rounding.

a. Includes medical schools.

b. Includes public liberal arts, private two-year, and other specialized institutions except medical schools.

Table A-28 ⇜ **Other Instructional Methods Used by Gender, Institutional Type, and Program Area**

	Computational tools / software	Computer-aided instruction	Student presentations	Student evaluations
By gender				
New faculty				
Males	27.4	21.6	36.1	20.4
Females	28.4	26.8	51.2	32.4
Senior faculty				
Males	31.8	22.8	42.1	22.0
Females	33.0	31.2	55.6	35.2
By institutional type				
New faculty				
All research universities	12.8	10.1	20.0	11.6
All other doctorate-granting institutions[a]	20.2	14.3	28.5	14.3
All comprehensive institutions	36.2	28.4	58.0	35.7
Private liberal arts institutions	33.4	30.1	68.8	43.5
Public two-year institutions	43.2	42.8	56.7	33.5
All other institutions[b]	32.1	27.2	47.2	32.8
Senior faculty				
All research universities	17.0	10.8	27.6	14.5
All other doctorate-granting institutions	23.7	17.5	35.2	19.0
All comprehensive institutions	39.5	29.3	56.7	31.1
Private liberal arts institutions	35.7	31.1	71.2	40.1
Public two-year institutions	44.9	40.5	53.2	32.1
All other institutions	40.6	31.3	50.5	30.9
By program area				
New faculty				
Professions	32.0	23.6	38.1	20.3
Liberal arts and sciences	27.6	24.1	45.7	29.3
Fine arts	22.3	32.6	68.5	58.2
Humanities	19.8	25.3	65.2	49.0
Natural sciences	36.9	25.2	26.7	13.2
Social sciences	22.5	17.0	46.9	21.9
All other program areas	24.4	27.8	49.9	29.7
Senior faculty				
Professions	38.5	28.2	44.3	26.0
Liberal arts and sciences	30.9	24.9	48.3	26.7
Fine arts	21.1	28.5	67.5	52.2
Humanities	19.2	22.5	60.7	38.8
Natural sciences	45.6	28.8	31.7	12.9
Social sciences	26.0	19.2	50.0	20.0
All other program areas	25.5	21.2	43.6	23.2

Note: Percent represents faculty who responded "some" or "all." The questionnaire item read, "In how many of the undergraduate courses that you taught for credit did you use. . . ."
a. Includes medical schools.
b. Includes public liberal arts, private two-year, and other specialized institutions except medical schools.

Multiple-choice exams	Essay exams	Short-answer exams	Term/research papers	Multiple drafts of written work	Grading on a curve	Competency-based grading
32.1	37.3	36.0	35.0	18.4	25.5	32.9
41.7	43.0	41.0	41.6	28.9	18.8	42.5
37.3	43.9	38.8	40.3	21.5	26.5	37.7
45.3	44.7	40.9	44.7	31.3	17.4	44.2
14.7	21.9	21.7	20.0	11.6	19.1	19.9
29.6	30.4	29.2	29.1	14.8	24.0	27.5
46.8	56.0	50.3	51.6	30.7	28.5	45.2
43.3	64.0	57.8	68.2	43.9	29.8	51.0
57.2	44.4	46.9	42.3	27.3	18.5	52.9
38.8	42.5	41.2	40.5	25.8	20.8	43.3
20.4	29.8	23.8	26.8	14.5	20.2	26.3
32.3	36.3	31.0	34.4	18.9	20.1	29.1
46.7	55.4	47.7	54.8	30.9	29.2	44.4
37.9	63.2	49.4	62.2	41.1	26.5	47.7
60.0	46.3	50.9	41.7	26.0	23.2	54.5
42.8	45.1	41.0	39.3	26.5	25.8	41.7
38.9	29.8	31.4	32.1	16.2	19.5	34.6
34.4	49.7	44.3	43.6	29.2	27.0	40.2
37.6	55.8	47.7	51.6	28.8	27.0	63.9
27.6	70.1	47.6	59.2	55.3	18.8	50.8
32.6	31.6	42.7	23.7	12.2	29.6	32.2
44.4	55.6	41.6	57.8	29.7	32.0	31.2
42.7	39.8	42.6	39.6	21.4	22.6	39.6
45.7	33.6	33.8	38.3	19.0	20.9	39.8
36.5	52.5	43.9	45.4	28.8	26.5	41.6
29.4	45.2	44.3	37.7	20.9	21.2	55.8
26.9	72.1	43.3	61.2	50.8	18.8	44.4
37.6	34.8	45.8	26.7	13.8	32.0	36.8
51.7	62.1	41.3	61.6	30.4	30.0	38.3
40.3	37.5	37.1	37.2	20.3	22.5	33.4

Table A-29A Involvement in Research and Publication by Gender

	Engaged in research/ writing	Engaged in funded research	Published in refereed journals	Published in nonrefereed journals	Created work in juried media	Created work in nonjuried media	Published book reviews	Published chapters
New faculty								
Males	75.5	38.9	62.9	35.5	6.2	12.0	23.1	31.6
Females	63.1	25.0	41.9	25.2	5.3	13.1	16.9	21.3
Senior faculty								
Males	72.7	30.1	65.0	41.6	6.9	13.4	35.7	35.3
Females	61.2	19.9	46.7	31.0	6.2	14.2	25.0	26.0

	Published textbooks	Published books	Published monographs	Published technical reports	Presented at conferences	Gave exhibitions or performances	Held patents or copyrights	Published computer software
New faculty								
Males	6.9	11.8	9.0	31.7	68.2	7.5	7.1	8.2
Females	3.7	8.0	6.2	20.8	65.4	9.1	4.5	2.0
Senior faculty								
Males	15.7	18.5	15.1	32.0	69.8	9.1	10.2	7.4
Females	9.2	12.8	9.4	25.8	67.7	9.1	5.9	3.1

Note: Percents represent percentage of all faculty.

Table A-29B Involvement in Research and Publication: Tenured and Tenure-Track Faculty at Research Universities by Gender

	Engaged in research/ writing	Engaged in funded research	Published in refereed journals	Published in nonrefereed journals	Created work in juried media	Created work in nonjuried media	Published book reviews	Published chapters
New faculty								
Males	96.4	72.1	89.1	52.0	4.1	8.1	34.3	57.4
Females	93.5	61.4	77.4	46.1	4.9	12.5	34.5	50.8
Senior faculty								
Males	92.9	60.0	86.2	53.6	7.5	13.4	50.2	57.0
Females	90.7	51.2	81.1	53.8	11.5	17.3	51.3	59.6

	Published textbooks	Published books	Published monographs	Published technical reports	Presented at conferences	Gave exhibitions or performances	Held patents or copyrights	Published computer software
New faculty								
Males	9.0	17.7	11.8	37.5	82.6	3.9	9.4	12.3
Females	4.2	16.6	14.9	30.0	82.7	8.2	9.5	2.6
Senior faculty								
Males	22.4	26.5	24.1	39.4	78.7	8.2	14.2	9.1
Females	20.1	25.9	20.3	43.2	84.9	10.7	10.0	5.0

Note: Percents represent percentage of all faculty.

Table A-29C ⇌ Involvement in Research and Publication by Institutional Type

	Engaged in research/ writing	Engaged in funded research	Published in refereed journals	Published in nonrefereed journals
New faculty				
All research universities	91.7	62.0	77.1	43.8
All other doctorate-granting institutions[a]	83.6	45.2	73.4	35.7
All comprehensive institutions	71.8	20.6	50.9	33.4
Private liberal arts institutions	66.2	17.7	47.3	25.6
Public two-year institutions	32.5	5.7	17.1	10.4
All other institutions[b]	52.4	15.2	33.0	23.7
Senior faculty				
All research universities	91.5	53.9	83.1	52.0
All other doctorate-granting institutions	82.4	35.9	77.3	47.3
All comprehensive institutions	71.2	18.4	61.9	42.1
Private liberal arts institutions	65.4	14.4	54.4	31.9
Public two-year institutions	33.1	5.7	20.3	13.7
All other institutions	58.0	13.4	42.9	33.8

	Published textbooks	Published books	Published monographs	Published technical reports
New faculty				
All research universities	6.3	14.8	10.6	33.5
All other doctorate-granting institutions	6.0	9.4	9.1	29.2
All comprehensive institutions	5.6	10.3	7.7	28.6
Private liberal arts institutions	3.7	11.9	10.1	22.5
Public two-year institutions	4.9	4.0	2.6	16.7
All other institutions	5.1	7.6	6.0	25.5
Senior faculty				
All research universities	20.1	24.4	21.7	38.9
All other doctorate-granting institutions	15.9	21.5	16.3	33.4
All comprehensive institutions	13.0	16.4	12.8	32.6
Private liberal arts institutions	7.1	15.0	12.0	24.0
Public two-year institutions	8.1	5.8	3.7	16.5
All other institutions	12.8	13.9	6.8	28.6

Note: Percents represent percentage of all faculty.

a. Includes medical schools.

b. Includes public liberal arts, private two-year, and other specialized institutions except medical schools.

Created work in juried media	Created work in nonjuried media	Published book reviews	Published chapters
4.6	9.3	27.7	47.1
6.5	11.1	23.8	35.2
7.1	16.4	19.6	18.6
7.4	16.0	23.1	22.3
5.1	11.5	7.5	6.8
4.9	15.3	19.4	15.1
7.8	13.8	47.4	55.4
7.0	13.2	38.8	46.7
7.2	15.0	32.2	27.2
8.1	14.2	33.5	22.3
4.3	11.5	10.6	6.5
5.9	15.5	26.8	21.8

Presented at conferences	Gave exhibitions or performances	Held patents or copyrights	Published computer software
77.7	5.3	9.0	8.4
76.8	5.4	6.9	6.9
70.5	10.2	4.3	5.2
68.0	14.2	7.0	3.1
42.5	8.4	2.9	2.9
53.1	13.9	5.4	3.0
78.2	8.2	12.5	7.7
79.4	7.0	10.1	6.7
74.0	10.1	9.1	6.2
68.6	16.6	5.7	3.9
46.2	7.5	4.8	4.8
61.3	10.5	7.8	5.9

Table A-29D ⇌ Involvement in Research and Publication by Program Area

	Engaged in research/ writing	Engaged in funded research	Published in refereed journals	Published nonrefereed journals	Created work in juried media	Created work in nonjuried media
New faculty						
Professions	66.2	34.0	54.8	32.4	4.7	12.5
Liberal arts and sciences	75.1	32.3	55.6	28.1	6.6	11.1
Fine arts	82.8	5.6	22.2	16.6	10.6	14.5
Humanities	69.7	12.7	41.3	23.8	11.0	15.0
Natural sciences	74.9	49.8	70.9	32.4	3.7	7.7
Social sciences	78.5	31.3	60.1	30.6	5.1	11.0
All other program areas	64.5	29.4	47.2	39.4	6.7	18.0
Senior faculty						
Professions	63.8	29.3	59.4	41.1	4.5	13.1
Liberal arts and sciences	73.7	25.9	62.3	34.9	8.0	13.0
Fine arts	83.1	17.9	29.8	22.4	17.8	18.4
Humanities	73.0	12.8	59.1	35.0	12.4	16.3
Natural sciences	68.3	37.7	68.8	29.6	3.0	8.3
Social sciences	78.8	27.3	73.9	51.2	5.5	13.8
All other program areas	65.7	26.4	51.2	48.3	6.4	18.3

	Published textbooks	Published books	Published monographs	Published technical reports	Presented at conferences	Gave exhibitions or perfor- mances
New faculty						
Professions	6.8	6.8	8.6	31.6	65.8	3.3
Liberal arts and sciences	5.2	12.1	7.3	23.3	68.7	11.4
Fine arts	2.7	8.9	4.9	9.7	59.6	65.8
Humanities	5.7	18.6	8.4	13.7	66.8	10.1
Natural sciences	5.5	8.0	5.3	28.4	70.4	2.5
Social sciences	5.1	13.2	10.7	31.5	72.1	4.0
All other program areas	4.9	12.0	8.3	31.0	63.3	9.6
Senior faculty						
Professions	14.1	11.4	12.5	35.4	70.6	3.3
Liberal arts and sciences	13.6	20.4	14.3	26.0	69.3	13.4
Fine arts	6.4	11.7	7.2	10.3	54.8	74.2
Humanities	15.3	29.1	18.5	17.8	73.3	9.6
Natural sciences	12.8	10.8	7.4	28.2	65.9	2.5
Social sciences	17.1	30.7	24.9	42.2	78.4	3.2
All other program areas	15.0	16.4	13.3	35.7	66.9	5.5

Note: Percents represent percentage of all faculty.

Published book reviews	Published chapters
16.4	27.5
24.0	28.1
18.0	9.3
30.9	24.4
17.1	30.6
31.5	36.5
21.4	24.9
24.9	32.4
37.2	33.1
25.5	13.0
48.9	34.9
23.2	28.3
52.8	50.5
33.4	33.2

Held patents or copyrights	Published computer software
6.0	8.1
5.8	4.4
9.8	1.1
5.0	1.5
6.6	8.0
3.6	2.9
6.4	4.6
9.3	7.9
9.1	5.7
12.2	2.8
8.0	2.2
10.0	9.3
7.4	5.7
7.5	4.3

Table A-30 ⇌ Concurrent Employment by Gender, Institutional Type, and Program Area

	Total	Full-time	Part-time
By Gender			
New faculty			
Males	24.4	2.9	21.4
Females	22.8	1.8	21.0
Senior faculty			
Males	26.7	1.9	24.8
Females	21.3	1.3	20.0
By institutional type			
New faculty			
All research institutions	18.8	1.3	17.5
All other doctorate-granting institutions[a]	19.7	1.7	18.0
All comprehensive institutions	24.4	2.0	22.7
Private liberal arts institutions	24.0	3.0	21.0
Public two-year institutions	27.2	3.4	23.8
All other institutions[b]	26.2	3.3	22.9
Senior faculty			
All research institutions	25.6	1.6	23.9
All other doctorate-granting institutions	25.1	1.4	23.7
All comprehensive institutions	23.6	1.4	22.2
Private liberal arts institutions	23.9	1.9	22.0
Public two-year institutions	25.3	2.2	23.0
All other institutions	27.6	1.9	25.8
By program area			
New faculty			
Professions	29.1	2.8	26.3
Liberal arts and sciences	19.8	1.9	17.9
Fine arts	39.7	5.5	34.2
Humanities	16.4	1.4	15.0
Natural sciences	14.6	1.0	13.5
Social sciences	23.6	2.1	21.5
All other program areas	26.3	3.2	23.1
Senior faculty			
Professions	29.8	2.0	27.8
Liberal arts and sciences	22.0	1.5	20.6
Fine arts	42.2	3.6	38.6
Humanities	15.6	1.2	14.4
Natural sciences	18.8	0.9	17.9
Social sciences	27.7	1.6	26.1
All other program areas	24.8	2.0	22.7

Note: Percents represent percentage of total number of faculty within cohort. Details may not add to total because of rounding.

a. Includes medical schools.

b. Includes public liberal arts, private two-year, and other specialized institutions except medical schools.

Table A-31 ⇒ Concurrent Employment Sector by Gender, Institutional Type, and Program Area

	Four-year college or university	Two-year college	Elementary or secondary school
By gender			
New faculty			
Males	3.0	1.1	0.3
Females	2.3	0.9	0.6
Senior faculty			
Males	2.9	0.7	0.3
Females	2.3	0.8	0.5
By institutional type			
New faculty			
All research universities	1.6	0.0	0.1
All other doctorate-granting institutions[a]	2.9	0.6	0.0
All comprehensive institutions	3.0	1.2	0.7
Private liberal arts institutions	1.5	1.7	0.2
Public two-year institutions	2.9	1.6	0.7
All other institutions[b]	4.0	0.7	0.0
Senior faculty			
All research universities	1.6	0.1	0.4
All other doctorate-granting institutions	2.4	0.6	0.3
All comprehensive institutions	2.2	0.4	0.4
Private liberal arts institutions	4.1	1.1	0.3
Public two-year institutions	3.3	1.4	0.4
All other institutions	4.4	1.2	0.5
By program area			
New faculty			
Professions	1.9	0.7	0.6
Liberal arts and sciences	3.3	1.3	0.3
Fine arts	2.7	0.0	0.7
Humanities	3.1	2.3	0.4
Natural sciences	2.9	0.9	0.3
Social sciences	4.5	0.9	0.0
All other program areas	2.8	0.9	0.3
Senior faculty			
Professions	2.1	0.5	0.6
Liberal arts and sciences	3.0	0.9	0.3
Fine arts	2.7	0.6	0.1
Humanities	2.9	0.9	0.3
Natural sciences	2.8	1.2	0.3
Social sciences	4.0	0.7	0.2
All other program areas	2.5	0.3	0.5

Note: The questionnaire item read, "Not counting any employment at this institution, what was the employment sector of the main other job you held during Fall 1992?" Details may not add to total because of rounding.

a. Includes medical schools.

b. Includes public liberal arts, private two-year, and other specialized institutions except medical schools.

Consulting, freelance, private business, or private practice	Hospital, health care, or clinical practice	Foundation or nonprofit	For-profit business or industry	Federal, state, local government or military	Other
13.3	1.1	0.7	2.0	1.1	1.8
9.5	5.6	0.6	0.9	0.7	1.6
15.4	1.0	1.1	1.9	1.2	2.2
9.4	4.0	0.7	1.1	0.9	1.6
11.9	1.7	0.5	1.2	0.7	1.1
10.3	3.0	0.2	0.6	0.6	1.4
12.8	2.8	0.8	1.3	1.0	1.2
9.4	2.6	1.9	1.5	1.7	3.4
10.8	5.7	0.5	2.3	0.9	1.9
13.5	1.5	0.7	2.2	0.4	3.3
16.6	1.4	1.6	1.0	1.6	1.4
14.4	2.2	0.9	1.4	1.3	1.6
13.6	1.5	0.7	1.6	1.2	2.0
10.7	1.4	1.0	1.5	1.0	2.7
11.0	3.3	1.0	2.2	0.7	2.0
14.8	0.9	0.7	0.7	0.9	3.5
13.1	8.6	0.5	1.4	1.2	1.1
9.6	0.6	0.8	1.0	0.8	2.0
22.9	0.0	3.8	1.7	0.3	7.5
6.5	0.4	0.3	1.2	0.7	1.5
6.9	0.5	0.2	0.7	0.8	1.2
12.2	1.4	1.2	0.7	1.4	1.2
15.1	1.1	0.4	3.1	0.5	2.1
15.5	6.0	0.6	1.7	1.3	1.4
11.5	0.5	1.2	1.4	1.0	2.1
23.7	0.4	3.3	1.8	0.4	9.1
6.7	0.1	1.2	1.5	0.6	1.4
10.1	0.4	0.5	1.1	1.4	0.9
15.9	1.1	1.2	1.6	1.4	1.7
16.1	0.2	0.8	2.3	1.0	2.8

Table A-32A ⇌ Perceptions of Faculty Roles and Rewards by Gender, Institutional Type, and Program Area

| | Teaching should be promotion criterion | |
	Mean	Percent somewhat/ strongly agree
By gender		
New faculty		
Males	3.0	74.2
Females	3.2	81.9
Senior faculty		
Males	3.1	75.5
Females	3.3	83.2
By institutional type		
New faculty		
All research universities	2.6	54.2
All other doctorate-granting institutions[a]	2.9	70.1
All comprehensive institutions	3.3	87.3
Private liberal arts institutions	3.5	94.3
Public two-year institutions	3.6	95.8
All other institutions[b]	3.5	92.8
Senior faculty		
All research universities	2.5	52.1
All other doctorate-granting institutions	2.9	67.6
All comprehensive institutions	3.4	87.9
Private liberal arts institutions	3.6	92.1
Public two-year institutions	3.6	96.0
All other institutions	3.6	93.4
By program area		
New faculty		
Professions	3.2	79.5
Liberal arts and sciences	3.1	74.5
Fine arts	3.3	86.4
Humanities	3.3	83.0
Natural sciences	2.9	66.8
Social sciences	3.0	73.3
All other program areas	3.3	82.0
Senior faculty		
Professions	3.2	79.3
Liberal arts and sciences	3.1	76.1
Fine arts	3.4	88.9
Humanities	3.2	81.0
Natural sciences	3.0	71.3
Social sciences	3.0	70.9
All other program areas	3.2	79.7

Note: The questionnaire items read, "Indicate the extent to which you agree or disagree with these statements: 1 = disagree strongly; 2 = disagree somewhat; 3 = agree somewhat; 4 = agree strongly." Teaching as promotion criterion: "Teaching effectiveness should be the primary criterion for promotion of college teachers at this institution." Research as promotion criterion: "Research/publications should be the primary criterion for promotion of college teachers at this institution." Research rewarded more than teaching: "At this institution, research is rewarded more than teaching." Assessment will improve quality of education: "State or federally mandated assessment requirements will improve the quality of under-

Research should be promotion criterion		Research rewarded more than teaching		Assessment will improve quality of education	
Mean	Percent somewhat/ strongly agree	Mean	Percent somewhat/ strongly agree	Mean	Percent somewhat/ strongly agree
2.2	40.2	2.5	52.0	2.1	33.9
1.9	25.4	2.3	43.5	2.2	39.3
2.1	36.4	2.6	52.9	1.9	29.4
1.9	23.6	2.3	44.8	2.1	36.0
2.5	54.1	3.4	86.9	2.0	36.1
2.4	47.7	3.0	71.1	2.1	30.5
2.0	26.7	2.2	35.6	2.2	33.0
1.8	21.2	1.6	14.8	2.0	39.7
1.6	10.2	1.4	8.2	2.3	29.6
1.8	22.5	1.7	20.8	2.2	43.5
2.6	57.5	3.5	90.0	1.9	26.1
2.3	44.4	3.1	72.6	1.9	28.3
1.9	26.0	2.4	44.7	2.0	32.3
1.8	20.3	1.7	16.5	1.9	27.4
1.5	8.7	1.4	9.4	2.2	40.0
1.7	18.7	1.8	24.5	2.0	32.7
2.1	32.8	2.5	51.9	2.2	39.2
2.1	36.2	2.4	46.1	2.1	32.7
1.9	25.7	2.1	34.5	2.1	35.3
2.0	28.4	2.1	37.2	2.1	35.7
2.2	40.9	2.6	52.4	2.1	32.4
2.3	41.7	2.5	50.5	2.0	28.6
2.0	28.0	2.4	44.6	2.2	36.9
2.0	31.8	2.6	55.2	2.1	34.7
2.1	34.2	2.4	48.5	1.9	29.0
2.0	29.4	2.3	39.6	2.0	30.9
2.0	29.5	2.4	46.5	1.9	27.4
2.1	35.3	2.5	50.9	2.0	30.3
2.3	41.6	2.5	51.7	1.9	27.6
2.0	28.5	2.5	48.3	2.0	32.8

graduate education." Percent somewhat/strongly agree represents cumulative percentage of those who responded "somewhat agree" or "strongly agree." Means and percents were calculated using only those faculty who responded in each category; thus the number of valid responses is different for each category. Details may not add to total because of rounding.

a. Includes medical schools.

b. Includes public liberal arts, private two-year, and other specialized institutions except medical schools.

Table A-32B Perceptions of Faculty Roles and Rewards: Tenured and Tenure-Track Faculty at Research and Doctoral Universities by Gender

	Teaching should be promotion criterion		Research should be promotion criterion	
	Mean	Percent somewhat/ strongly agree	Mean	Percent somewhat/ strongly agree
New faculty				
Males	2.5	53.5	2.6	57.0
Females	2.7	56.3	2.4	50.1
Senior faculty				
Males	2.6	55.2	2.6	56.2
Females	2.6	56.3	2.4	47.1

Note: The questionnaire items read, "Indicate the extent to which you agree or disagree with these statements: 1 = disagree strongly; 2 = disagree somewhat; 3 = agree somewhat; 4 = agree strongly." Teaching as promotion criterion: "Teaching effectiveness should be the primary criterion for promotion of college teachers at this institution." Research as promotion criterion: "Research/ publications should be the primary criterion for promotion of college teachers at this institution." Research rewarded more than teaching: "At this institution, research is rewarded more than teaching." Assessment will improve quality of education: "State or federally mandated assessment requirements will improve the quality of undergraduate education." Percent somewhat/strongly agree represents cumulative percentage of those who responded "somewhat agree" or "strongly agree." Means and percents were calculated using only those faculty who had responded in each category; thus the number of valid responses is different for each category. Details may not add to total because of rounding.

Research rewarded more than teaching		Assessment will improve quality of education	
Mean	Percent somewhat/ strongly agree	Mean	Percent somewhat/ strongly agree
3.3	80.9	1.9	26.4
3.3	83.4	2.0	26.9
3.3	84.0	1.9	25.2
3.3	84.3	1.9	25.4

Table A-33 ⇌ Perceptions of Instructional Duties by Gender, Institutional Type, and Program Area

	Course content and methods	
	Mean	Percent somewhat/ very satisfied
By gender		
New faculty		
Males	3.7	94.6
Females	3.6	93.1
Senior faculty		
Males	3.7	95.0
Females	3.7	94.1
By institutional type		
New faculty		
All research universities	3.7	95.3
All other doctorate-granting institutions[a]	3.6	92.1
All comprehensive institutions	3.7	94.6
Private liberal arts institutions	3.7	92.7
Public two-year institutions	3.6	93.5
All other institutions[b]	3.7	94.2
Senior faculty		
All research universities	3.7	95.0
All other doctorate-granting institutions	3.7	93.7
All comprehensive institutions	3.8	95.2
Private liberal arts institutions	3.8	95.5
Public two-year institutions	3.7	94.6
All other institutions	3.7	93.2
By program area		
New faculty		
Professions	3.6	93.1
Liberal arts and sciences	3.7	94.1
Fine arts	3.7	94.8
Humanities	3.7	93.9
Natural sciences	3.6	93.3
Social sciences	3.7	95.2
All other program areas	3.7	96.0
Senior faculty		
Professions	3.7	93.7
Liberal arts and sciences	3.8	95.0
Fine arts	3.7	94.2
Humanities	3.8	95.5
Natural sciences	3.7	94.1
Social sciences	3.8	96.6
All other program areas	3.8	96.3

Note: The questionnaire items read, "How satisfied are you with each of these aspects of your instructional duties: 1 = very dissatisfied; 2 = somewhat dissatisfied; 3 = somewhat satisfied; 4 = very satisfied." Content and methods: "Authority I have to make decisions about content and methods in the courses I teach." Noninstructional aspects: "Authority I have to make decisions about other (non-instructional) aspects of my job." Course choice: "Authority I have to make decisions about what courses I teach." Time for students: "Time available for working with students as an advisor, mentor, etc."

Noninstructional aspects		Course choice		Time for students	
	Percent somewhat/		Percent somewhat/		Percent somewhat/
Mean	very satisfied	Mean	very satisfied	Mean	very satisfied
3.1	77.5	3.2	84.4	3.1	79.5
3.0	74.0	3.2	81.3	3.0	73.6
3.1	76.7	3.4	88.1	3.2	83.9
2.9	70.2	3.3	83.9	3.0	73.5
3.1	79.6	3.2	85.3	3.0	77.5
3.0	76.2	3.2	81.3	3.0	76.7
3.0	73.7	3.1	79.4	3.1	78.6
3.0	76.1	3.1	82.0	3.0	75.0
3.0	73.9	3.3	85.4	3.0	76.3
3.0	77.0	3.3	87.4	3.1	75.0
3.1	77.6	3.4	88.6	3.2	83.0
3.1	78.5	3.3	83.8	3.1	82.1
3.0	74.1	3.3	86.3	3.1	80.0
3.1	78.6	3.5	89.4	3.2	83.1
2.9	70.2	3.4	87.3	3.1	78.6
2.9	69.5	3.4	85.5	3.1	79.7
3.0	77.9	3.2	83.5	3.0	74.8
3.0	75.0	3.2	82.0	3.0	78.8
2.9	69.2	3.2	82.4	3.0	75.2
3.0	72.2	3.2	81.3	3.1	79.4
3.0	77.2	3.1	80.1	3.1	80.8
3.0	77.2	3.3	85.9	3.0	76.1
3.1	75.7	3.3	85.7	3.1	76.4
3.0	74.8	3.3	85.3	3.1	78.4
3.0	74.1	3.4	87.4	3.2	82.8
2.9	70.2	3.4	86.7	3.1	82.3
2.9	69.6	3.4	85.8	3.2	82.8
3.1	76.0	3.4	87.3	3.2	82.3
3.1	78.7	3.5	90.3	3.2	83.9
3.1	78.2	3.4	89.0	3.1	79.8

Percent somewhat/very satisifed represents cumulative percentage of those who responded "somewhat satisfied" or "very satisfied." Means and percents were calculated using only those faculty who responded in each category; thus the number of valid responses is different for each category. Details may not add to total because of rounding.
a. Includes medical schools.
b. Includes public liberal arts, private two-year, and other specialized institutions except medical schools.

Table A-34 ⇌ Perceptions of Campus Environment: Undergraduate Education by Gender, Institutional Type, and Program Area

	Quality of undergraduates	
	Mean	Percent somewhat/ very satisfied
By gender		
New faculty		
Males	2.8	66.9
Females	2.9	70.5
Senior faculty		
Males	2.8	66.5
Females	2.9	69.6
By institutional type		
New faculty		
All research institutions	2.9	71.6
All other doctorate-granting institutions[a]	2.9	69.7
All comprehensive institutions	2.8	66.0
Private liberal arts institutions	2.9	74.1
Public two-year institutions	2.8	65.9
All other institutions[b]	2.9	63.3
Senior faculty		
All research institutions	3.0	73.2
All other doctorate-granting institutions	2.9	69.2
All comprehensive institutions	2.7	63.9
Private liberal arts institutions	3.0	75.9
Public two-year institutions	2.7	61.0
All other institutions	2.9	70.9
By program area		
New faculty		
Professions	3.0	73.9
Liberal arts and sciences	2.8	64.7
Fine arts	2.7	59.7
Humanities	2.8	65.4
Natural sciences	2.7	63.4
Social sciences	2.8	68.6
All other program areas	2.8	68.1
Senior faculty		
Professions	3.0	73.5
Liberal arts and sciences	2.7	62.8
Fine arts	2.9	68.8
Humanities	2.7	62.9
Natural sciences	2.7	60.9
Social sciences	2.7	62.5
All other program areas	2.9	72.8

Note: The first questionnaire item read, "How satisfied are you with each of the following aspects of your instructional duties at this institution? 1 = very dissatisfied; 2 = somewhat dissatisfied; 3 = somewhat satisfied; 4 = very satisfied." For "Quality of undergraduate students whom I have taught here," percent somewhat/very satisfied represents cumulative percentage of those who responded "somewhat satisfied" or "very satisfied." Means and percents were calculated using only those faculty who responded. The second questionnaire item read, "Please indicate your opinion regarding whether each of the following has worsened, stayed the same, or

	Institution is meeting the educational needs of students		
Worsened	Stayed the same	Improved	Don't know
20.5	35.6	35.0	8.9
18.5	29.9	38.0	13.6
24.3	35.6	37.3	2.7
21.9	29.4	45.1	3.6
23.8	38.9	22.7	14.6
19.4	34.7	35.7	10.2
22.8	30.8	37.2	9.2
14.3	31.7	43.1	11.0
13.8	29.6	49.2	7.5
13.5	24.1	51.8	10.6
29.8	38.2	27.5	4.5
23.4	37.0	36.4	3.2
25.2	32.0	40.4	2.5
13.0	36.2	48.5	2.4
19.1	28.4	50.7	1.8
16.2	30.3	50.4	3.1
18.4	33.2	40.1	8.3
20.5	34.5	33.5	11.5
23.8	25.3	39.8	11.2
21.5	32.1	35.2	11.2
19.9	38.0	32.0	10.2
19.0	35.1	31.3	14.6
21.2	31.3	37.0	10.5
20.4	33.5	42.3	3.8
25.8	34.1	37.7	2.4
21.0	34.5	41.7	2.8
29.5	30.6	37.4	2.6
24.0	36.6	37.1	2.3
26.8	34.3	37.0	1.8
22.5	32.7	42.0	2.7

improved in recent years at this institution." For "Ability of this institution to meet the educational needs of entering students," percents represent row percentages totaling 100 percent. Details may not add to total because of rounding.

a. Includes medical schools.

b. Includes public liberal arts, private two-year, and other specialized institutions except medical schools.

Table A-35A ⇌+ Perceptions of Campus Environment: Equity Issues by Race

	Female faculty		Minority faculty	
	Mean	Percent somewhat/strongly agree	Mean	Percent somewhat/strongly agree
All faculty				
American Indian / Alaskan Native	3.1	76.5	3.0	73.6
Asian / Pacific Islander	3.2	81.1	2.9	70.4
Black not Hispanic	2.9	67.4	2.8	65.6
Hispanic	3.0	71.7	2.8	66.9
White not Hispanic	3.1	76.0	3.2	83.5
New faculty				
American Indian / Alaskan Native	3.1	79.2	2.9	68.9
Asian / Pacific Islander	3.1	80.3	2.9	69.0
Black not Hispanic	2.8	63.5	2.8	66.9
Hispanic	3.0	71.8	2.9	68.0
White not Hispanic	3.0	74.3	3.2	81.3
Senior faculty				
American Indian / Alaskan Native	3.1	75.6	3.1	76.5
Asian / Pacific Islander	3.2	81.9	2.9	71.5
Black not Hispanic	2.9	69.9	2.8	64.6
Hispanic	3.1	72.5	2.8	66.1
White not Hispanic	3.1	76.9	3.3	84.6

ote: The questionnaire items read, "Please indicate the extent to which you agree or disagree with each of the following statements: 1 = disagree strongly; 2 = disagree somewhat; 3 = agree somewhat; 4 = agree strongly." Female faculty: "Female faculty members are treated fairly at this institution." Minority faculty: "Faculty who are members of racial or ethnic minorities are treated fairly at this institution." Percent somewhat/strongly agree represents cumulative percentage of those who responded "somewhat agree" or "strongly agree." Means and percents were calculated using only those faculty who had responded in each category; thus the number of valid responses is different for each category. Details may not add to total because of rounding.

Table A-35B ⇌ Perceptions of Campus Environment: Equity Issues by Gender, Institutional Type, and Program Area

	Female faculty		Minority faculty	
	Mean	Percent somewhat/strongly agree	Mean	Percent somewhat/strongly agree
By gender				
New faculty				
Males	3.2	81.5	3.2	83.2
Females	2.8	63.2	3.0	73.1
Senior faculty				
Males	3.3	84.4	3.3	86.6
Females	2.6	57.2	3.0	72.4
By institutional type				
New faculty				
All research institutions	2.9	70.0	3.0	74.7
All other doctorate-granting institutions[a]	2.9	73.0	3.0	76.6
All comprehensive institutions	2.9	70.2	3.1	77.4
Private liberal arts institutions	3.1	77.6	3.1	81.1
Public two-year institutions	3.2	82.3	3.4	87.5
All other institutions[b]	3.2	79.8	3.3	84.0
Senior faculty				
All research institutions	3.0	74.1	3.1	80.5
All other doctorate-granting institutions	3.0	74.6	3.2	81.3
All comprehensive institutions	3.1	74.0	3.2	81.1
Private liberal arts institutions	3.3	81.6	3.3	86.2
Public two-year institutions	3.3	82.5	3.4	86.4
All other institutions	3.2	79.5	3.3	84.9
By program area				
New faculty				
Professions	3.0	74.4	3.2	80.4
Liberal arts and sciences	3.0	73.5	3.1	78.4
Fine arts	2.9	65.0	3.0	73.0
Humanities	2.9	68.3	3.1	75.8
Natural sciences	3.1	79.2	3.2	83.5
Social sciences	3.0	73.3	3.0	74.6
All other program areas	3.0	74.3	3.1	77.3
Senior faculty				
Professions	3.1	75.1	3.2	81.4
Liberal arts and sciences	3.1	77.8	3.2	83.6
Fine arts	3.0	73.3	3.2	83.4
Humanities	3.0	73.0	3.2	80.1
Natural sciences	3.3	84.3	3.4	89.9
Social sciences	3.1	75.3	3.1	77.5
All other program areas	3.1	75.6	3.2	81.5

Note: The questionnaire items read, "Please indicate the extent to which you agree or disagree with each of the following statements: 1 = disagree strongly; 2 = disagree somewhat; 3 = agree somewhat; 4 = agree strongly." Female faculty: "Female faculty members are treated fairly at this institution." Minority faculty: "Faculty who are members of racial or ethnic minorities are treated fairly at this institution." Percent somewhat/strongly agree represents cumulative percentage of those who responded "somewhat agree" or "strongly agree." Means and percents were calculated using only those faculty who had responded in each category; thus the number of valid responses is different for each category. Details may not add to total because of rounding.

a. Includes medical schools.

b. Includes public liberal arts, private two-year, and other specialized institutions except medical schools.

Table A-36 ⇒ Perceptions of Campus Environment: Work Pressures by Gender, Institutional Type, and Program Area

| | Pressure to increase faculty workload | | | |
	Worsened	Stayed the same	Improved	Don't know
By gender				
New faculty				
Males	48.9	33.7	8.1	9.3
Females	50.9	29.3	6.8	13.0
Senior faculty				
Males	49.9	38.1	8.7	3.4
Females	56.1	31.0	8.7	4.2
By institutional type				
New faculty				
All research institutions	55.4	27.7	5.6	11.3
All other doctorate-granting institutions[a]	51.4	29.4	8.3	11.0
All comprehensive institutions	47.8	32.8	8.5	10.8
Private liberal arts institutions	39.6	38.6	10.8	11.0
Public two-year institutions	46.4	36.8	7.0	9.8
All other institutions[b]	48.3	32.0	9.2	10.5
Senior faculty				
All research institutions	57.9	31.9	7.1	3.0
All other doctorate-granting institutions	53.5	33.5	9.3	3.6
All comprehensive institutions	49.2	37.0	10.3	3.5
Private liberal arts institutions	41.6	40.3	14.4	3.8
Public two-year institutions	50.4	39.9	5.9	3.8
All other institutions	44.4	38.5	10.8	6.3
By program area				
New faculty				
Professions	51.6	31.8	7.9	8.7
Liberal arts and sciences	48.9	32.6	7.4	11.1
Fine arts	50.1	32.4	5.3	12.2
Humanities	47.9	31.5	9.6	11.0
Natural sciences	48.4	35.5	6.9	9.2
Social sciences	50.4	28.8	6.6	14.3
All other program areas	51.6	29.9	7.3	11.2
Senior faculty				
Professions	53.1	34.5	8.8	3.5
Liberal arts and sciences	51.5	37.1	8.3	3.1
Fine arts	49.9	35.0	11.4	3.7
Humanities	52.4	35.1	8.9	3.6
Natural sciences	49.7	40.8	6.6	2.9
Social sciences	54.5	34.6	8.7	2.2
All other program areas	49.1	35.2	10.5	5.2

Note: The questionnaire items read, "Please indicate your opinion regarding whether each of the following has worsened, stayed the same, or improved in recent years at this institution." Item: "Pressure to increase faculty workload at this institution." Item: "The ability of faculty to obtain external funding." Percents represent row percentage totaling 100 percent. Details may not add to total because of rounding.

a. Includes medical schools.

b. Includes public liberal arts, private two-year, and other specialized institutions except medical schools.

	Ability of faculty to obtain external funding		
Worsened	Stayed the same	Improved	Don't know
39.9	26.5	17.2	16.3
31.7	22.5	15.6	30.2
39.9	29.8	19.2	11.1
34.3	25.8	19.5	20.4
48.8	21.2	15.8	14.2
41.1	21.6	20.8	16.6
32.5	24.9	18.5	24.1
25.9	30.0	17.2	26.8
27.4	29.4	11.9	31.3
22.4	31.0	15.7	30.9
51.1	25.0	16.8	7.2
43.5	25.3	20.3	10.8
32.5	30.8	23.9	12.8
28.8	32.4	20.1	18.8
31.7	30.9	14.9	22.5
26.9	32.4	21.6	19.1
36.7	25.9	17.8	19.7
38.6	24.6	14.0	22.8
33.1	23.2	15.9	27.7
27.7	25.8	14.7	31.8
50.5	21.1	14.4	13.9
32.2	30.1	11.6	26.2
30.7	24.8	20.6	24.0
38.3	28.6	20.5	12.6
39.7	28.6	18.0	13.7
33.1	33.0	16.7	17.2
34.8	26.4	18.6	20.2
45.9	25.9	18.4	9.8
39.1	33.6	17.3	9.9
32.7	30.0	21.8	15.5

Table A-37 ⇒ Perceptions of Campus Facilities: Space Issues by Gender, Institutional Type, and Program Area

	Laboratory space and supplies	
	Mean	Percent good/ very good
By gender		
New faculty		
Males	2.8	68.0
Females	2.7	61.0
Senior faculty		
Males	2.8	67.3
Females	2.7	61.7
By institutional type		
New faculty		
All research universities	3.0	74.3
All other doctorate-granting institutions[a]	2.8	66.5
All comprehensive institutions	2.5	52.7
Private liberal arts institutions	2.5	54.8
Public two-year institutions	2.8	67.2
All other institutions[b]	2.8	65.5
Senior faculty		
All research universities	2.9	73.1
All other doctorate-granting institutions	2.8	68.3
All comprehensive institutions	2.5	55.2
Private liberal arts institutions	2.7	62.8
Public two-year institutions	2.8	68.2
All other institutions	2.8	67.7
By program area		
New faculty		
Professions	2.8	65.8
Liberal arts and sciences	2.7	63.3
Fine arts	2.6	58.9
Humanities	2.7	60.5
Natural sciences	2.8	65.5
Social sciences	2.7	62.2
All other program areas	2.8	66.7
Senior faculty		
Professions	2.8	66.6
Liberal arts and sciences	2.7	64.8
Fine arts	2.6	59.8
Humanities	2.6	58.2
Natural sciences	2.9	71.4
Social sciences	2.6	55.8
All other program areas	2.8	67.2

Note: The questionnaire items read, "How would you rate each of the following facilities or resources at this institution that were available for your own use during the 1992 Fall term? 1 = very poor; 2 = poor; 3 = good; 4 = very good." Percent good/very good represents cumulative percentage of those who responded "good" or "very good." Means and percents were calculated using only those faculty who had responded in each category; thus the number

Classroom space		Office space		Studio/performance space	
Mean	Percent good/ very good	Mean	Percent good/ very good	Mean	Percent good/ very good
2.9	72.1	2.8	69.1	2.7	62.8
2.8	68.3	2.7	65.0	2.6	60.5
2.9	72.4	2.9	74.0	2.7	65.2
2.8	67.3	2.8	69.0	2.6	61.4
2.8	68.4	2.9	70.1	2.7	64.0
2.8	71.6	2.8	70.4	2.7	61.2
2.8	69.3	2.8	67.0	2.6	58.0
2.9	75.8	2.8	68.7	2.7	57.6
2.8	69.6	2.7	60.7	2.7	63.3
3.1	80.5	2.8	67.6	2.9	70.8
2.8	66.4	2.9	72.7	2.7	66.0
2.9	71.9	3.0	77.5	2.8	66.6
2.8	68.7	2.9	71.5	2.7	62.0
3.0	78.8	3.1	80.3	2.8	63.8
2.9	73.8	2.8	67.9	2.7	62.5
3.0	80.0	2.9	71.8	2.8	69.8
2.8	71.8	2.8	68.0	2.7	62.4
2.8	69.3	2.8	66.6	2.7	60.6
2.7	66.5	2.7	65.1	2.6	57.9
2.8	72.1	2.7	61.8	2.6	56.6
2.8	69.7	2.8	69.7	2.7	60.4
2.8	66.7	2.8	67.4	2.9	72.7
2.8	70.3	2.8	69.1	2.6	59.6
2.9	72.0	2.9	72.4	2.7	66.5
2.8	69.1	2.9	71.7	2.7	61.2
2.7	66.4	2.9	71.5	2.7	59.5
2.8	70.0	2.9	70.4	2.6	60.8
2.8	70.8	2.9	74.1	2.7	65.8
2.8	66.6	2.9	69.2	2.7	58.1
2.9	75.2	3.0	75.1	2.8	68.0

of valid responses is different for each category. Details may not add to total because of rounding.

a. Includes medical schools.

b. Includes public liberal arts, private two-year, and other specialized institutions except medical schools.

Table A-38 ⇒ Perceptions of Campus Facilities: Computing Resources by Gender, Institutional Type, and Program Area

	Personal computers	
	Mean	Percent good/ very good
By gender		
New faculty		
Males	3.1	80.8
Females	2.9	71.1
Senior faculty		
Males	3.1	80.1
Females	2.9	70.9
By institutional type		
New faculty		
All research universities	3.2	84.6
All other doctorate-granting institutions[a]	3.1	81.8
All comprehensive institutions	2.9	72.5
Private liberal arts institutions	2.8	67.3
Public two-year institutions	2.9	69.3
All other institutions[b]	3.0	75.5
Senior faculty		
All research universities	3.2	84.3
All other doctorate-granting institutions	3.2	82.0
All comprehensive institutions	3.0	76.1
Private liberal arts institutions	3.0	74.3
Public two-year institutions	2.9	68.7
All other institutions	3.0	76.6
By program area		
New faculty		
Professions	3.1	79.4
Liberal arts and sciences	3.0	75.2
Fine arts	2.7	63.4
Humanities	2.9	71.0
Natural sciences	3.1	79.0
Social sciences	3.1	78.0
All other program areas	3.0	74.5
Senior faculty		
Professions	3.1	79.3
Liberal arts and sciences	3.0	76.3
Fine arts	2.7	64.0
Humanities	2.9	71.6
Natural sciences	3.1	82.1
Social sciences	3.1	77.9
All other program areas	3.0	76.9

Note: The questionnaire items read, "How would you rate each of the following facilities or resources at this institution that were available for your own use during the 1992 Fall term? 1 = very poor; 2 = poor; 3 = good; 4 = very good." Percent good/very good represents cumulative percentage of those who responded "good" or "very good." Means and percents were calculated using only those faculty who had responded in each category; thus the number

Centralized computer facilities		Computer networks with other institutions		Audiovisual equipment	
Mean	Percent good/ very good	Mean	Percent good/ very good	Mean	Percent good/ very good
2.9	74.0	2.8	67.7	2.9	77.5
2.9	73.1	2.7	62.1	2.9	76.6
3.1	81.8	2.9	71.7	3.0	77.7
3.0	75.7	2.7	63.6	3.0	78.2
3.2	82.3	3.1	80.1	2.9	73.9
2.9	74.3	2.8	68.6	3.0	81.0
2.9	73.0	2.7	64.3	2.9	75.1
2.6	59.7	2.3	48.4	2.9	77.0
2.7	66.0	2.3	44.8	3.0	81.4
2.7	61.3	2.5	52.2	3.0	75.8
3.3	89.5	3.2	85.7	2.9	74.7
3.2	85.4	3.0	76.1	3.0	79.2
3.0	78.1	2.7	66.1	2.9	75.1
2.8	69.7	2.6	57.7	3.0	79.4
2.8	71.0	2.4	48.8	3.1	83.3
2.8	69.4	2.6	62.1	3.0	79.7
2.9	72.9	2.7	62.0	3.0	79.9
2.9	72.8	2.8	68.4	2.9	75.0
2.7	60.3	2.5	55.9	2.7	68.0
2.9	73.7	2.7	63.4	3.0	78.3
2.9	75.3	2.9	71.5	2.8	75.1
2.9	71.9	2.9	72.1	2.9	74.3
2.9	75.3	2.7	61.7	3.0	76.3
3.1	81.2	2.9	69.4	3.0	79.2
3.0	79.1	2.8	69.1	2.9	76.3
2.9	70.9	2.7	60.3	2.8	72.5
3.0	77.7	2.8	68.1	2.9	77.2
3.0	80.6	2.9	71.4	2.9	77.1
3.1	81.6	2.9	70.1	2.9	75.7
3.1	80.3	2.8	69.6	3.1	80.6

of valid responses is different for each category. Details may not add to total because of rounding.

a. Includes medical schools.

b. Includes public liberal arts, private two-year, and other specialized institutions except medical schools.

Table A-39 ⇌ Perceptions of Campus Facilities: Other Support by Gender, Institutional Type, and Program Area

| | Basic research equipment/ instruments | |
	Mean	Percent good/ very good
By gender		
New faculty		
Males	2.9	71.5
Females	2.7	63.5
Senior faculty		
Males	2.8	69.8
Females	2.7	61.6
By institutional type		
New faculty		
All research institutions	3.1	84.5
All other doctorate-granting institutions[a]	2.9	73.9
All comprehensive institutions	2.5	56.0
Private liberal arts institutions	2.5	49.7
Public two-year institutions	2.6	58.9
All other institutions[b]	2.7	64.1
Senior faculty		
All research institutions	3.1	83.4
All other doctorate-granting institutions	2.9	75.5
All comprehensive institutions	2.6	57.6
Private liberal arts institutions	2.6	59.0
Public two-year institutions	2.6	56.8
All other institutions	2.7	61.7
By program area		
New faculty		
Professions	2.8	67.6
Liberal arts and sciences	2.8	67.1
Fine arts	2.7	62.8
Humanities	2.6	61.3
Natural sciences	2.9	70.7
Social sciences	2.8	67.2
All other program areas	2.8	70.7
Senior faculty		
Professions	2.8	68.9
Liberal arts and sciences	2.8	66.5
Fine arts	2.7	62.8
Humanities	2.7	64.5
Natural sciences	2.8	69.1
Social sciences	2.7	65.5
All other program areas	2.8	70.3

Note: The questionnaire items read, "How would you rate each of the following facilities or resources at this institution that were available for your own use during the 1992 Fall term? 1 = very poor; 2 = poor; 3 = good; 4 = very good." Percent good/very good represents cumulative percentage of those who responded "good" or "very good."

Availability of research assistants		Secretarial support		Library holdings	
Mean	Percent good/ very good	Mean	Percent good/ very good	Mean	Percent good/ very good
2.4	49.7	2.8	65.8	2.8	65.2
2.1	36.4	2.7	62.2	2.6	60.5
2.3	43.7	2.8	65.5	2.8	68.9
2.1	35.2	2.7	60.5	2.8	66.9
2.6	60.0	2.7	60.5	3.0	75.4
2.4	46.0	2.8	66.4	2.7	63.3
2.0	29.9	2.8	67.1	2.4	49.7
2.0	30.1	2.6	59.5	2.5	50.6
2.0	31.5	2.8	66.4	2.7	65.7
2.2	37.6	2.8	66.4	2.7	64.6
2.7	60.0	2.8	66.1	3.1	79.0
2.4	46.5	2.8	66.4	2.8	69.1
1.9	24.6	2.7	61.2	2.6	58.4
2.1	34.4	2.8	65.7	2.8	66.0
1.8	24.6	2.7	62.9	2.8	68.4
2.1	35.2	2.7	65.4	2.8	67.1
2.3	43.9	2.7	63.1	2.8	68.5
2.3	43.0	2.7	64.6	2.6	57.1
2.0	26.4	2.6	61.3	2.6	57.6
2.0	32.1	2.7	63.0	2.5	53.1
2.4	47.2	2.8	68.2	2.7	60.2
2.4	49.6	2.7	61.6	2.6	56.1
2.3	48.0	2.8	64.4	2.8	67.1
2.3	42.1	2.8	65.3	2.9	72.5
2.2	38.8	2.7	63.4	2.7	65.0
2.0	30.1	2.6	56.7	2.8	70.7
1.9	28.0	2.7	64.7	2.7	62.2
2.3	45.4	2.7	64.2	2.8	68.6
2.3	42.1	2.7	63.9	2.6	59.2
2.4	49.1	2.7	62.9	2.9	71.6

Means and percents were calculated using only those faculty who responded in each category; thus the number of valid responses is different for each category. Details may not add to total because of rounding.

a. Includes medical schools.

b. Includes public liberal arts, private two-year, and other specialized institutions except medical schools.

SELECTED COMPARISONS OF NEW- AND SENIOR-FACULTY COHORTS

	Senior-faculty cohort	New-faculty cohort	Table reference
1. Size of cohort	342,657	172,319	1
2. Percent of all full-time faculty	66.5	33.5	1
3. Percent by institution type			1
Research universities, private	58.6	41.4	
Comprehensive institutions, public	70.2	29.8	
4. Percent by program area (aggregated)			2
Liberal arts and sciences	69.5	30.5	
Fine arts	73.0	27.0	
Humanities	71.2	28.8	
Natural sciences	67.9	32.1	
Social sciences	68.4	31.6	
Professions	63.7	36.3	
5. Percent by program area (disaggregated)			A-2
Communications	58.0	42.0	
Chemical engineering	47.1	52.9	
History	79.0	21.0	
Mathematics	71.7	28.3	
Mechanical engineering	69.0	31.0	
6. Age (mean)	51	42	3
7. Percent in ladder ranks			
(ladder ranks: professor, associate professor, assistant professor)*	84.1	69.5	4
Males	87.6	76.0	A-4
Females	75.1	60.0	A-4
Humanities	82.2	62.1	A-4
Social scientists	91.3	79.1	A-4
Males—full professors only	49.6	16.6	A-4
Females—full professors only	23.9	5.2	A-4
8. Percent by gender			5
Males	71.5	59.2	
Females	28.5	40.8	
New-cohort females as percent of all female faculty			A-5
Research universities	47.9		
Other doctorate-granting institutions, public	43.2		
Other doctorate-granting institutions, private	36.0		
Public two-year institutions	38.7		
Percent of women by program area			
Education	44.1[†]	64.4	A-5A
Humanities	36.2	53.9	A-5
Natural sciences	16.7	28.7	A-5
Social sciences	21.9	38.4	A-5
Engineering	2.4[†]	12.0	A-5A
Professions	37.9	44.0	A-5
9. Percent by race			
Nonwhite	11.7	17.0	6
Asians / Pacific Islanders	4.4	7.7	
As percent of all minority faculty in new cohort		45.6	6[‡]
10. Percent by nativity			
Not U.S. native born	11.5	16.9	7
At research universities	17.0	26.7	A-7
Among natural scientists	14.4	24.7	A-7

	Senior-faculty cohort	New-faculty cohort	Table reference
11. Combined characteristics			
White women	24.9	34.3	A-6[‡]
White males	63.5	48.8	A-6[‡]
Native-born white males	58.6	43.2	11
Native-born white males in the liberal arts	33.5	20.5	12
12. Type of appointment			
Percent tenured or tenure eligible	83.5	66.8	21
Percent tenured or tenure eligible (excluding faculty at campuses for which no tenure system exists)[§]	90.1	73.6	
Males	92.6	78.0	
Females	83.2	67.2	
Percent tenured or tenure eligible			A-21
By institutional type			
Research universities	87.8	71.1	
All other doctorate-granting institutions	85.7	71.2	
Comprehensive institutions	91.3	71.2	
Private liberal arts institutions	80.0	63.5	
Public two-year institutions	74.8	62.0	
By program area			
Professions	80.6	65.2	
Liberal arts and sciences	85.9	71.1	
Fine arts	79.9	66.1	
Humanities	84.1	63.9	
Natural sciences	86.8	74.5	
Social sciences	89.7	75.5	

*If instructor rank is added: 93.9 percent of senior cohort, 89.6 percent of new cohort.
[†]Derived from data not shown in tables.
[‡]Derived from this table.
[§]See Chapter 4, note 10.

1993 NATIONAL STUDY OF POSTSECONDARY FACULTY: FACULTY QUESTIONNAIRE

U.S. Department of Education
Office of Educational Research and Improvement

National Center for Education Studies

Co-sponsored by: National Science Foundation
National Endowment for the Humanities

Contractor: National Opinion Research Center (NORC)
University of Chicago
Mailing Address:
1525 East 55th Street
Chicago, Illinois 60615
Toll-Free Number: 1-800-733-NORC

All information on this form will be kept confidential and will not be
disclosed or released to your institution or any other group or individual.

NATIONAL STUDY OF POSTSECONDARY FACULTY
Instructions for Completing Faculty Questionnaire

Many of our questions ask about your activities during the 1992 Fall Term. By this, we mean whatever academic term was in progress on October 15, 1992.

All questions that ask about your position at "this institution" refer to your position during the 1992 Fall Term at the institution listed on the label on the back cover of the questionnaire.

This questionnaire was designed to be completed by both full-time and part-time instructional faculty and staff, and non-instructional faculty, in 2- and 4-year (and above) higher education institutions of all types and sizes. Please read each question carefully and follow all instructions. Some of the questions may not appear to fit your situation precisely; if you have a response other than those listed for a particular question, write in that response.

Most questions ask you to circle a number to indicate your response. Circle the number in front of your response and not the response itself. Other questions ask you to fill in information; write in the information in the space provided.

Mailing instructions for returning the completed questionnaire are on page 26.

If you have any questions on how to proceed, please call NORC toll-free at 1-800-733-NORC.

1. During the 1992 Fall Term, did you have any <u>instructional</u> duties at this institution (e.g., teaching one or more courses, or advising or supervising students' academic activities)? *(CIRCLE ONE NUMBER)*

   1. Yes (ANSWER 1A)   2. No (SKIP TO QUESTION 2)

   1A. During the 1992 Fall Term, were . . .
   (CIRCLE ONE NUMBER)

   1. *all* of your instructional duties related to credit courses,

   2. some of your instructional duties related to credit courses or advising or supervising academic activities for credit, <u>or</u>

   3. *all* of your instructional duties related to *non*credit courses or advising or supervising *non*credit academic activities?

2. What was your principal activity at this institution during the 1992 Fall Term? If you have equal responsibilities, please select one. *(CIRCLE ONE NUMBER)*

   1. Teaching

   2. Research

   3. Technical activities (e.g., programmer, technician, chemist, engineer, etc.)

   4. Clinical service

   5. Community/public service

   6. Administration
   (WRITE IN TITLE OR POSITION) _____

   7. On sabbatical from this institution

   8. Other (subsidized performer, artist-in-residence, etc.)

3. During the 1992 Fall Term, did you have faculty status at this institution? *(CIRCLE ONE NUMBER)*

   1. Yes

   2. No, I did not have faculty status

   3. No, no one has faculty status at this institution

2

4. During the 1992 Fall Term, did this institution consider you to be employed part-time or full-time? *(CIRCLE ONE NUMBER)*

1. Part-time **(ANSWER 4A)**   2. Full-time **(SKIP TO QUESTION 5)**

    4A. Did you hold a part-time position at this institution during the 1992 Fall Term because . . . *(CIRCLE "1" OR "2" FOR EACH REASON)*

Yes	No	
1	2	a. you preferred working on a part-time basis?
1	2	b. a full-time position was not available?
1	2	c. you were supplementing your income from other employment?
1	2	d. you wanted to be part of an academic environment?
1	2	e. you were finishing a graduate degree?
1	2	f. of other reasons?

5. Were you chairperson of a department or division at this institution during the 1992 Fall Term? *(CIRCLE ONE NUMBER)*

1. Yes

2. No

6. In what year did you begin the job you held at this institution during the 1992 Fall Term? Include promotions in rank as part of your Fall 1992 job. *(WRITE IN YEAR)*

19 ☐☐

7. What was your tenure status at this institution during the 1992 Fall Term? *(CIRCLE ONE NUMBER)*

1. Tenured → 7A. In what year did you achieve tenure at this institution? 19 ☐☐

2. On tenure track but not tenured   **(SKIP TO QUESTION 9)**

3. Not on tenure track

4. No tenure system for my faculty status

5. No tenure system at this institution

8. During the 1992 Fall Term, what was the duration of your contract or appointment at this institution? *(CIRCLE ONE NUMBER)*

1. One academic term

2. One academic/calendar year

3. A limited number of years (i.e., two or more academic/calendar years)

4. Unspecified duration

5. Other

3

186

9. **Which of the following best describes your academic rank, title, or position at this institution during the 1992 Fall Term?** *(CIRCLE ONE NUMBER, OR "NA")*

NA. Not applicable: no ranks designated at this institution **[SKIP TO QUESTION 11]**

1. Professor

2. Associate Professor

3. Assistant Professor

4. Instructor

5. Lecturer

6. Other *(WRITE IN)*_____

10. **In what year did you first achieve this rank?**
(WRITE IN YEAR)

19 ☐☐

11. **During the 1992 Fall Term, which of the following kinds of appointments did you hold at this institution?**
(CIRCLE ALL THAT APPLY)

1. Acting

2. Affiliate or adjunct

3. Visiting

4. Assigned by religious order

5. Clinical
(WRITE IN TITLE OR POSITION) _____

6. Research
(WRITE IN TITLE OR POSITION) _____

7. None of the above

4

12. **What is your <u>principal</u> field or discipline of teaching?** *(REFER TO THE LIST OF MAJOR FIELDS OF STUDY ON PAGES 5 AND 6 AND ENTER THE APPROPRIATE CODE NUMBER AND NAME BELOW. IF YOU HAVE NO FIELD OF TEACHING, CIRCLE "NA")*

NA. Not Applicable

CODE FOR FIELD
OR DISCIPLINE: _____   NAME OF PRINCIPAL FIELD/DISCIPLINE

13. **What is your <u>principal</u> area of research?** **If equal areas, select one.** *(IF YOU HAVE NO RESEARCH AREA, CIRCLE "NA")*

NA. Not Applicable

CODE FOR FIELD
OR DISCIPLINE: _____   NAME OF PRINCIPAL FIELD/DISCIPLINE

CODES FOR MAJOR FIELDS OF STUDY AND ACADEMIC DISCIPLINES

AGRICULTURE

101	Agribusiness & Agricultural Production
102	Agricultural, Animal, Food, & Plant Sciences
103	Renewable Natural Resources, including Conservation, Fishing, & Forestry.
110	Other Agriculture

ARCHITECTURE & ENVIRONMENTAL DESIGN

121	Architecture & Environmental Design
122	City, Community, & Regional Planning
123	Interior Design
124	Land Use Management & Reclamation
130	Other Arch. & Environmental Design

ART

141	Art History & Appreciation
142	Crafts
143	Dance
144	Design (other than Arch. or Interior)
145	Dramatic Arts
146	Film Arts
147	Fine Arts
148	Music
149	Music History & Appreciation
150	Other Visual & Performing Arts

BUSINESS

161	Accounting
162	Banking & Finance
163	Business Administration & Management
164	Business Administrative Support (e.g., Bookkeeping, Office Management, Secretarial)
165	Human Resources Development
166	Organizational Behavior
167	Marketing & Distribution
170	Other Business

COMMUNICATIONS

181	Advertising
182	Broadcasting & Journalism
183	Communications Research
184	Communication Technologies
190	Other Communications

COMPUTER SCIENCE

201	Computer & Information Sciences
202	Computer Programming
203	Data Processing
204	Systems Analysis
210	Other Computer Science

EDUCATION

221	Education, General
222	Basic Skills
223	Bilingual/Cross-cultural Education
224	Curriculum & Instruction
225	Education Administration
226	Education Evaluation & Research
227	Educational Psychology
228	Special Education
229	Student Counseling & Personnel Svcs.
230	Other Education

TEACHER EDUCATION

241	Pre-Elementary
242	Elementary
243	Secondary
244	Adult & Continuing
245	Other General Teacher Ed. Programs
250	Teacher Education in Specific Subjects

ENGINEERING

261	Engineering, General
262	Civil Engineering
263	Electrical, Electronics, & Communication Engineering
264	Mechanical Engineering
265	Chemical Engineering
270	Other Engineering
280	Engineering-Related Technologies

ENGLISH AND LITERATURE

291	English, General
292	Composition & Creative Writing
293	American Literature
294	English Literature
295	Linguistics
296	Speech, Debate, & Forensics
297	English as a Second Language
300	English, Other

5

FOREIGN LANGUAGES
311 Chinese (Mandarin, Cantonese, or Other Chinese)
312 French
313 German
314 Italian
315 Latin
316 Japanese
317 Other Asian
318 Russian or Other Slavic
319 Spanish
320 Other Foreign Languages

HEALTH SCIENCES
331 Allied Health Technologies & Services
332 Dentistry
333 Health Services Administration
334 Medicine, including Psychiatry
335 Nursing
336 Pharmacy
337 Public Health
338 Veterinary Medicine
340 Other Health Sciences

350 HOME ECONOMICS

360 INDUSTRIAL ARTS

370 LAW

380 LIBRARY & ARCHIVAL SCIENCES

NATURAL SCIENCES: BIOLOGICAL SCIENCES
391 Biochemistry
392 Biology
393 Botany
394 Genetics
395 Immunology
396 Microbiology
397 Physiology
398 Zoology
400 Biological Sciences, Other

NATURAL SCIENCES: PHYSICAL SCIENCES
411 Astronomy
412 Chemistry
413 Physics
414 Earth, Atmosphere, and Oceanographic (Geological Sciences)
420 Physical Sciences, Other

430 MATHEMATICS

440 STATISTICS

450 MILITARY STUDIES

460 MULTI/INTERDISCIPLINARY STUDIES

470 PARKS & RECREATION

480 PHILOSOPHY AND RELIGION

490 THEOLOGY

500 PROTECTIVE SERVICES (e.g., Criminal Justice, Fire Protection)

510 PSYCHOLOGY

520 PUBLIC AFFAIRS (e.g., Community Services, Public Administration, Public Works, Social Work)

530 SCIENCE TECHNOLOGIES

SOCIAL SCIENCES AND HISTORY
541 Social Sciences, General
542 Anthropology
543 Archeology
544 Area & Ethnic Studies
545 Demography
546 Economics
547 Geography
548 History
549 International Relations
550 Political Science & Government
551 Sociology
560 Other Social Sciences

VOCATIONAL TRAINING

CONSTRUCTION TRADES
601 Carpentry
602 Electrician
603 Plumbing
610 Other Construction Trades

CONSUMER, PERSONAL, & MISC. SERVICES
621 Personal Services (e.g., Barbering, Cosmetology)
630 Other Consumer Services

MECHANICS AND REPAIRERS
641 Electrical & Electronics Equipment Repair
642 Heating, Air Conditioning, & Refrigeration Mechanics & Repairers
643 Vehicle & Mobile Equipment Mechanics & Repairers
644 Other Mechanics & Repairers

PRECISION PRODUCTION
661 Drafting
662 Graphic & Print Communications
663 Leatherworking & Upholstering
664 Precision Metal Work
665 Woodworking
670 Other Precision Production Work

TRANSPORTATION AND MATERIAL MOVING
681 Air Transportation (e.g., Piloting, Traffic Control, Flight Attendance, Aviation Management)
682 Land Vehicle & Equipment Operation
683 Water Transportation (e.g., Boat & Fishing Operations, Deep Water Diving, Marina Operations, Sailors & Deckhands)
690 Other Transportation & Material Moving

900 OTHER *(IF YOU USE THIS CODE, BE SURE TO WRITE IN A COMPLETE DESCRIPTION AT QUESTIONS 12-13, AND 16)*

14. Which of the following undergraduate academic honors or awards, if any, did you receive?
(CIRCLE ALL THAT APPLY)

    1. National academic honor society, such as Phi Beta Kappa, Tau Beta Pi,
       or other field-specific national honor society

    2. Cum laude or honors

    3. Magna cum laude or high honors

    4. Summa cum laude or highest honors

    5. Other undergraduate academic achievement award

    6. None of the above

15. When you were in graduate school, which of the following forms of financial assistance, if any, did you
receive? *(CIRCLE ALL THAT APPLY, OR CIRCLE "NA")*

    NA. Not applicable; did not attend graduate school   **(GO TO QUESTION 16)**

    1. Teaching assistantship

    2. Research assistantship

    3. Program or residence hall assistantship

    4. Fellowship

    5. Scholarship or traineeship

    6. Grant

    7. G.I. Bill or other veterans' financial aid

    8. Federal or state loan

    9. Other loan

    10. None of the above

7

190

16. Please list below the degrees or other formal awards that you hold, the year you received each one, the field code (from pages 5-6) that applies, name of the field, and the name and location of the institution from which you received each degree or award. Do not list honorary degrees. *(COMPLETE ALL COLUMNS FOR EACH DEGREE)*

CODES FOR TYPE OF DEGREE

1 Professional degree (M.D., D.D.S., L.L.B., etc.)
2 Doctoral degree (Ph.D., Ed.D., etc.)
3 Master's degree or equivalent
4 Bachelor's degree or equivalent
5 Certificate, diploma, or degree for completion of undergraduate program of more than 2 years but less than 4 years in length
6 Associate's degree or equivalent
7 Certificate, diploma, or degree for completion of undergraduate program of at least 1 year but less than 2 years in length

A. Degree Code (see above)	B. Year Received	C. Field Code (from pp. 5-6)	D. Name of Field (from pp. 5-6)	E. Name of Institution (a) and City and State/Country of Institution (b)
(1) Highest _____	19_____	_____	_____	a. _____
				b. _____
(2) Next Highest _____	19_____	_____	_____	a. _____
				b. _____
(3) Next Highest _____	19_____	_____	_____	a. _____
				b. _____
(4) Next Highest _____	19_____	_____	_____	a. _____
				b. _____

8

17. During the 1992 Fall Term, were you employed <u>only</u> at this institution, or did you also have other employment including any outside consulting or other self-owned business, or private practice? *(CIRCLE ONE NUMBER)*

    1. Employed only at this institution   **(SKIP TO QUESTION 19)**

    2. Had other employment, consulting, self-owned business, or private practice

        17A. How many different jobs, other than your employment at this institution, did you have during the 1992 Fall Term? Include all outside consulting, self-owned business, and private practice. *(WRITE IN NUMBER)*

            _____ Number of Jobs

18. Not counting any employment at this institution, what was the employment sector of the main <u>other</u> job you held during Fall 1992? *(CIRCLE ONE NUMBER)*

    1. 4-year college or university, graduate or professional school

    2. 2-year or other postsecondary institution

    3. Elementary or secondary school

    4. Consulting, freelance work, self-owned business, or private practice

    5. Hospital or other health care or clinical setting

    6. Foundation or other nonprofit organization other than health care organization

    7. For-profit business or industry in the private sector

    8. Federal government, including military, or state or local government

    9. Other *(WRITE IN)* _____

      18A. What year did you begin that job?
          (WRITE IN YEAR)
          19 ☐☐

      18B. What was your primary responsibility in that job?
          (CIRCLE ONE NUMBER)

          1. Teaching

          2. Research

          3. Technical activities (e.g., programmer, technician, chemist, engineer, etc.)

          4. Clinical service

          5. Community/public service

          6. Administration

          7. Other

      18C. Was that job full-time or part-time? *(CIRCLE ONE NUMBER)*

          1. Full-time

          2. Part-time

9

19. The next questions ask about jobs that ended <u>before</u> the beginning of the 1992 Fall Term. For the three most recent and significant <u>main</u> jobs that you held during the past 15 years, indicate below the year you began and the year you left each job, the employment sector, your primary responsibility, and whether you were employed full-time or part-time.

- Do not list promotions in rank at one place of employment as different jobs.
- Do not include temporary positions (i.e., summer positions) or work as a graduate student.
- List each job (other than promotion in rank) separately.

If not applicable, circle "NA" ⟶	NA	NA	NA
	A.	**B.**	**C.**
(1) YEARS JOB HELD	MOST RECENT MAIN JOB (PRIOR TO FALL 1992)	NEXT MOST RECENT MAIN JOB	NEXT MOST RECENT MAIN JOB
FROM:	19_____	19_____	19_____
TO:	19_____	19_____	19_____
(2) EMPLOYMENT SECTOR	*(CIRCLE ONE)*	*(CIRCLE ONE)*	*(CIRCLE ONE)*
4-year college or university, graduate or professional school	1	1	1
2-year or other postsecondary institution	2	2	2
Elementary or secondary school	3	3	3
Consulting, freelance work, self-owned business, or private practice	4	4	4
Hospital or other health care or clinical setting	5	5	5
Foundation or other nonprofit organization other than health care organization	6	6	6
For-profit business or industry in the private sector	7	7	7
Federal government, including military, or state or local government	8	8	8
Other	9	9	9
(3) PRIMARY RESPONSIBILITY	*(CIRCLE ONE)*	*(CIRCLE ONE)*	*(CIRCLE ONE)*
Teaching	1	1	1
Research	2	2	2
Technical activities (e.g., programmer, technician, chemist, engineer, etc.)	3	3	3
Clinical service	4	4	4
Community/public service	5	5	5
Administration	6	6	6
Other	7	7	7
(4) FULL-TIME/PART-TIME	*(CIRCLE ONE)*	*(CIRCLE ONE)*	*(CIRCLE ONE)*
Full-time	1	1	1
Part-time	2	2	2

10

20. About how many of each of the following have you presented/published/etc. during your entire career and during the last 2 years? For publications, please include only works that have been accepted for publication. Count multiple presentations/publications of the same work only once. *(CIRCLE "NA" IF YOU HAVE NOT PUBLISHED OR PRESENTED)*

NA. No presentations/publications/etc. (GO TO QUESTION 21)

(WRITE IN A NUMBER ON EACH LINE; IF NONE, WRITE IN "0")

Type of Presentation/Publication/etc.	A. Total during career	B. Number in past 2 years
(1) Articles published in refereed professional or trade journals		
(2) Articles published in nonrefereed professional or trade journals		
(3) Creative works published in juried media		
(4) Creative works published in nonjuried media or in-house newsletters		
(5) Published reviews of books, articles, or creative works		
(6) Chapters in edited volumes		
(7) Textbooks		
(8) Other books		
(9) Monographs		
(10) Research or technical reports disseminated internally or to clients		
(11) Presentations at conferences, workshops, etc.		
(12) Exhibitions or performances in the fine or applied arts		
(13) Patents or copyrights (excluding thesis or dissertation)		
(14) Computer software products		

11

21. During the 1992 Fall Term, how many undergraduate or graduate thesis or dissertation committees, comprehensive exams, orals committees, or examination or certification committees did you chair and/or serve on at this institution? *(CIRCLE "NA" IF YOU DID NOT SERVE ON ANY COMMITTEES)*

NA. Did not serve on any undergraduate or graduate committees **(GO TO QUESTION 22)**

(WRITE IN A NUMBER ON EACH LINE; IF NONE, WRITE IN "0")

Type of Committee	A. Number served on	B. Of that number, how many did you chair?
(1) Undergraduate thesis or dissertation committees	_____	_____
(2) Undergraduate comprehensive exams or orals committees (other than as part of thesis/dissertation committees)	_____	_____
(3) Undergraduate examination/certification committees	_____	_____
(4) Graduate thesis or dissertation committees	_____	_____
(5) Graduate comprehensive exams or orals committees (other than as part of thesis/dissertation committees)	_____	_____
(6) Graduate examination/certification committees	_____	_____

22. During the 1992 Fall Term, what was the total number of classes or sections you taught at this institution? Do not include individualized instruction, such as independent study or individual performance classes. Count multiple sections of the same course as a separate class, but not the lab section of a course. *(WRITE IN A NUMBER, OR CIRCLE "0")*

0. No classes taught **(SKIP TO QUESTION 25)**

_____ Number of classes/sections **(ANSWER 22A)**

22A. How many of those classes were classes for credit?

0. No classes for credit **(SKIP TO QUESTION 25)**

_____ Number of classes/sections for credit **(ANSWER QUESTION 23 ON THE NEXT PAGE)**

12

23. For each class or section that you taught for credit at this institution during the 1992 Fall Term, please answer the following items. Do not include individualized instruction, such as independent study or individual one-on-one performance classes.

If you taught multiple sections of the same course, count them as separate classes, but do not include the lab section of the course as a separate class. For each class, enter the code for the academic discipline of the class. (Refer to pages 5-6 for the codes. Please enter the code rather than the course name.)

		A. FIRST FOR-CREDIT CLASS	B. SECOND FOR-CREDIT CLASS
(1)	CODE FOR ACADEMIC DISCIPLINE OF CLASS (from pp. 5-6)		
(2)	DURING 1992 FALL TERM		
	Number of weeks the class met?	a. _____	a. _____
	Number of credit hours?	b. _____	b. _____
	Number of hours the class met per week?	c. _____	c. _____
	Number of teaching assistants, readers?	d. _____	d. _____
	Number of students enrolled?	e. _____	e. _____
	Was this class team taught?	f. 1. Yes 2. No	f. 1. Yes 2. No
	Average # hours per week *you* taught the class?	g. _____	g. _____
(3)	PRIMARY LEVEL OF STUDENTS	*(CIRCLE ONE)*	*(CIRCLE ONE)*
	Lower division students (first or second year postsecondary) or	1	1
	Upper division students (third or fourth year postsecondary) or	2	2
	Graduate or any other post-baccalaureate students, or	3	3
	All other students?	4	4
(4)	PRIMARY INSTRUCTIONAL METHOD USED	*(CIRCLE ONE)*	*(CIRCLE ONE)*
	Lecture	1	1
	Seminar	2	2
	Discussion group or class presentations	3	3
	Lab, clinic or problem session	4	4
	Apprenticeship, internship, field work, or field trips	5	5
	Role playing, simulation, or other performance (e.g., art, music, drama)	6	6
	TV or radio	7	7
	Group projects	8	8
	Cooperative learning groups	9	9

13

196

C.	D.	E.	
THIRD FOR-CREDIT CLASS	FOURTH FOR-CREDIT CLASS	FIFTH FOR-CREDIT CLASS	
a. _____	a. _____	a. _____	a. Number of weeks the class met
b. _____	b. _____	b. _____	b. Number of credit hours
c. _____	c. _____	c. _____	c. Number of hours the class met per week
d. _____	d. _____	d. _____	d. Number of teaching assistants, readers
e. _____	e. _____	e. _____	e. Number of students enrolled
f. 1. Yes 2. No	f. 1. Yes 2. No	f. 1. Yes 2. No	f. Was this class team taught
g. _____	g. _____	g. _____	g. Average # hours per week *you* taught
(CIRCLE ONE)	(CIRCLE ONE)	(CIRCLE ONE)	
1	1	1	Lower division students
2	2	2	Upper division students
3	3	3	Graduate, post-baccalaureate students
4	4	4	All other students
(CIRCLE ONE)	(CIRCLE ONE)	(CIRCLE ONE)	
1	1	1	Lecture
2	2	2	Seminar
3	3	3	Discussion group or class presentations
4	4	4	Lab, clinic or problem session
5	5	5	Apprenticeship, internship, etc.
6	6	6	Role playing, simulation, performance, etc.
7	7	7	TV or radio
8	8	8	Group projects
9	9	9	Cooperative learning groups

14

24. Did you teach any undergraduate courses <u>for</u> <u>credit</u> during the 1992 Fall Term at this institution?

    1. Yes (ANSWER 24A)   2. No (SKIP TO QUESTION 25)

        24A.   In how many of the undergraduate courses that you taught <u>for</u> <u>credit</u> during the 1992 Fall Term did you use . . . *(CIRCLE ONE NUMBER FOR EACH ITEM)*

None	Some	All		
1	2	3	a.	Computational tools or software?
1	2	3	b.	Computer-aided or machine-aided instruction?
1	2	3	c.	Student presentations?
1	2	3	d.	Student evaluations of each other's work?
1	2	3	e.	Multiple-choice midterm and/or final exam?
1	2	3	f.	Essay midterm and/or final exams?
1	2	3	g.	Short-answer midterm and/or final exams?
1	2	3	h.	Term/research papers?
1	2	3	i.	Multiple drafts of written work?
1	2	3	j.	Grading on a curve?
1	2	3	k.	Competency-based grading?

25. For each type of student listed below, please indicate how many students received individual instruction from you during the 1992 Fall Term, (e.g., independent study or one-on-one instruction, including working with individual students in a clinical or research setting), and the total number of contact hours with these students per week. Do not count regularly scheduled office hours. *(WRITE IN A NUMBER ON EACH LINE; IF NONE, WRITE IN "0")*

Type of students receiving Formal Individualized Instruction	A. Number of students	B. Total contact hours per week
(1) Lower division students (first or second year postsecondary)	_____	_____
(2) Upper division students (third or fourth year postsecondary)	_____	_____
(3) Graduate or any other post-baccalaureate students	_____	_____
(4) All other students	_____	_____

26. During the 1992 Fall Term, how many regularly scheduled office hours did you have per week? *(WRITE IN A NUMBER; IF NONE, WRITE IN "0")*

_____ Number of hours per week

27. During the 1992 Fall Term, how much informal contact with students did you have each week outside of the classroom? Do <u>not</u> count individual instruction, independent study, etc., <u>or</u> regularly scheduled office hours. *(WRITE IN A NUMBER; IF NONE, WRITE IN "0")*

_____ Number of hours per week

28. During the 1992 Fall Term, were you engaged in any professional research, writing, or creative works?

    1. Yes (ANSWER QUESTION 29)   2. No (SKIP TO QUESTION 34)

15

29. How would you describe your <u>primary</u> professional research, writing, or creative work during the 1992 Fall Term? *(CIRCLE ONE NUMBER)*

1. Pure or basic research
2. Applied research
3. Policy-oriented research or analysis

4. Literary or expressive
5. Program/Curriculum design and development
6. Other

30. During the 1992 Fall Term, were you engaged in any <u>funded</u> research or <u>funded</u> creative endeavors? Include any grants, contracts, or institutional awards. Do not include consulting services. *(CIRCLE ONE NUMBER)*

1. Yes   2. No   {SKIP TO QUESTION 34}

31. During the 1992 Fall Term, were you a principal investigator (PI) or co-principal investigator (Co-PI) for any grants or contracts? *(CIRCLE ONE NUMBER)*

1. Yes   2. No   {SKIP TO QUESTION 33}

32. During the 1992 Fall Term, how many individuals other than yourself were supported by all the grants and contracts for which you were PI or Co-PI? *(WRITE IN NUMBER; IF NONE, WRITE IN "0")*

_____ Number of individuals

33. Fill out the information below for each funding source during the 1992 Fall Term. If not sure, give your best estimate.

A. Funding source *(CIRCLE "1" OR "2" FOR EACH SOURCE)*		B. Number of Grants/ Contracts	C. Work done as . . . *(CIRCLE ALL THAT APPLY)*	D. Total funds for 1992-93 academic year	E. How funds were used *(CIRCLE ALL THAT APPLY)*
(1) This institution?	1. Yes → 2. No	_____	1. PI 2. Co-PI 3. Staff	$ _____	1. Research 2. Program/curriculum development 3. Other
(2) Foundation or other nonprofit organization?	1. Yes → 2. No	_____	1. PI 2. Co-PI 3. Staff	$ _____	1. Research 2. Program/curriculum development 3. Other
(3) For profit business or industry in the private sector?	1. Yes → 2. No	_____	1. PI 2. Co-PI 3. Staff	$ _____	1. Research 2. Program/curriculum development 3. Other
(4) State or local government?	1. Yes → 2. No	_____	1. PI 2. Co-PI 3. Staff	$ _____	1. Research 2. Program/curriculum development 3. Other
(5) Federal Government?	1. Yes → 2. No	_____	1. PI 2. Co-PI 3. Staff	$ _____	1. Research 2. Program/curriculum development 3. Other
(6) Other source? *(WRITE IN)* _____	1. Yes → 2. No	_____	1. PI 2. Co-PI 3. Staff	$ _____	1. Research 2. Program/curriculum development 3. Other

16

34. How would you rate each of the following facilities or resources at this institution that were available for your own use during the 1992 Fall Term? *(CIRCLE ONE NUMBER, OR "NA," ON EACH LINE)*

Not Available/ Not Applicable	Very Poor	Poor	Good	Very Good	
NA	1	2	3	4	a. Basic research equipment/instruments
NA	1	2	3	4	b. Laboratory space and supplies
NA	1	2	3	4	c. Availability of research assistants
NA	1	2	3	4	d. Personal computers
MA	1	2	3	4	e. Centralized (main frame) computer facilities
NA	1	2	3	4	f. Computer networks with other institutions
NA	1	2	3	4	g. Audio-visual equipment
NA	1	2	3	4	h. Classroom space
NA	1	2	3	4	i. Office space
NA	1	2	3	4	j. Studio/performance space
NA	1	2	3	4	k. Secretarial support
NA	1	2	3	4	l. Library holdings

35. Listed below are some ways that institutions and departments may use internal funds for the professional development of faculty.

A. Was institutional or department funding available for your use during the past two years for . . .	B. Did you use any of those funds at <u>this</u> institution?	C. Were those funds adequate for your purposes?
(1) tuition remission at this <u>or</u> other institutions? 1. Yes ⟶ 2. No DK. Don't know	1. Yes ⟶ 2. No	1. Yes 2. No
(2) professional association memberships and/or registration fees? 1. Yes ⟶ 2. No DK. Don't know	1. Yes ⟶ 2. No	1. Yes 2. No
(3) professional travel? 1. Yes ⟶ 2. No DK. Don't know	1. Yes ⟶ 2. No	1. Yes 2. No
(4) training to improve research or teaching skills? 1. Yes ⟶ 2. No DK. Don't know	1. Yes ⟶ 2. No	1. Yes 2. No
(5) retraining for fields in higher demand? 1. Yes ⟶ 2. No DK. Don't know	1. Yes ⟶ 2. No	1. Yes 2. No
(6) sabbatical leave? 1. Yes ⟶ 2. No DK. Don't know	1. Yes ⟶ 2. No	1. Yes 2. No

17

200

36. On the average, how many hours per week did you spend at each of the following kinds of activities during the 1992 Fall Term? *(IF NOT SURE, GIVE YOUR BEST ESTIMATES)*

Average number hours per week
during the 1992 Fall Term

_____ a. All paid activities at this institution (teaching, research, administration, etc.)

_____ b. All unpaid activities at this institution

_____ c. Any other paid activities outside this institution (e.g., consulting, working on other jobs)

_____ d. Unpaid (pro bono) professional service activities outside this institution

37. In column A, we ask you to allocate your <u>total</u> work time in the Fall of 1992 (as reported in Question 36) into several categories. We realize that they are not mutually exclusive categories (e.g., research may include teaching; preparing a course may be part of professional growth). We ask, however, that you allocate as best you can the proportion of your time spent in activities whose primary focus falls within the indicated categories. In column B, indicate what percentage of your time you would <u>prefer</u> to spend in each of the listed categories.

A. % of Work Time Spent	*(WRITE IN A PERCENTAGE ON EACH LINE.* *IF NOT SURE, GIVE YOUR BEST ESTIMATE; IF NONE, WRITE IN "0")*	B. % of Work Time Preferred
_____%	a. **Teaching** (including teaching, grading papers, preparing courses; developing new curricula; advising or supervising students; working with student organizations or intramural athletics)	_____%
_____%	b. **Research/Scholarship** (including research; reviewing or preparing articles or books; attending or preparing for professional meetings or conferences; reviewing proposals; seeking outside funding; giving performances or exhibitions in the fine or applied arts, or giving speeches)	_____%
_____%	c. **Professional Growth** (including taking courses, pursuing an advanced degree; other professional development activities, such as practice or activities to remain current in your field)	_____%
_____%	d. **Administration**	_____%
_____%	e. **Outside Consulting or Freelance Work**	_____%
_____%	f. **Service/Other Non-Teaching Activities** (including providing legal or medical services or psychological counseling to clients or patients; paid or unpaid community or public service, service to professional societies/associations; other activities or work not listed in a-e)	_____%
100%	PLEASE BE SURE THAT THE PERCENTAGES YOU PROVIDE ADD UP TO 100% OF THE TOTAL TIME.	100%

18

38. **Are you a member of the union (or other bargaining association) that represents faculty at this institution?**

1. Union is available, but I am not eligible
2. I am eligible, but not a member
3. I am eligible, and a member
4. Union is not available at this institution

SECTION D. JOB SATISFACTION ISSUES

39. **How satisfied or dissatisfied are you with each of the following aspects of your instructional duties at this institution?** *(CIRCLE "NA" IF YOU HAD NO INSTRUCTIONAL DUTIES)*

NA. No instructional duties **(GO TO QUESTION 40)**

(CIRCLE ONE NUMBER FOR EACH ITEM; IF AN ITEM DOES NOT APPLY TO YOU, WRITE IN "NA" NEXT TO THE ITEM)

Very Dissatisfied	Somewhat Dissatisfied	Somewhat Satisfied	Very Satisfied	
1	2	3	4	a. The authority I have to make decisions about content and methods in the courses I teach
1	2	3	4	b. The authority I have to make decisions about other (non-instructional) aspects of my job
1	2	3	4	c. The authority I have to make decisions about what courses I teach
1	2	3	4	d. Time available for working with students as an advisor, mentor, etc.
1	2	3	4	e. Quality of undergraduate students whom I have taught here
1	2	3	4	f. Quality of graduate students whom I have taught here

40. **How satisfied or dissatisfied are you with the following aspects of your job at this institution?** *(CIRCLE ONE NUMBER FOR EACH ITEM)*

Very Dissatisfied	Somewhat Dissatisfied	Somewhat Satisfied	Very Satisfied	
1	2	3	4	a. My work load
1	2	3	4	b. My job security
1	2	3	4	c. Opportunity for advancement in rank at this institution
1	2	3	4	d. Time available for keeping current in my field
1	2	3	4	e. Freedom to do outside consulting
1	2	3	4	f. My salary
1	2	3	4	g. My benefits, generally
1	2	3	4	h. Spouse or partner employment opportunities in this geographic area
1	2	3	4	i. My job here, overall

19

41. During the next three years, how likely is it that you will leave this job to . . .
(CIRCLE ONE NUMBER FOR EACH ITEM)

Not At All Likely	Somewhat Likely	Very Likely		
1	2	3	a.	accept a <u>part-time</u> job at a <u>different</u> postsecondary institution?
1	2	3	b.	accept a <u>full-time</u> job at a <u>different</u> postsecondary institution?
1	2	3	c.	accept a <u>part-time</u> job <u>not at a</u> postsecondary institution?
1	2	3	d.	accept a <u>full-time</u> job <u>not at a</u> postsecondary institution?
1	2	3	e.	retire from the labor force?

42. At what age do you think you are most likely to stop working at a postsecondary institution?
(WRITE IN AGE, OR CIRCLE "DK")

_____ Years of age

DK. Don't know

43. If you were to leave your current position in academia to accept another position inside or outside of academia, how important would each of the following be in your decision? *(CIRCLE ONE NUMBER FOR EACH ITEM)*

Not Important	Somewhat Important	Very Important		
1	2	3	a.	Salary level
1	2	3	b.	Tenure-track/tenured position
1	2	3	c.	Job security
1	2	3	d.	Opportunities for advancement
1	2	3	e.	Benefits
1	2	3	f.	No pressure to publish
1	2	3	g.	Good research facilities and equipment
1	2	3	h.	Good instructional facilities and equipment
1	2	3	i.	Good job or job opportunities for my spouse or partner
1	2	3	j.	Good geographic location
1	2	3	k.	Good environment/schools for my children
1	2	3	l.	Greater opportunity to teach
1	2	3	m.	Greater opportunity to do research
1	2	3	n.	Greater opportunity for administrative responsibilities

20

44. If you could elect to draw on your retirement and still continue working at your institution on a part-time basis, would you do so? *(CIRCLE ONE)*

   1. Yes

   2. No

   DK. Don't know

45. If an early retirement option were offered to you at your institution, would you take it? *(CIRCLE ONE)*

   1. Yes

   2. No

   DK. Don't know

46. At which age do you think you are most likely to retire from all paid employment? *(WRITE IN AGE, OR CIRCLE "DK")*

   _____ Years of age

   DK. Don't know

Note: Your responses to these items as with all other items in this questionnaire are voluntary and strictly confidential. They will be used only in statistical summaries, and will not be disclosed to your institution or to any individual or group. Furthermore, all information that would permit identification of individuals or institutions will be removed from the survey files.

47. For the calendar year 1992, estimate your gross compensation before taxes from each of the sources listed below.

    (IF NOT SURE, GIVE YOUR BEST ESTIMATES; IF NO COMPENSATION FROM A SOURCE, WRITE IN '0')

    Compensation from this institution:

    $ _____ a. Basic salary ⟶ b. **Type of appointment** (e.g., 9 months) [   ] # of months

    $ _____ c. Other teaching at this institution not included in basic salary (e.g., for summer session)

    $ _____ d. Supplements not included in basic salary (for administration, research, coaching sports, etc.)

    $ _____ e. Non-monetary compensation, such as food, housing, car (Do not include employee benefits such as medical, dental, or life insurance)

    $ _____ f. Any other income from this institution

    Compensation from other sources:

    $ _____ g. Employment at another academic institution

    $ _____ h. Legal or medical services or psychological counseling

    $ _____ i. Outside consulting, consulting business or freelance work

    $ _____ j. Self-owned business (other than consulting)

    $ _____ k. Professional performances or exhibitions

    $ _____ l. Speaking fees, honoraria

    $ _____ m. Royalties or commissions

    $ _____ n. Any other employment

    $ _____ o. Non-monetary compensation, such as food, housing, car (Do not include employee benefits such as medical, dental, or life insurance)

    Other sources of earned income *(WRITE IN BELOW):*

    $ _____ p. _____

    $ _____ q. _____

48. For the calendar year 1992, how many persons were in your household including yourself?

    _____ Total number in household

49. For the calendar year 1992, what was your total household income?

    $ _____ Total household income

50. For the calendar year 1992, how many dependents did you have? Do not include yourself. (A dependent is someone receiving at least half of his or her support from you.)

    _____ Number of dependents

51. Are you . . .

    1. male, or

    2. female?

52. In what month and year were you born?
(WRITE IN MONTH AND YEAR)

☐☐ 19 ☐☐

  MONTH   YEAR

53. What is your race? *(CIRCLE ONE NUMBER)*

    1. American Indian or Alaskan Native

    2. Asian or Pacific Islander **(ANSWER 53A)** ⟶ **53A.** What is your Asian or Pacific Islander origin? If more than one, circle the one you consider the most important part of your background. *(CIRCLE ONE NUMBER)*

    3. African American/Black

    4. White

    5. Other *(WRITE IN BELOW)*

                         1. Chinese

                         2. Filipino

54. Are you of Hispanic descent?
(CIRCLE ONE NUMBER)

                         3. Japanese

                         4. Korean

    1. Yes **(ANSWER 54A)**

    2. No **(SKIP TO QUESTION 55)**

                         5. Southeast Asian (Vietnamese, Laotian, Cambodian/Kampuchean, etc.)

                         6. Pacific Islander

    54A. What is your Spanish/Hispanic origin? If more than one, circle the one you consider the most important part of your background.

                         7. Other *(WRITE IN BELOW)*

        1. Mexican, Mexican-American, Chicano

        2. Cuban, Cubano

                         (SKIP TO QUESTION 55)

        3. Puerto Rican, Puertorriqueno, or Bouricuan

        4. Other *(WRITE IN BELOW)*

55. What is your current marital status?
(CIRCLE ONE NUMBER)

    1. Single, never married

    2. Married

    3. Living with someone in a marriage-like relationship

    4. Separated

    5. Divorced

    6. Widowed

56. In what country were you born?
(CIRCLE ONE NUMBER)

1. USA

2. Other *(WRITE IN)*_____

57. What is your citizenship status?
(CIRCLE ONE NUMBER)

1. United States citizen, native

2. United States citizen, naturalized

3. Permanent resident of the United States (immigrant visa)

_____
COUNTRY OF PRESENT CITIZENSHIP

4. Temporary resident of United States (non-immigrant visa)

_____
COUNTRY OF PRESENT CITIZENSHIP

58. What is the highest level of formal education completed by your mother and your father?
(CIRCLE ONE FOR EACH PERSON)

A. Mother	B. Father		
1	1	a.	Less than high school diploma
2	2	b.	High school diploma
3	3	c.	Some college
4	4	d.	Associate's degree
5	5	e.	Bachelor's degree
6	6	f.	Master's degree
7	7	g.	Doctorate or professional degree (e.g., Ph.D., M.D., D.V.M., J.D./L.L.B.)
8	8	h.	Other
DK	DK	i.	Don't know

24

59. Please indicate the extent to which you agree or disagree with each of the following statements.
(CIRCLE ONE NUMBER FOR EACH STATEMENT)

Disagree Strongly	Disagree Somewhat	Agree Somewhat	Agree Strongly	
1	2	3	4	a. Teaching effectiveness should be the primary criterion for promotion of college teachers at this institution.
1	2	3	4	b. Research/publications should be the primary criterion for promotion of college teachers at this institution.
1	2	3	4	c. At this institution, research is rewarded more than teaching.
1	2	3	4	d. State or federally mandated assessment requirements will improve the quality of undergraduate education.
1	2	3	4	e. Female faculty members are treated fairly at this institution.
1	2	3	4	f. Faculty who are members of racial or ethnic minorities are treated fairly at this institution.
1	2	3	4	g. If I had it to do over again, I would still choose an academic career.

60. Please indicate your opinion regarding whether each of the following has worsened, stayed the same, or improved in recent years at this institution. *(CIRCLE ONE FOR EACH ITEM)*

Worsened	Stayed the Same	Improved	Don't Know	
1	2	3	DK	a. The quality of students who choose to pursue academic careers in my field
1	2	3	DK	b. The opportunities junior faculty have for advancement in my field
1	2	3	DK	c. The professional competence of individuals entering my academic field
1	2	3	DK	d. The ability of this institution to meet the educational needs of entering students
1	2	3	DK	e. The ability of faculty to obtain external funding
1	2	3	DK	f. Pressure to increase faculty workload at this institution
1	2	3	DK	g. The quality of undergraduate education at this institution
1	2	3	DK	h. The atmosphere for free expression of ideas
1	2	3	DK	i. The quality of research at this institution

25

THANK YOU VERY MUCH FOR YOUR PARTICIPATION

Return this completed questionnaire in the enclosed prepaid envelope to:

National Opinion Research Center (NORC)
University of Chicago
1525 East 55th Street
Chicago, Illinois 60615

NOTES

ONE   Context: The Faculty at a Crossroads

1. Burton R. Clark, *Academic Life: Small Worlds, Different Worlds* (Princeton, N.J.: Carnegie Foundation for the Advancement of Teaching, 1987).

2. "Not So Good: The Annual Report of the American Association of University Professors, 1996–97," *Academe* 83, no. 2 (1997): 14–39, especially Table 1 (16) and Fig. 1 (17); Denise K. Magner, "Increases in Faculty Salaries Fail to Keep Pace With Inflation," *Chronicle of Higher Education* 43, no. 43 (1997): A8–A13.

3. Indeed, Altbach and Lewis (1996) describe economic constraints and resultant strategies for achieving staffing flexibility as a "common denominator" among fourteen countries surveyed by the Carnegie Foundation for the Advancement of Teaching.

4. Ernest L. Boyer, *Scholarship Reconsidered: Priorities of the Professoriate* (Princeton, N.J.: Carnegie Foundation for the Advancement of Teaching, 1990).

5. Indeed, the Carnegie Foundation for the Advancement of Teaching issued a follow-up report setting out a framework within which campuses could assess faculty "scholarship" broadly conceived (Glassick, Huber, and Maeroff 1997).

6. Rice, R. Eugene, "Making a Place for the New American Scholar." New Pathways Working Papers Series, No. 1 (Washington, D.C.: American Association for Higher Education, 1996). See also Rice, "Heeding New Voices." New Pathways Working Papers Series, No. 7 (Washington, D.C.: American Association for Higher Education, 1997).

7. National Center for Education Statistics. Instructional Faculty and Staff in Higher Education Institutions: Fall 1987 and Fall 1992. National Center for Education Statistics No. 97-470 (Washington, D.C.: U.S. Department of Education,

Office of Educational Research and Improvement, 1997a). Table 2.1 (14) reports the proportion of part-time faculty in fall 1992 as 41.6 percent (compared with 33.1 percent for fall 1987). An earlier NCES report on NSOPF-93 places the proportion of part-time faculty at 40.6 percent (National Center for Education Statistics. *Institutional Policies and Practices Regarding Faculty in Higher Education.* National Center for Education Statistics No. 97-080 [Washington, D.C.: U.S. Department of Education, Office of Educational Research and Improvement, 1996], Table 2.2 [8]).

TWO   Taking the Measure of a New Academic Generation

1. The NSOPF-93 initially projected the number of part-timers at about 292,000 or 32.9 percent of the entire faculty (National Center for Education Statistics 1994, 11). Using the method we employed to determine the number of full-time faculty, as explained in this chapter, the number of part-time faculty would constitute 41.0 percent of the faculty by headcount. Or if those whom the survey lists as part-time faculty whose principal activity is *not* teaching are subtracted, the remaining part-timers would number approximately 243,000 or 33.5 percent of the faculty. At this writing, there is evidence, including NCES's own reassessment, to establish that the proportion of faculty who were part-timers at the time of the survey, and who are now part-time, is substantially higher than the 33.5 percent figure, probably closer to 42 or 43 percent.

2. Following the criteria and process described in the text, we eliminated 83,255 "faculty members" from the total NSOPF-93 population of 598,231 full-time "faculty" (which total included faculty teaching either for-credit or not-for-credit courses). This yielded a balance of 514,976 faculty members. (As explained in Chapter 3, we further sorted these 514,976 individuals into 342,658 faculty making up our senior cohort and 172,319 in our new-entry cohort.) Thus 13.9 percent of the NSOPF sample of faculty did not qualify for inclusion in accordance with our criteria. Because all of our tables are derived from our adjusted base of 514,976 full-time faculty members, it is important to understand what kinds of persons were eliminated from our analysis. Most of the 83,255 had faculty status of some sort, but they were not functioning essentially as faculty members.

- The largest proportion of them, 29,250 (35.1 percent of the total), were engaged principally in clinical service activities. Of these almost 26,000 held appointments at research universities or doctoral institutions with medical schools.
- Another 17,787 (21.4 percent) identified their principal activity as "administration" but not basically as *academic* administration; their positions ranged from presidents or chancellors to vice presidents to managers to coaches to chaplains to clerical workers.
- An additional 2,572 (3.1 percent) were librarians, another 6,295 (7.6 percent) were principally engaged in technical activity, and about 4,467 (5.4 percent) were primarily involved in public service.
- A considerable number of respondents who failed to meet our criteria—10,641 or 12.8 percent—checked "other" as their principal activity on the questionnaire. (The only examples provided on the questionnaire were "subsidized performer, artist in residence, etc.")

Together the foregoing six categories account for 71,012 of the excluded persons (or 85.3 percent of those excluded). To repeat, they were excluded because they failed to meet our criteria of having faculty status *and* a full-time appointment *and* a principal activity that they identified as teaching *or* research *or* administration in the form of being a program director, department chair, or academic dean.

This process yielded the subset of 514,976 persons who we believe best represent the "working faculty." It is their characteristics and activities we have undertaken to analyze.

One further note. The faculty in our sample whose only teaching in the fall of 1992 was of not-for-credit courses but who nevertheless survived the cut by meeting our other criteria constituted 3.1 percent of our sample. (They numbered 15,713 weighted or 359 unweighted cases.) The substantial majority of them (78.5 percent) listed their principal activity as teaching (43.7 percent) or research (34.8 percent), whereas another one-fifth (19.6 percent) identified their principal activity as administration.

3. It might be argued that using seven years to demarcate the two cohorts exaggerates the differences between them because, plausibly, disproportionately larger percentages of nonwhite and women faculty will subsequently fail to clear the tenure hurdle. If it is the case that larger proportions of women and minority academics are being denied tenure (or not having term contracts renewed or departing voluntarily), the intercohort differences that we have reported would thereby be exaggerated because fewer of the new faces will have made it into senior faculty ranks. However, we do not know the extent to which that is the case—or, indeed, if it is the case at all. It is clear that the "pure" AAUP-prescribed probationary period of seven years is adhered to less and less (1) as probationary periods are more frequently extended (Sibley-Fries 1986; Chait 1997) and (2) as larger numbers of full-time appointments are made off the tenure track (see Chapter 4). This situation suggests that the seven-year cutoff is no longer as much a career marker—perhaps not nearly so much—as it once was.

4. Both the 1988 and 1993 NSOPFs were funded by the U.S. Department of Education, but the latter survey received supplemental support from the National Endowment for the Humanities and the National Science Foundation.

5. The NSOPF-93 survey employed techniques of weighting in order to produce national estimates of faculty. (This methodology is described in National Center for Education Statistics 1994 [see especially the Technical Notes, 19–25].) The methodology is described in greater detail in National Center for Education Statistics (1997b). This method ultimately yielded "best estimate" weighted projections of 1,033,966 total faculty (composed of faculty teaching for-credit and not-for-credit courses), including 598,232 full time and 435,735 part time (Exhibit 10-10, 139).

THREE   Demographic Contours of the New Academic Generation

1. Note that these totals are larger than the total number of cases appearing in individual tables. This is because the totals reported here are based on the total number of usable responses to the NSOPF-93 questionnaire (as weighted and projected). The n for each table, by contrast, omits the "missing cases," that is, subtracts from the totals the number of cases for the particular item for which respondents either did not answer or did not provide a usable (codable) answer. Note also that

for *all* tables the category "all faculty" refers only to all *full-time* core faculty as defined in Chapter 2.

2. Historically, about 4 percent of faculty leave higher education employment annually, including voluntary and involuntary separations. Many factors influence that attrition rate, including most prominently the age distribution of the faculty. In any event, the number of new-entry faculty we have identified in our analysis is consistent with the historical pattern of job openings created through faculty departures. For a detailed discussion of the steady out-migration of faculty, see the section on "Faculty Attrition" in Bowen and Schuster (1986, 169–72 and Appendix C, 294–96).

3. For the NSOPF-93 survey, the NCES coded institutions according to a modified Carnegie classification scheme (see Carnegie Foundation for the Advancement of Teaching 1994, 20–21, and National Center for Education Statistics 1997a, 3–4). In the interest of simplifying comparisons we have collapsed categories for most purposes; this results in six main categories:

    a. *Research Universities:* consists of Research Universities I and II.

    b. *Doctoral:* includes Doctoral Universities I and II.

    c. *Comprehensive:* consists of Comprehensives I and II; this category includes institutions that confer master's degrees but not doctorates (or only a very few). (The name for this category was changed to "Masters" in the most recent [1994] Carnegie classification, that is, subsequent to NSOPF-93.)

    d. *Liberal Arts:* includes Liberal Arts I and II; this category includes institutions that confer baccalaureate degrees but not graduate degrees. (The name for this category was changed to "Baccalaureate" in the most recent Carnegie classification.)

    e. *Two-year:* includes public two-year institutions.

    f. *Other:* consists of public liberal arts and private two-year institutions (both categories are small in numbers) and "other specialized institutions," except medical.

4. A word of explanation is in order regarding the last category of institutions in Table 1, namely "all other." This is a catchall category used by NCES for the NSOPF survey. As explained in note b to the table, it encompasses faculty at public liberal arts colleges and private two-year institutions (both categories account for relatively few faculty) as well as an array of specialized institutions ranging from freestanding engineering and law schools to schools of theology and from art and music schools to some types of health-related institutions. Because this potpourri of institutions is so varied, generalizations about their faculties are not very meaningful, and accordingly we have chosen not to include the category "all other" in most of our analyses that compare faculty across types of institutions.

5. For purposes of this analysis, we have aggregated the following NSOPF-93 program areas into a category we label "Professional and Vocational": agriculture/home economics, business, communications, education, engineering, health sciences, law, occupationally specific programs, and all other programs (except fine arts, humanities, natural sciences, and social sciences).

These aggregated categories are a convenience, a shorthand for a wide variety of fields, and accordingly they obfuscate important demographic and cultural differences across the component groups. Thus the lumping together under "professions" of, say, engineering and education blurs important demographic and cultural differences. These aggregated categories also tend to muddy important distinctions *within* liberal arts fields, for instance differences within the social sciences between, say, economics and sociology. Disaggregations are shown on occasion, when they are deemed to be especially relevant, but for most purposes aggregated data must suffice.

6. For analytical purposes, scholars sometimes distinguish the fine arts from the humanities and natural and social sciences. Thus faculty in the fine arts, emphasizing visual and performance arts, can be readily distinguished from other liberal arts faculty members, for instance in terms of their training (a master of fine arts degree very often suffices as a terminal degree) or the applicable promotion criteria (performance, such as on a musical instrument or in the creation of a sculpture, rather than publication is often most relevant). We have chosen to include the fine arts among the liberal arts but have routinely broken out the fine arts in the same way that the humanities and natural and social sciences are shown separately.

7. A cautionary note is needed here. To speak of increasing or decreasing "market share," whether by institutional type or program area or another variable, addresses the number and distribution of new faculty and thereby depicts domains of high (or low) activity as reckoned by new hires. However, these numbers, derived from the 1993 NSOPF survey, constitute a single "snapshot" rather than data points measured at different times. Accordingly, this single survey does not per se measure change, although strong inferences can be drawn from differences in frequency distributions between the new and senior cohorts about trends in faculty characteristics, activity, and attitudes.

8. We use the terms *academic field* and *program area* interchangeably.

9. We have collapsed the category "<25" into the 25–29 band and similarly the category ">74" into the 70–74 band. In neither instance are the results affected in a substantial way. For the under-25 category, the total for all faculty is 0.2 percent (0.0 percent for senior cohort and 0.5 percent for new cohort). For the over-74 category, the total for all faculty is likewise 0.2 percent (0.2 percent for senior cohort and 0.1 percent for new cohort). Breakouts by gender, institutional type, and program area reveal quite even frequency distributions at each end of the age spectrum.

10. Community college faculty in the rank of instructor often have tenure or occupy tenure-eligible academic lines. The difference between the community college cohorts in the proportion of faculty in the rank of instructor may be explained in part by the wording of the questionnaire item: "Which of the following *best* describes your academic rank, title, or position . . ." (emphasis added). In many instances—commonly the case, for example in California's community colleges—faculty members on a particular campus may all technically or legally hold the rank of instructor, but institutional policies (sometimes negotiated as part of collective bargaining agreements) authorize faculty members, depending on level of seniority, to use a different (arguably more impressive) title (e.g., professor or associate professor) in signing their correspondence or on their business cards. Thus a more senior respondent to the NSOPF questionnaire may appropriately have marked "professor" as the rank "best" describing her situation though she is offi-

cially an "instructor," whereas her junior counterpart, without benefit of a "paper" rank, would be obliged to check "instructor." Accordingly, the difference between cohorts in the proportion of "off-ladder" faculty must be viewed cautiously because the protocol just described may serve to exaggerate the difference.

11. This 1.6 percent figure is derived from data not shown in Table A-5A.

12. Our analysis of frequency distributions by race necessarily relies on the categories used in the NSOPF-93 questionnaire: (1) American Indian or Alaskan Native, (2) Asian or Pacific Islander, (3) African American / Black, (4) White, (5) Other. A separate item asks, "Are you of Hispanic descent?"

13. These calculations are derived from Table 6.

14. These calculations are derived from Table A-6.

15. Direct comparisons between cohorts of the percentage of faculty who are temporary residents, permanent residents, and naturalized U.S. citizens are problematic. This is because over time some proportion of those with temporary resident status will become permanent residents and some of those, in turn, will become naturalized U.S. citizens. Because many of the new-cohort faculty will have been in the United States for a shorter period of time than their senior-cohort colleagues, the distribution of these new faculty among the temporary and permanent resident and naturalized citizen groups will not have "matured" sufficiently to be directly comparable with that of the senior faculty.

16. The NCES questionnaire asked, "In what country were you born?" In coding the responses, countries of origin that no longer exist, such as "West Germany" and "the USSR" were tabulated as given by the respondents.

17. But countervailing factors—such as the declining attractiveness (according to some observers) of careers in the historically "competing" vocations (for instance, law, medicine, and business)—undoubtedly play an influential role in guiding career preferences.

18. In some instances, federal government policy prohibits federal agencies from seeking information about questionnaire respondents' religious beliefs or affiliations; this proscription applied to NSOPF-93.

FOUR   **The Preparation and Careers of the New Academic Generation**

1. The NSOPF-93 survey included a number of items regarding faculty compensation. We elected not to undertake an analysis of compensation by cohorts on two grounds. First, our interest, for purposes of this study, was to compare the two cohorts. Differences in compensation between the senior- and new-faculty cohorts obviously will be substantial because of significant differences between the cohorts in their professional experience (and in their respective ages, ranks, and so forth); accordingly, analyses of the differences would be difficult at best to interpret. Second, of all categories of data gathered regularly on faculty, the amount of annual reporting on faculty salaries or compensation is perhaps the most voluminous, including comparisons by faculty rank, gender, and field. Accordingly, reasonably reliable periodic data on compensation exist.

2. It is not clear whether Trow and the National Education Association included professional degrees in their reporting of faculty doctorates. Thus the 1992 National Center for Education Statistics (NCES) data may represent a pattern of relative stability (assuming earlier studies report only on Ph.D.'s) over the past twenty years,

or, assuming that earlier studies included professional degrees (such as J.D.'s) as doctorates, the data may reflect a continued escalation of faculty qualifications. Bayer's 1973 analysis appears to support the latter alternative.

3. We use the term *highest degree* instead of *terminal degree*. For a number of faculty members, their *current* highest degree is not terminal in that, for example, some who hold master's degrees are at work on and will earn doctoral degrees. NCES includes Ph.D.'s and Ed.D.'s in the "doctoral" category, counting other doctorates (e.g., J.D., M.D., D.B.A.) as "professional" degrees.

4. There is a major issue of data comparability here. Berelson (1960) focuses on Ph.D.'s awarded generally (and is not limited to Ph.D.'s on full-time academic appointments). Moreover, Trow (1975) and National Center for Education Statistics (1994) do not share the same classification of "major" research universities.

5. Some undetermined but probably small number of senior-cohort faculty members received their highest degrees from institutions that were subsequently reclassified according to Carnegie criteria (usually upgraded from, say, Doctoral I to Research II), thereby rendering the two cohorts not strictly comparable on this variable.

6. A further caveat is in order. The appreciable number of missing data for new-cohort faculty members' source of highest degrees (10.0 percent of the total) is likely to be attributable in part to the considerable number of nonnatives in the new cohort. Some (perhaps many) of these earned their degrees outside the United States from institutions that do not fit into the Carnegie classification scheme (which is restricted to U.S. institutions), and accordingly those degree sources are probably not reported.

7. This narrowing of the gap between the genders no doubt reflects in part the larger proportion of males who appear to earn doctorates outside the United States (see Table A-7) and, as indicated in note 6, are not tallied according to the Carnegie classification.

8. The questionnaire item asks about jobs held within the previous fifteen years, and thus direct intercohort comparisons are not possible.

9. Strictly speaking, it is not known what proportion of the senior cohort held ladder-rank appointments during the first seven years of their careers. Although it is possible, it is highly unlikely that a large percentage of senior faculty initially did not hold ladder ranks but were moved into the ladder ranks later in their careers.

10. For the senior-faculty cohort, 92.7 percent are at institutions with tenure systems and 83.5 percent are either tenured or on the tenure track: $83.5 \div 92.7 = 90.1$ percent. For the new-faculty cohort, the corresponding numbers are $66.8 \div 90.8 = 73.6$ percent who are either tenured or on the tenure track.

11. The picture for the two-year colleges is complex because so many of their faculty (more than 20 percent) are at institutions that do not have a tenure system. If those faculty are deleted from the calculations, the remaining proportion of two-year college faculty who are on the tenure track (including those who are already tenured) is quite high: 93.5 percent of the senior cohort and 80.1 percent of the new cohort.

12. Table 22 reports levels of faculty satisfaction for eight component issues, both as mean scores for responses on the four-point scale of satisfaction and as the percentage of faculty members who say that they are "very satisfied" or "somewhat

satisfied." Comparing the mean issue scores in Table 22 with the global mean score in Table 21, which measures satisfaction with "my job here, overall," it can be seen that for the senior faculty, six of the eight component mean scores are lower than the global score, one is the same, and one, regarding job security (unsurprisingly), is higher. For the new faculty, all eight mean component scores are lower than the global score (although two scores are only 0.1 lower than the global measure). For both cohorts combined, seven scores are lower and one is the same.

An examination of the percentages of faculty reporting that they are "very satisfied" or "somewhat satisfied" shows the same pattern. For senior faculty, seven component scores are lower than the global measure and one (again regarding job security) is higher. For new faculty, once more all eight scores are lower, and all scores are also lower in the case of both cohorts combined.

FIVE   The New Academic Generation at Work

1. Many of the earlier data, preceding Baldridge's 1978 study, are not strictly comparable since those studies focus on *hours* spent in various work roles rather than on self-reported *percentages* of time. Moreover, either approach, relying on self-reported effort, has its limitations.

2. The categories of activity are defined in the questionnaire as follows:

   a. *Teaching* (including teaching, grading papers, preparing courses; developing new curricula; advising or supervising students; working with student organizations or intramural athletics)

   b. *Research/scholarship* (including research; reviewing or preparing articles or books; attending or preparing for professional meetings or conferences; reviewing proposals; seeking outside funding; giving performances or exhibitions in the fine or applied arts, or giving speeches)

   c. *Professional growth* (including taking courses; pursuing an advanced degree; other professional development activities, such as practice or activities to remain current in your field)

   d. *Administration*

   e. *Outside consulting or freelance work*

   f. *Service/other nonteaching activities* (including providing legal or medical services or psychological counseling to clients or patients; paid or unpaid community or public service, service to professional societies/associations; other activities or work not listed in a–e)

3. Strictly speaking, it is difficult to discern historical trends here. Whereas earlier studies, such as that by Gaff and Wilson (1975), focus on the number of interactions over a specified time period, current surveys, such as NSOPF-93, typically focus on number of hours of contact per week, irrespective of number of students or number of contacts.

4. As a caution, it should be noted that these estimates are based on samples of universities, the institutional type wherein lecturing is the predominant mode of instruction (Gaff and Wilson 1975).

5. The data unfortunately are not strictly comparable. The 1969 data are based on publications (of any kind) in the last two years. The National Center for Education Statistics data disaggregate total publications into ten specific types over the last two years.

6. Our Tables 29 and A-29A–D record the extent to which faculty report *any* activity in a given category rather than the *number* of incidents in a given category. For example, the faculty's mean number of articles published in refereed journals or the mean number of conference presentations is not included in our tables.

SIX   The Attitudes and Values of the New Academic Generation

1. It is curious that some proportion of faculty members, roughly 7–14 percent in each category (cohort, gender, institutional type, and program area) selected *both* research *and* teaching as the criterion that should serve as the *primary* basis for promotion at their institution. Since logic rejects the possibility of two "primary" criteria, we leave to others the task of interpreting this anomaly (see Tables 32, A-32A, and A-32B).

2. This category is not defined in the survey.

3. These percentages are derived from Table 6 and the number of faculty in each cohort.

4. For convenience of display, the audiovisual equipment item is included with Tables 38 and A-38 rather than with Tables 39 and A-39.

SEVEN   The New Academic Generation and the Future of American Higher Education

1. This has been especially the case in the wake of the Education Amendments of 1972, which channeled federal student financial aid to students, rather than to institutions, and thereby provided great momentum to student consumerism.

2. Although accurate measurements of the number of part-time faculty are notoriously difficult, part-timers appear to have constituted 22 percent of the faculty in 1970–71 (Bowen and Schuster, 1986, 62).

3. See, for example, Frederick F. Reichheld, *The Loyalty Effect: The Hidden Force Behind Growth, Profits, and Lasting Value* (Boston: Harvard Business School Press, 1996).

REFERENCES

Altbach, Philip G., and Lionel Lewis. 1996. "The Academic Profession in International Perspective." In *The International Academic Profession*, edited by Philip G. Altbach. Princeton, N.J.: Carnegie Foundation for the Advancement of Teaching, 3–48.

American Association of University Professors. 1992. "On the Status of Non-Tenure-Track Faculty." A Report of Committee G on Part-Time and Non-Tenure-Track Appointments. *Academe* 80, no. 6: 39–48.

———. 1995. "Academic Freedom and Tenure—Statement of Principles, 1940." In *AAUP Policy, Documents and Reports*. Washington, D.C.: American Association of University Professors, 3–7.

Atelsek, Frank J., and Irene Gomberg. 1978. *New Full-Time Faculty 1976–77: Hiring Patterns by Field and Educational Attainment*. Higher Education Panel Reports, No. 38. Washington, D.C.: American Council on Education.

Austin, Ann E., and Zelda F. Gamson. 1983. *Academic Workplace: New Demands, Heightened Tensions*. ASHE-ERIC Higher Education Research Report No. 10. Washington, D.C.: Association for the Study of Higher Education.

Baldridge, J. Victor, David V. Curtis, George Ecker, and Gary L. Riley. 1978. *Policy Making and Effective Leadership*. San Francisco: Jossey-Bass.

Baldwin, Roger, and Robert T. Blackburn. 1981. "The Academic Career as a Developmental Process." *Journal of Higher Education* 52, no. 6: 598–614.

Bayer, Alan E. 1973. *Teaching Faculty in Academe: 1972–73*. ACE Research Reports, Vol. 8, No. 2. Washington, D.C.: American Council on Education.

Berelson, Bernard. 1960. *Graduate Education in the United States*. New York: McGraw-Hill.

Bess, James L. 1973. "Integrating Faculty and Student Life Cycles." *Review of Educational Research* 43, no. 4: 371–407.

Biglan, Anthony. 1973. "The Characteristics of Subject Matter in Different Academic Areas." *Journal of Applied Psychology* 57, no. 3: 195–203.

Blackburn, Robert T., and Janet H. Lawrence. 1995. *Faculty at Work: Motivation, Expectation, Satisfaction*. Baltimore: Johns Hopkins University Press.

Bouvier, Leon F., and David Simcox. 1995. "Foreign-Born Professionals in the United States." *Population and Environment: A Journal of Interdisciplinary Studies* 16, no. 5: 429–44.

Bowen, Howard R., and Jack H. Schuster. 1986. *American Professors: A National Resource Imperiled.* New York: Oxford University Press.

Bowen, William G., and Neil L. Rudenstine. 1992. *In Pursuit of the Ph.D.* Princeton, N.J.: Princeton University Press.

Boyer, Carol M., and Darrell R. Lewis. 1985. *And on the Seventh Day: Faculty Consulting and Supplemental Income.* ASHE-ERIC Higher Education Research Report No. 3. Washington, D.C.: Association for the Study of Higher Education.

Boyer, Ernest L. 1990. *Scholarship Reconsidered: Priorities of the Professoriate.* Princeton, N.J.: Carnegie Foundation for the Advancement of Teaching.

Braxton, John M., and Lowell L. Hargens. 1996. "Variation Among Academic Disciplines: Analytical Frameworks and Research." In *Higher Education: Handbook of Theory and Research,* Vol. 11, edited by John C. Smart. New York: Agathon Press, 1–46.

Breneman, David W. 1994. *Liberal Arts Colleges: Thriving, Surviving, or Endangered?* Washington, D.C.: Brookings Institution.

Carnegie Foundation for the Advancement of Teaching. 1986. "The Satisfied Faculty." *Change* 18, no. 2: 31–34.

——. 1989. *The Condition of the Professoriate: Attitudes and Trends, 1989.* Princeton, N.J.: Carnegie Foundation for the Advancement of Teaching.

——. 1994. *A Classification of Institutions of Higher Education.* Princeton, N.J.: Carnegie Foundation for the Advancement of Teaching.

Cartter, Allan M. 1976. *Ph.D.'s and the Academic Labor Market.* New York: McGraw-Hill.

Chait, Richard. 1997. "Innovative Modifications of Traditional Tenure Systems." New Pathways Working Paper Series, No. 9. Washington, D.C.: American Association for Higher Education.

Chronister, Jay L., Roger G. Baldwin, and Theresa Bailey. 1992. "Full-Time Non-Tenure-Track Faculty: Current Status, Conditions, and Attitudes." *Review of Higher Education* 15, no. 4: 383–400.

Clark, Burton R. 1987. *Academic Life: Small Worlds, Different Worlds.* Princeton, N.J.: Carnegie Foundation for the Advancement of Teaching.

Cohen, Arthur M., and Florence B. Brawer. 1977. *The Two-Year College Instructor Today.* New York: Praeger.

Corcoran, Mary, and Shirley M. Clark. 1984. "Professional Socialization and Contemporary Career Attitudes of Three Faculty Generations." *Research in Higher Education* 20, no. 2: 131–54.

Creswell, John. 1985. *Faculty Research Performance: Lessons from the Sciences and the Social Sciences.* ASHE-ERIC Higher Education Research Report No. 4. Washington, D.C.: Association for the Study of Higher Education.

Creutz, Alan. 1981. "From College Teacher to University Scholar: The Evolution and Professionalization of Academics at the University of Michigan, 1841–1900." Unpublished Ph.D. dissertation, University of Michigan.

Davis, Geoff. 1997. "Mathematicians and the Market." *Notices of the AMS* 44, no. 10: 1307–15.

Dolence, Michael G., and Donald M. Norris. 1995. *Transforming Higher Education: A Vision for Learning in the 21st Century.* Ann Arbor, Mich.: Society for College and University Planning.

Dwyer, Mary M., Arlene A. Flynn, and Patricia A. Inman. 1991. "Differential Progress of Women Faculty: Status, 1980–1990." In *Higher Education: Handbook of Theory and Research,* Vol. 7, edited by John C. Smart. New York: Agathon Press, 173–222.

Eckert, Ruth E., and Howard Y. Williams. 1972. *College Faculty View Themselves and Their Jobs.* Minneapolis: University of Minnesota, College of Education.

El-Khawas, Elaine. 1986. *Campus Trends, 1986.* Higher Education Panel Report No. 73. Washington, D.C.: American Council on Education.

Exum, William H. 1983. "Climbing the Crystal Stair: Values, Affirmative Action and Minority Faculty." *Social Problems* 30, no. 4: 383–99.

Fairweather, James S. 1996. *Faculty Work and Public Trust: Restoring the Value of Teaching and Public Service in American Academic Life.* Needham Heights, Mass.: Allyn and Bacon.

Farley, Jennie. 1982. *Academic Women and Employment Discrimination: A Critical Annotated Bibliography.* Cornell Industrial and Labor Relations Bibliography Series, No. 16. Ithaca, N.Y.: Cornell University.

Finkelstein, Martin J. 1984. *The American Academic Profession: An Analysis of Social Science Research since World War II.* Columbus: Ohio State University Press.

———. 1995. "College Faculty as Teachers." In *The NEA 1995 Almanac of Higher Education.* Washington, D.C.: National Education Association, 33–47.

Finkelstein, Martin J., and Mark W. LaCelle Peterson. 1992. "New and Junior Faculty: A Review of the Literature." In *Developing New and Junior Faculty,* edited by Mary Dean Sorcinelli and Ann Austin. New Directions in Teaching and Learning, No. 50. San Francisco: Jossey-Bass, 5–14.

Finkelstein, Martin J., and Jack H. Schuster. 1992. "College and University Faculty." In *Encyclopedia of Educational Research,* 6th ed., Vol. 1, edited by Marvin C. Alkin. New York: Macmillan, 190–97.

Finnegan, Dorothy E. 1993. "Segmentation in the Academic Labor Market: Hiring Cohorts in Comprehensive Universities." *Journal of Higher Education* 64, no. 6: 621–56.

Freeman, Bonnie C. 1977. "Faculty Women in the American University: Up the Down Staircase." *Higher Education* 6, no. 2: 165–88.

Fulton, Oliver. 1975. "Rewards and Fairness: Academic Women in the United States." In *Teachers and Students,* edited by Martin Trow. New York: McGraw-Hill, 199–248.

Gaff, Jerry G., and Robert C. Wilson. 1975. "Faculty Impact on Students." In *College Professors and Their Impact on Students,* edited by Robert C. Wilson, Jerry G. Gaff, Evelyn R. Dienst, Lynn Wood, and James L. Bavry. New York: John Wiley, 85–198.

Gappa, Judith M., and David W. Leslie. 1993. *The Invisible Faculty.* San Francisco: Jossey-Bass.

———. 1997. "Two Faculties or One? The Conundrum of Part-Timers in a Bifurcated Workforce." New Pathways Working Paper Series, No. 6. Washington, D.C.: American Association for Higher Education.

Gappa, Judith M., and Barbara S. Uehling. 1979. *Women in Academe: Steps to Greater Equality.* ASHE-ERIC Higher Education Research Report No. 1. Washington, D.C.: Association for the Study of Higher Education.

Geiger, Roger L. 1986. *To Advance Knowledge: The Growth of American Research Universities, 1900–1940.* New York: Oxford University Press.

Gilford, Dorothy M., and Joan Snyder. 1977. *Women and Minority Ph.D.'s in the 1970's: A Data Book.* Washington, D.C.: National Academy of Sciences.

Glassick, Charles E., Mary Taylor Huber, and Gene I. Maeroff. 1997. *Scholarship Assessed: Evaluation of the Professoriate.* San Francisco: Jossey-Bass and Carnegie Foundation for the Advancement of Teaching.

Green, Kenneth C. 1996. "Technology Use Jumps on College Campuses." The Campus Computing Project. Claremont, Calif.: Claremont Graduate University.

Green, Kenneth C., and Steven W. Gilbert. 1995. "Great Expectations: Content, Communications, Productivity, and the Role of Information Technology in Higher Education." *Change* 27, no. 2: 8–18.

Heller, Scott. 1987. "Fewer and Fewer Americans Take Graduate Work in Mathematics." *Chronicle of Higher Education* 33, no. 44: A11–A12.

Hesseldenz, Jon S., and Samuel A. Rodgers. 1976. "An Analysis of Predictors of Instruction Work Effort." *Research in Higher Education* 4, no. 3: 219–34.

Jencks, Christopher, and David Riesman. 1968. *The Academic Revolution*. New York: Doubleday.

Kennedy, Donald. 1995. "Another Century's End, Another Revolution for Higher Education." *Change* 27, no. 3: 8–15.

Kerr, Clark. 1994. *Troubled Times for American Higher Education*. Buffalo: State University of New York Press.

———. 1997. "Speculations about the Increasingly Indeterminate Future of Higher Education in the United States." *Review of Higher Education* 20, no. 4: 345–56.

Ladd, Everett C., Jr. 1979. "The Work Experience of American College Professors: Some Data and an Argument." In *Faculty Career Development*. Current Issues in Higher Education, No. 2. Washington, D.C.: American Association for Higher Education, 1–4.

Lenzner, Robert, and Stephen S. Johnson. 1997. "Seeing Things as They Really Are." An interview with Peter Drucker. *Forbes* 159, no. 5: 122–28.

Lipset, Seymour M., and Everett C. Ladd, Jr. 1979. "The Changing Social Origins of American Academics." In *Qualitative and Quantitative Social Research*, edited by Robert K. Merton, James S. Coleman, and Peter H. Rossi. New York: Free Press, 319–38.

McCaughey, Robert A. 1974. "The Transformation of American Academic Life: Harvard University 1821–1892." *Perspectives in American History* 8: 239–334.

Magner, Denise K. 1996. "The New Generation." *Chronicle of Higher Education* 42, no. 21: A17–A18.

———. 1997. "Increases in Faculty Salaries Fail to Keep Pace with Inflation." *Chronicle of Higher Education* 43, no. 43: A8–A13.

National Center for Education Statistics. 1990. *Faculty in Higher Education Institutions, 1988.* Washington, D.C.: U.S. Department of Education, Office of Educational Research and Improvement.

———. 1994. *Faculty and Instructional Staff: Who Are They and What Do They Do?* National Center for Education Statistics No. 94-346. Washington, D.C.: U.S. Department of Education, Office of Educational Research and Improvement.

———. 1995. *Digest of Educational Statistics, 1995.* Washington, D.C.: U.S. Department of Education, Office of Educational Research and Improvement.

———. 1996. *Institutional Policies and Practices Regarding Faculty in Higher Education.* National Center for Education Statistics No. 97-080. Washington, D.C.: U.S. Department of Education, Office of Educational Research and Improvement.

———. 1997a. *Instructional Faculty and Staff in Higher Education Institutions: Fall 1987 and Fall 1992.* National Center for Education Statistics No. 97-470. Washington, D.C.: U.S. Department of Education, Office of Educational Research and Improvement.

———. 1997b. *Methodology Report.* National Center for Education Statistics No. 97-467. Washington, D.C.: U.S. Department of Education, Office of Educational Research and Improvement.

National Education Association. 1979. *Higher Education Faculty: Characteristics and Opinions.* Washington, D.C.: National Education Association.

———. 1996. "Full-Time Non-Tenure-Track Faculty." *Research Center Update* 2, no. 5: 1–4.

National Research Council. 1978. *A Century of Doctorates.* Washington, D.C.: National Academy of Sciences.

———. 1989. *Summary Report 1987: Doctoral Recipients from United States Universities.* Washington, D.C.: National Academy of Sciences.

Noam, Eli M. 1995. "Electronics and the Dim Future of the University." *Science* 270, no. 5234: 247–49.

"Not So Good: The Annual Report of the American Association of University Professors, 1996–97." *Academe* 83, no. 2: 14–39.

Olsen, Deborah, and Mary Dean Sorcinelli. 1992. "The Pretenure Years: A Longitudinal Perspective." In *Developing New and Junior Faculty*, edited by Mary Dean Sorcinelli and Ann Austin. New Directions in Teaching and Learning, No. 50. San Francisco: Jossey-Bass, 5–25.

Packard, Alpheus S., ed. 1882. *History of Bowdoin College*. Boston: James Ripley Osgood.

Parsons, Talcott, and Gerald M. Platt. 1968. *The Academic Profession: A Pilot Study*. Cambridge, Mass.: Harvard University.

Reichheld, Frederick F. 1996. *The Loyalty Effect: The Hidden Force Behind Growth, Profits, and Lasting Value*. Boston: Harvard Business School Press.

Rice, R. Eugene. 1980. "Danforth Fellows at Mid-Career." *AAHE Bulletin* 32 (April): 4.

———. 1996. "Making a Place for the New American Scholar." New Pathways Working Paper Series, No. 1. Washington, D.C.: American Association for Higher Education.

———. 1997. "Heeding New Voices." New Pathways Working Paper Series, No. 7. Washington, D.C.: American Association for Higher Education.

Riesman, David. 1980. *On Higher Education*. San Francisco: Jossey-Bass.

Rudolph, Frederick. 1956. *Mark Hopkins and the Log*. New Haven, Conn.: Yale University Press.

———. 1977. *Curriculum: A History of the American Undergraduate Course of Study since 1636*. San Francisco: Jossey-Bass.

Russell, Alene B. 1992. *Faculty Workload: State and System Perspectives*. Denver: Education Commission of the States.

Ryan, Jake, and Charles Sackrey. 1984. *Strangers in Paradise: Academics from the Working Class*. Boston: South End.

Schuster, Jack H. 1994. "Emigration, Internationalization, and `Brain Drain': Propensities among British Academics." *Higher Education* 28, no. 4: 437–52.

———. 1995. "Whither the Faculty? The Changing Academic Labor Market." *Education Record* 76, no. 4: 28–33.

———. 1998. "Reconfiguring the Professoriate: An Overview." *Academe* 84, no. 1: 48–53.

Seidman, Earl. 1985. *In the Words of the Faculty*. San Francisco: Jossey-Bass.

Sibley-Fries, Marilyn. 1986. "Extended Probation at Research Universities." *Academe* 72, no. 1: 37–40.

Smelser, Neil J., and Robin Content. 1980. *The Changing Academic Market: General Trends and a Berkeley Case Study*. Berkeley: University of California Press.

Stadtman, Verne A. 1980. *Academic Adaptations*. San Francisco: Jossey-Bass.

Steinberg, Stephen. 1974. *The Academic Melting Pot*. New York: McGraw-Hill.

Stetar, Joseph M., and Martin J. Finkelstein. 1997. "The Influences of Faculty Backgrounds on the Motivation to Teach." In *Teaching Well and Liking It: Motivating Faculty to Teach Effectively*, edited by James L. Bess. Baltimore: Johns Hopkins University Press, 287–313.

Thielens, Wagner. 1987. "The Disciplines and Undergraduate Lecturing." Paper presented at the annual meeting of the American Educational Research Association, Washington, D.C., April 20–24.

Tobias, Marilyn. 1982. *Old Dartmouth on Trial: The Transformation of the Academic Community in Nineteenth-Century America*. New York: New York University Press.

Tokarczyk, Michelle M., and Elizabeth A. Fay, eds. 1993. *Working Class Women in the Academy*. Amherst: University of Massachusetts Press.

Trow, Martin, ed. 1975. *Teachers and Students*. New York: McGraw-Hill.

Tuckman, Howard P. 1978. "Who Is Part-Time in Academe?" *AAUP Bulletin* 64, no. 4: 305–15.

Tuckman, Howard P., and Karen L. Pickerill. 1988. "Part-Time Faculty and Part-Time Academic Careers." In *Academic Labor Markets and Faculty Careers,* edited by David W. Breneman and Ted I. K. Youn. New York: Falmer Press, 98–113.

Youn, Ted K. 1984. "Changing Academic Labor Markets: Effects of Expansion and Contraction of Higher Education." Paper presented at the annual meeting of the American Sociological Association, San Antonio, Texas, August 28, 1984.

Yuker, Harold E. 1984. *Faculty Workload: Research, Theory, and Interpretation.* ASHE-ERIC Higher Education Research Report No. 10. Washington, D.C.: Association for the Study of Higher Education.

Zumeta, William M. 1985. *Extending the Educational Ladder.* Boston: D. C. Heath.

INDEX

Page numbers for entries occurring in figure captions are followed by an *f* and those for entries occurring in tables by a *t*.

AAUP. *See* American Association of University Professors

ABD (all but dissertation), origin of term, 43

Academic appointment(s): age of faculty upon, 50*t*, 50–51; changing patterns of, 5; cost containment at institutions, and increase in number of off-track appointments, 2–3; nonacademic employment prior to, 51–53, 52*t*, 53*t*, 54*t*–55*t*; normal path of, in post–World War II period, 43; number of, in recent years, 18–19; supply versus demand for, 102

Academic degree. *See* Degree

Academic life, traditional, disruptions of, 1–4

Academic program areas. *See* Program areas, comparisons by

Academic rank: by gender, institutional type, and program area, 120t–21*t*; of new-faculty cohort, 24*t*, 24–26; of tenured new faculty, 135*t*; traditional ladder, diminished number of appointments to, 25

Administration, time spent by faculty in, 65–70, 66*t*

Administrators, reaction of, to limited resources, 2, 3

Advancement opportunities, faculty satisfaction with, 59, 60t; by gender, 136*t*–37*t*; by institutional type, 138*t*–39*t*; by program area, 140*t*–41*t*

Affirmative action programs, resistance to, 104

African American faculty. *See* Black faculty

Age of faculty: at appointment to current position, 50*t*, 50–51; at award of highest degree, 50*t*, 50–51; and father's level of education, 129*t*; at full professor rank in new cohort, 122*t*; by gender, institutional type, and program area, 118*t*–19*t*; and marital status, 131*t*; and mother's level of education, 130*t*; in new cohort, 23*t*, 23–24; of tenured new faculty, 135*t*

Agriculture/home economics, gender of new hires in, 28

American Association for Higher Education: Conference on Faculty Roles and Rewards, xii; New Pathways project, 5

American Association of University Professors (AAUP): founding of, 9; statement on academic freedom and tenure, 54; tenure policy of, 13

American faculty, internationalization of, 105. *See also* Foreign-born faculty

American Indians, as percentage of faculty, 29t

Appointments. *See* Academic appointment(s)

Asian faculty: country of birth, by program area, 128t; ghettoization of, 31; increased number of, in new academic cohort, 102; as percentage of faculty, 29t, 30–31, 34–35; top five program areas for, 126t. *See also* Minority faculty

Assessment movement, 109; as threat to traditional academic life, 1, 88

Attitudes and values analyzed in study, 11

Autonomy, faculty satisfaction with, 90–91

Benefits, faculty satisfaction with, 59, 60t; by gender, 136t–37t; by institutional type, 138t–39t; by program area, 140t–41t

Black faculty: ghettoization of, 31; as percentage of faculty, 29t, 30; top five program areas for, 126t. *See also* Minority faculty

Bowdoin College, historical shifts in faculty composition, 9

Boyer, Ernest L., 4

California Civil Rights Initiative (CCRI), 104

Campus environment, faculty satisfaction with, 91–96, 92t, 93t, 95t; by gender, institutional type, and program area, 166t–71t; by race, 168t

Campus facilities, faculty satisfaction with, 96t–98t, 96–99; by gender, institutional type, and program area, 172t–77t

Career characteristics analyzed in study, 10

Career experience of new-faculty cohort, 50t, 50–63, 52t–55t, 60t

Career path, normal, in post–World War II period, 43

Career satisfaction, by gender, institutional type, and program area, 142t

Carnegie Foundation for the Advancement of Teaching, 46

Catholics, first appearance in American academe, 10

CCRI. *See* California Civil Rights Initiative

Citizenship of faculty, by gender, institutional type, and program area, 127t. *See also* Foreign-born faculty; National origin of faculty

Civil Rights Initiative in California, 104

Classroom space, faculty satisfaction with, 96t, 96–97; by gender, institutional type, and program area, 172t–73t

Communications, as growth field, 23

Community college(s): faculty opinions of promotion criteria at, 87; faculty satisfaction with treatment of minorities at, 94; gender of new hires at, 27; number of new hires at, 102; percentage of faculty employed by, 19–21, 21t; percentage of faculty holding doctorates at, 45; percentage of white male faculty at, 41; race/ethnicity of new hires at, 30–31; use of computer-aided instruction at, 76; use of multiple-choice examinations at, 76; women and tenure at, 57–58. *See also* Institutional type, comparisons by

Community college faculty: job satisfaction of, 61, 63, 110; concurrent employment of, 81–83; satisfaction with students, 91; satisfaction with support services, 99; time worked per week, 71–72. *See also* Faculty; Institutional type, comparisons by

Compensation for faculty, in 1990s, 2

Competency-based grading, percentage of faculty using, 75t, 151t

Comprehensive institutions: faculty opinions of promotion criteria at, 87; faculty satisfaction with support services at, 99;

faculty turnover at, 20–21; gender of new hires at, 27; number of new hires at, 102; percentage of faculty employed by, 19–21, 21t; race/ethnicity of new hires at, 30–31; women and tenure at, 57. *See also* Institutional type, comparisons by

Computer facilities, faculty satisfaction with, 96–98, 97t; by gender, institutional type, and program area, 174t–75t

Computers, frequency of use for instruction, 74–76, 75t, 150t

Computer science, as growth field, 23

Concurrent employment of faculty. *See* Employment, concurrent, of faculty

Consulting, faculty freedom for. *See* Freedom for outside consulting, faculty satisfaction with

Contact hours of faculty. *See* Office hours held per week by faculty

Currency in field, faculty satisfaction with time to maintain, 59, 60t; by gender, 136t–37t

Curve, percentage of faculty grading on, 74, 75t, 151t

Dartmouth College, historical shifts in faculty composition, 9

Degree(s): doctorate, percentage of faculty holding, 44–46, 45t; faculty age at receipt of, 50t, 50–51; highest received, 44–46, 45t; highest received, by gender, institutional type, and program area, 133t; source of, 46–47, 47t

Demographic characteristics analyzed in study, 10

Demographic shifts, and increased emphasis on multiculturalism, 7

Discussion-style classes, percentage of faculty conducting, 73t, 73–74, 149t

Diversity of faculty: increasing, 41–42; increasing, by place of birth, 33; likelihood of increasing in future, 104; in new cohort, 102

Divorce and women faculty, 38

Doctorate, percentage of faculty holding, 44–46, 45t

Doctorate-granting universities: expansion of, in 1960s, 46; gender of new hires at, 27; increase in number of foreign-born

faculty at, 32; instructional tools used in, 76; number of new hires at, 102; as organizational form, origin of, 9; percentage of faculty employed by, 19–21, 21t; percentage of white male hires by, 40–41; as primary source of Ph.D.'s before 1960s, 46; race/ethnicity of new hires at, 30–31; service work in, for women versus men, 70; turnover at, 20–21. *See also* Institutional type, comparisons by

Doctorate-granting university faculty: increased workload pressures on, 95; office hours held per week by, 72, 72t; opinions of promotion criteria, 87; percentage holding doctorates, 45, 45t; satisfaction with students, 91; satisfaction with support services, 99; time worked per week by, 71–72; women and tenure at, 57. *See also* Faculty; Institutional type, comparisons by

Educational background of faculty, 44–50, 45t, 47t, 48t. *See also* Degree(s)

Education faculty, gender of new hires, 27–28

Educational level of faculty's parents, 35–37, 36t, 129t–30t

Effort, actual versus preferred distribution of, 65–70, 66t; by gender, 145t, 146t; by institutional type, 143t; by program area, 144t

Employment, concurrent, of faculty: by institutional type, 80t, 80–83, 82t; by sector, gender, institutional type, and program area, 157t–59t

Employment of faculty prior to current position, 51–53, 52t–55t

Employment opportunities for spouse. *See* Spouse employment opportunities, faculty satisfaction with

Engineering faculty, gender of new hires, 28

English, as international first language of higher learning, 106

Equity issues, faculty satisfaction with, 93t, 93–95; by gender, institutional type, and program area, 169t; by race, 168t

Essay examinations, percentage of faculty using, 75*t*, 76, 151*t*

Ethnicity of faculty. *See* Race/ethnicity of faculty

European faculty, emigration to United States by, 105. *See also* Foreign-born faculty

Examination types, percentage use by faculty, 75*t*, 76, 151*t*

External funding. *See* Funding, ability to obtain

Faculty: attitude of, toward work, 85–90, 86*t*; attitudes and values analyzed in study, 11; career chacteristics analyzed in study, 10; as central to educational venture, 3–4; compensation for, in 1990s, 2; demographic changes in, xi; demographic characteristics analyzed in study, 10; diminished loyalty of, 107; forces shaping life of, 4–5; full-time, institutional venues of, 19; graying of, 23; historic periods of change in, 9–10; interests in conflict with institutional interests, 3; internationalization of, 105; percentage in new cohort, 101–2; percentage of full- versus part-time, in NCES study, 12; pessimism of, 58–59; as privileged individuals, 2; by program area, 116*t*–17*t*; recent transformation in careers of, 108; research-oriented, as shapers of current system, 7; satisfaction of, by institutional type, 110. *See also* Institutional type, comparisons by; Part-time faculty

Faculty, minority. *See* Minority faculty; *specific minority groups*

Faculty, new generation of. *See* New-faculty cohort

Faculty, senior. *See* Senior faculty

Faculty and Instructional Staff: Who Are They and What Do They Do? (NCES), 15

Father's level of education, 36*t*; by gender and age, 129*t*

Federally mandated assessment, faculty willingness to accept, 88

Female faculty. *See* Gender; Women faculty

Financing of higher education, 48–50, 49*t*

Fine arts: concurrent employment of faculty in, 81; percentage of white male faculty in, 42; women and tenure in, 58. *See also* Program areas, comparisons by

Fine arts faculty: opinions of students and institutions, 92; percentage of time spent teaching, 68

Flexibility of institutions: perceived need to maintain, 3; pros and cons of, 108

Foreign-born faculty, increased number of, 32, 32*t*; in new academic cohort, 102. *See also* Citizenship of faculty; National origin of faculty

Freedom for outside consulting, faculty satisfaction with, 59, 60*t*; by gender, 136*t*–37*t*; by institutional type, 138*t*–39*t*; by program area, 140*t*–41*t*

Full professors in new-faculty cohort, by gender, institutional type, program area, and age, 122*t*

Funded research, percentage of faculty involved in, 77–80, 78*t*

Funding, ability to obtain, 95*t*, 95–96; by gender, institutional type, and program area, 170*t*–71*t*

Gender, 18*f*, 25–28; and ability to obtain funding, 170*t*–71*t*; and academic rank, 120*t*–21*t*; and age, 118*t*–19*t*; and appointment to non–tenure track positions, 57; and career satisfaction, 142*t*; and citizenship, 127*t*; and concurrent employment, 157*t*–59*t*; and distribution of effort, actual versus preferred, 145*t*, 146*t*; of full professors in new-faculty cohort, 122*t*; and highest degree obtained, 133*t*; by institutional type and program area, 123*t*; and instructional method, 73–75, 149*t*, 150*t*–51*t*; and job satisfaction, 136*t*–37*t*; and level of graduate school support, 48–49, 49*t*; and marital status, 38, 131*t*; of new-faculty cohort, 26–28, 27*t*; and office hours per week, 148*t*; and concurrent employment, 81; and paid versus unpaid activities, 147*t*; and parents' level of education, 129*t*, 130*t*; and perception of faculty role, 160*t*–63*t*; and perception of rewards, 160*t*–63*t*; and race, 125*t*; and research activity, 77–79;

and satisfaction with autonomy, 90t, 90–91; and satisfaction with campus environment, 166t–67t, 169t–71t; and satisfaction with campus facilities, 172t–77t; and satisfaction with computer facilities, 98; and satisfaction with equity issues, 169t; and satisfaction with instructional duties, 164t–65t; and satisfaction with space availability, 97; and satisfaction with support services, 98–99; and satisfaction with undergraduate students, 166t–67t; and satisfaction with work pressure, 170t–71t; and tenure status, 134t; and time worked in paid and unpaid activities, 71. *See also* Women faculty; *specific attributes*

Generational replacement of faculty: ease of, 2; studies of, 9

Ghettoization of minority faculty, 31

Governance of institutions, faculty's diminishing role in, 2

Government-mandated assessment, faculty willingness to accept, 88

Grading methods, faculty use percentages for, 75t, 76, 151t

Graduate school support of faculty, 48–50, 49t

Harvard University, historical shifts in faculty composition, 9

Health sciences: gender of new hires in, 28; as growth field, 23

Hiring. *See* Academic appointment(s)

Hispanic faculty: ghettoization of, 31; as percentage of faculty, 29t; top five program areas for, 126t. *See also* Minority faculty

Humanities: decreasing faculty support for, 107; decreasing program share of, 21–23, 22t, 102–3; gender of new hires in, 28; instructional tools used in, 76; job satisfaction in, 61, 63; number of off-track appointments in, 58; percentage of faculty with doctorates in, 45; primary instructional method in, 74; promotion criteria in, 88; publication in, 79–80; women and tenure in, 58. *See also* Liberal arts; Program areas, comparisons by

Humanities faculty: opinions of students and institution, 92; concurrent employment of, 81; percentage of time spent teaching, 68; satisfaction with support services, 99

Immigration Act (1990), 106

Immigration Reform Act (1965), 32

Institutional type, comparisons by: ability to obtain funding, 170t–71t; academic rank, 120t–21t; actual versus preferred distribution of effort, 143t; age of faculty, 118t–19t; career satisfaction, 142t; citizenship of faculty, 127t; concurrent employ-ment, 157t–59t; full professors on faculty, percent, 122t; gender of faculty, 123t; highest degree, 133t; instructional methods, 149t; job satisfaction, 138t–39t; native-born white males, 132t; office hours held per week, 148t; opinions of work pressure, 170t–71t; paid versus unpaid activities, 147t; perception of faculty role, 160t–61t; perception of rewards for faculty, 160t–61t; race/ethnicity of faculty, 125t; satisfaction with campus environment, 166t–67t, 169t–71t; satisfaction with campus facilities, 172t–77t; satisfaction with equity issues, 169t; satisfaction with instructional duties, 164t–65t; satisfaction with undergraduate students, 166t–67t; supplemental instructional methods, 150t–51t; tenured new faculty, 135t; tenure status, 134t

Institutional venues of faculty, 19–21

Instructional duties, faculty satisfaction with, 90t, 90–91; by gender, institutional type, and program area, 164t–65t

Instructional methods of faculty, 73t, 73–76, 75t; by gender, institutional type, and program area, 149t

Instructional methods of faculty, supplemental, 74–76, 75t; by gender, institutional type, and program area, 150t–51t

Intercohort comparisons, 102–3, 180t–81t

Internationalization of American faculty, 105. *See also* Citizenship of faculty; Foreign-born faculty; National origin of faculty

Jews: emigration of, to United States, 105; first appearance of, in American academe, 10

Job market for faculty, weakness of, 2, 3; in 1970s, 43–44

Jobs. *See* Academic appointment(s)

Job satisfaction, 58–63, 60*t*, 62*t*; by gender, 136*t*–37*t*; by institutional type, 138*t*–39*t*; by program area, 140*t*–41*t*

Job security, faculty satisfaction with, 59, 60*t*; by gender, 136*t*–37*t*; by institutional type, 138*t*–39*t*; by program area, 140*t*–41*t*

Labor market for faculty. *See* Job market for faculty

Laboratory space, faculty satisfaction with, 96*t*, 96–97; by gender, institutional type, and program area, 172*tt*

Laboratory-style classes, percentage of faculty employing, 73*t*, 73–74, 149*t*

Law, gender of new hires in, 28

Lecture-style classes, percentage of faculty employing, 73*t*, 73–74, 149*t*

Liberal arts: percentage of white male faculty in, 41*t*, 41*f*, 41–42; shrinking program share of, 21–23, 22*t*. *See also* Humanities

Liberal arts college(s): faculty opinions of promotion criteria at, 87, 90; faculty satisfaction with treatment of minorities at, 94; gender of new hires at, 27; instructional tools used in, 76; lecture versus discussion classes in, 74; percentage of faculty employed by, 19–21, 21*t*; race/ethnicity of new hires at, 30–31; women and tenure at, 57–58. *See also* Institutional type, comparisons by

Liberal arts college faculty: increased workload pressures on, 95; job satisfaction of, 61, 63, 110; concurrent employment of, 83; percentage holding doctorates, 45; satisfaction with students, 91; satisfaction with support services, 99. *See also* Faculty; Institutional type, comparisons by

Library holdings, faculty satisfaction with, 96–99, 98*t*; by gender, institutional type, and program area, 176*t*–77*t*

Loans, pressure on faculty to repay, 48

Loyalty of faculty, diminished, 107

Marital status of faculty, 37–38, 38*t*; by gender and age, 131*t*

Market for faculty. *See* Job market for faculty

Minority faculty: faculty satisfaction with treatment of, 93*t*, 93–95; increased number of, in new academic cohort, 102; by institutional type, 30; perception of equity by, 93–94; satisfaction with campus environment, 168*t*; top five program areas for, 126*tt*. *See also specific minority groups*

Mother's level of education, 36*t*; by gender and age, 130*t*

Multiculturalism: increased emphasis on, 7; likely future increase in, 105

Multiple-choice examinations, percentage of faculty using, 75*t*, 76, 151*t*

National Center for Education Statistics (NCES), xi; estimates of full-time faculty by, 11–12

National Opinion Research Center, xii, 15

National origin of faculty, 32*t*, 32–35, 34*t*, 35*t*. *See also* Citizenship of faculty; Foreign-born faculty

National Research Council, 43

National Study of Postsecondary Faculty, 1988 (NSOPF-88), xi, 8

National Study of Postsecondary Faculty, 1993 (NSOPF-93), xi, 8; analysis method for data from, 15–16; description of, 15; questionnaire reproduced in full, 183–209

Native Americans, as percentage of faculty, 29*t*

Native-born white males. *See* White males, native-born

Natural sciences: changes in, in 1970s, 43–44; funded research in, 80; increased number of foreign-born faculty in, 32–33; instructional tools used in, 76; primary instructional method in, 74; promotion criteria in, 88; publication in, 79–80. *See also* Program areas, comparisons by

Natural sciences faculty: job satisfaction of, 61, 63; opinions of students and institution, 92; concurrent employment of, 81; percentage of time spent teaching, 68; satisfaction with support services, 99; time worked per week by, 72. *See also* Program areas, comparisons by

NCES. *See* National Center for Education Statistics

New Entrants to the Full-Time Faculty of Higher Education Institutions (Finkelstein et al.), xii

New-faculty cohort: characteristics of, 8–9, 11–15, 102–3; comparison with senior faculty, 180*t*–81*t*; demographic information on, 23–39; diversity of, 102; female faculty in, by program area, 124*t*; full professors in, by gender, institutional type, program area, and age, 122*t*; gender distribution of, 18*f*, 123*t*; as percentage of faculty, by institutional type, 19–21; as percentage of faculty, by program area, 116*t*; as percentage of women in specific fields, 28; percentage with doctorates, 44–46, 45*t*; race/ethnicity of, 125*t*; as shapers of future, 7–8, 104–10; size of, 18*f*, 18–19, 101–2; tenured, by institutional type, program area, rank, and age, 135*t*. *See also specific attributes*

New Pathways project, 5

1990s, as difficult decade for faculty, 1–6

1960s, expansion of American faculty during, 10

Nineteenth century, changes in faculty composition during, 9

Nonacademic employment of new-faculty cohort prior to appointment, 51–53, 52*t*–55*t*

NSOPF-88. *See* National Study of Postsecondary Faculty, 1988

NSOPF-93. *See* National Study of Postsecondary Faculty, 1993

Occupational programs, increased number of, 21–23, 22*t*

Office hours held per week by faculty, 72*t*, 72–73; by gender, institutional type, and program area, 148*t*

Office space, faculty satisfaction with, 96*t*, 96–97; by gender, institutional type, and program area, 172*t*–73*t*

Outside employment. *See* Employment, concurrent, of faculty

Paid versus unpaid activities of faculty, 70–72, 71*t*; by gender, institutional type, and program area, 147*t*

Parents' educational level, for faculty, 35–37, 36*t*, 129*t*–30*t*

Part-time faculty: exclusion from study, 11–12, 14; increased number of, 2, 5, 54, 107; number of, versus full-time, 11–12

Physical science programs, decrease in number of, 21–23, 22*t*. *See also* Natural sciences

Policymakers' opinion of faculty, 2

Postdoctoral appointments: growth of, 43–44; as holding pattern for employment, 44

Pressure at work, faculty opinions of. *See* Workload, pressure to increase

Productivity of faculty: new emphasis on, 2

Professional programs: increased number of, 21–23, 22*t*; instructional tools used in, 76

Professional program faculty: office hours per week held by, 72; opinions of students and institution, 92; concurrent employment of, 81; percentage of time spent teaching, 68

Program areas, comparisons by: ability to obtain funding, 170*t*–71*t*; academic rank, 120*t*–21*t*; actual versus preferred distribution of effort, 144*t*; age of faculty, 118*t*–19*t*; career satisfaction, 142*t*; citizenship of faculty, 127*t*; concurrent employment of faculty, 157*t*–59*t*; female new faculty, 124*t*; full professors in new faculty, 122*t*; gender of faculty, 123*t*; highest degree, 133*t*; instructional methods, 149*t*, 150*t*–51*t*; job satisfaction, 140*t*–41*t*; native born white males, 132*t*; office hours held per week, 148*t*; opinions of work pressure, 170*t*–71*t*; paid versus unpaid activities, 147*t*; percentages employed in, 22*t*;

Program areas, comparisons by *(cont'd.)*
perception of faculty role, 160*t*–61*t*;
perception of rewards, 160*t*–61*t*; race/
ethnicity of faculty, 125*t*; satisfaction
with campus environment, 166*t*–67*t*,
169*t*–71*t*; satisfaction with campus facilities, 172*t*–77*t*; satisfaction with equity
issues, 169*t*; satisfaction with instructional duties, 164*t*–65*t*; satisfaction with
undergraduate students, 166*t*–67*t*;
tenured faculty, 134*t*; tenured new
faculty, 135*t*; top five, in number of
minority faculty, 126*t*

Promotion criteria: faculty opinions of, 86*t*,
86–90

Proposition 209, 104

Publication by faculty. *See* Research and
publication

Public institutions, and increased pressure
to diversify faculty, 27

Public opinion of faculty, diminished, 2

Questionnaire for NSOPF-93, reproduced
in full, 183–209

Race/ethnicity: faculty satisfaction
with campus environment by, 168*t*;
faculty satisfaction with equity issues
by, 168*t*

Race/ethnicity of faculty, 28–32, 29*f*, 29*t*; by
gender, 125*t*; by gender, institutional
type, and program area, 125*t*; by institutional type, 125*t*; in new cohort, 125*t*;
newly hired, 30–31; by program area,
125*t*

Rank. *See* Academic rank

Religion, effect of, on higher education,
38–39

Replacement of faculty: ease of, 2; studies
of, 9

Research: expanded parameters of, 4–5;
funded, percentage of faculty involved
in, 77–80, 78*t*

Research and publication, faculty involved
in, 67, 76–80, 78*t*; by gender, 152*t*; by
institutional type, 154*t*–55*t*; by program
area, 156*t*–57*t*; at research universities,
by gender, 153*t*. *See also* Workload, pressure to increase

Research assistant availability, faculty satisfaction with, 96, 97–99, 98*t*; by gender,
institutional type, and program area,
176*t*–77*t*

Research assistant jobs, increased number
of, 48, 49*t*

Research equipment, faculty satisfaction
with, 96, 98*t*, 98–99; by gender, institutional type, and program area, 176*t*

Research-oriented faculty, as shapers of
current system, 7, 10

Research papers, percentage of faculty
assigning, 75*t*, 76, 151*t*

Research universities: declining share
of Ph.D.'s granted, 46; gender of new
hires at, 27; increases in foreign-born
faculty at, 32; instructional tools used
in, 76; number of new hires at, 102;
as organizational form, origin of, 9;
percentage of faculty employed by,
20–21, 21*t*; percentage of white males
hired by, 40–41; as primary source
of Ph.D.'s before 1960s, 46;
race/ethnicity of new hires at, 30;
service work in, for women versus
men, 70; turnover at, 20–21.
See also Institutional type,
comparisons by

Research university faculty: increased
workload pressures on, 95; office hours
held per week by, 72; opinions of
promotion criteria, 87; percent holding doctorates, 45; satisfaction with
students, 91; satisfaction with support
services, 99; time worked per week
by, 71–72; women and tenure, 57.
See also Faculty; Institutional type,
comparisons by

Research versus teaching: faculty opinions
of, 86*t*, 86–90, 109–10; faculty time spent
in, 5, 65–70, 66*t*

Resources, scarcity of, for higher
education, 3

Rewards, faculty perception of, by gender,
institutional type, and program area,
160*t*–63*t*

Role of faculty, perception of, by gender,
institutional type, and program area,
160*t*–63*t*

Salary, faculty satisfaction with, 59–60, 60*t*; by gender, 136*t*–37*t*; by institutional type, 138*t*–39*t*; by program area, 140*t*–41*t*

Scholarship, expanded parameters of, 4–5

Scholarship Reconsidered: Priorities of the Professoriate (Boyer), 4

Secretarial support, faculty satisfaction with, 98*t*, 99; by gender, institutional type, and program area, 176*t*–77*t*

Seminars, percentage of faculty employing, 73*t*, 73–74, 149*t*

Senior faculty: comparison with new-faculty cohort, 180*t*–81*t*; gender distribution of, 18*f*; as percentage of faculty, 117*t*. *See also* Faculty; *specific attributes*

Short-answer examinations, percentage of faculty using, 75*t*, 76

Social class background of faculty, 35–37, 103

Social sciences: instructional tools used in, 76; primary instructional method in, 74; promotion criteria in, 88; publication in, 79–80. *See also* Program areas, comparisons by

Social sciences faculty: percentage of time spent teaching, 68; time worked per week, 72. *See also* Program areas, comparisons by

Socioeconomic status of new-faculty cohort, 35–37, 36*t*

Software, frequency of use for instruction, 74–76, 75*t*

Soviet Union, dissolution of, and emigration of scholars to United States, 106

Spouse employment opportunities, faculty satisfaction with, 59, 60*t*; by gender, 136*t*–37*t*; by institutional type, 138*t*–39*t*; by program area, 140*t*–41*t*

State-mandated assessment, faculty willingness to accept, 88

Student contact by faculty per week, 72*t*, 72–73; by gender, institutional type, and program area, 148*t*

Student evaluations, percentage of faculty using, 75*t*, 76, 150*t*

Student loans, pressure of faculty to repay, 48

Student needs, faculty opinions of institution's meeting of, 91–93, 92*t*, 166*t*–67*t*

Student presentations, percentage of faculty using, 75*t*, 76, 150*t*

Students, foreign, studying in American schools, 105–6

Students, undergraduate. *See* Undergraduate students

Studio space, faculty satisfaction with, 96*t*, 96–97; by gender, institutional type, and program area, 172*t*–73*t*

Teaching: increasing importance of, 88; time spent in, 65–70, 66*t*. *See also* Effort, actual versus preferred distribution of

Teaching assistantships, decrease in, 48, 49*t*

Teaching duties, faculty satisfaction with, 90*t*, 90–91

Teaching strategies of faculty, 73*t*, 73–76, 75*t*

Teaching versus research: faculty opinions of, 86*t*, 86–90, 109–10; time spent in, 5, 65–70, 66*t*

Technology, as force reshaping higher education, 7

Tenure: attacks on, 2; decreased opportunity for, 44, 107; increased number of appointments not leading to, 2, 54–55, 55*t*, 56*f*; pros and cons of, 108; up-or-out policy in, 2

Tenure status of faculty, 54–58, 55*t*, 56*f*; by gender, institutional type, and program area, 134*t*

Term papers, percentage of faculty assigning, 75*t*, 76, 151*t*

Time spent by faculty: by gender, 145*t*, 146*t*; by institutional type, 143*t*; on keeping current in field, 59–60, 60*t*, 136*t*–37*t*; by program area, 144*t*; on various activities, 65–70, 66*t*; on working with students, 72*t*, 72–73, 90*t*, 90, 148*t*, 164*t*–65*t*

Top-down management in academic institutions, 2

Traditional academic life, disruption of, 1–4

Turnover at research universities, 20, 101–2

Two-year colleges. *See* Community college(s)

Undergraduate education, pressure to improve, 109

Undergraduate honors of new-faculty cohort, 47, 48t

Undergraduate students, faculty satisfaction with, 91–93, 92t; by gender, institutional type, and program area, 166t–67t

Universities. *See* Doctorate-granting universities; Research universities

University of Michigan, historical shifts in faculty composition, 9

Unpaid versus paid activities of faculty, 70–72, 71t; by gender, institutional type, and program area, 147t

U.S. Department of Education, xi

White males: shrinking share of faculty positions, 104

White males, native-born: as percentage of faculty, 39t, 39–42, 40f, 41f, 41t; by institutional type and program area, 132t

Whites, as percentage of faculty, 29t, 29–30. *See also* Race/ethnicity of faculty

Williams College, historical shifts in faculty composition, 9

Women faculty: age of, 24; age of, at appointment to current position, 50t; age of, at receipt of degree, 50t; faculty satisfaction with treatment of, 93t, 93–95; first appearance in academe, 10; and funding availability, 96; highest degree attained by, 46; increased number of, in new academic cohort, 102; and job satisfaction, 60–63; minority, as percentage of minority hires, 30; opinions of, on promotion criteria, 88–90; opinions of, on students and institution, 92–93; as percentage of tenured faculty, 57; and perception of increased workload, 96; satisfaction with campus environment, 168t; satisfaction with treatment of women and minorities, 94–95; source of highest degree, 47, 47t; surge in appointments of, 26–27; and teaching versus research, 68–70, 109–10; time allocation of, preferred and actual, 68–70; white, as percentage of new hires, 30. *See also* Gender; *specific attributes*

Work, attitude of faculty toward, 85–90, 86t. *See also* Effort, actual versus preferred distribution of

Work characteristics analyzed in study, 10

Workload, faculty satisfaction with, 59, 60t; by gender, 136t–37t; by institutional type, 138t–39t; by program area, 140t–41t

Workload, pressure to increase, 44, 95t, 95–96; perception of, by gender, institutional type, and program area, 170t–71t

Work week of new-faculty cohort, 70–73

Written work, multiple drafts of, as instructional tool, 75t, 76

Library of Congress Cataloging-in-Publication Data

Finkelstein, Martin J., 1949–
    The new academic generation: a profession in transformation /
Martin J. Finkelstein, Robert K. Seal, Jack H. Schuster.
        p.   cm.
    Includes bibliographical references (p.   ) and index.
    ISBN 0-8018-5886-0
    1. College teachers—United States.   2. College teaching—United
States.   I. Seal, Robert K.   II. Schuster, Jack H.   III. Title.
LB1778.2.F6   1998
378.1'2'0973—dc21   97-49368
                                                                     CIP